THE
SELLING
OF THE
GREEN

THE
SELLING
OF THE
GREEN

The Financial Rise and Moral Decline of the Boston Celtics

HARVEY ARATON
and FILIP BONDY

 HarperCollins*Publishers*

HarperCollins books may be purchased for educational, business, or sales promotional use. For information, please call or write: Special Markets Department, HarperCollins Publishers, Inc., 10 East 53rd Street, New York, NY 10022. Telephone: (212) 207-7528; Fax: (212) 207-7222.

FIRST EDITION

Designed by Fritz Metsch

Library of Congress Cataloging-in-Publication Data

Araton, Harvey.
The selling of the green: the financial rise and moral decline of the Boston Celtics/Harvey Araton & Filip Bondy.
    p.   cm.
    Includes index.
    ISBN 0-06-018301-2
    1. Boston Celtics (Basketball team)—History. I. Bondy, Filip. II. Title.
GV885.52.B67A73   1992
796.323'64'0974461—dc20   91-50453

---

92 93 94 95 96 MAC/RRD 10 9 8 7 6 5 4 3 2 1

To LynNell and Charlotte, non-sports fans   —F.B.

To Alexander and to the memory of his grandfather Gilbert   —H.A.

To the memory of Larry Fleisher   —H.A. and F.B.

Contents

Acknowledgments	ix
Introduction	xi
1. Romans and Vandals	1
2. Seeing Red	19
3. Pride and Prejudice	37
4. Green and White	59
5. Changing Faces	75
6. Bird Watching	87
7. Selling Out	107
8. From the Sidelines	128
9. Three Steals	143
10. A Tale of Two Bostons	170
11. The Outsiders	183
12. Building the Empire	200
13. Changing of the Guards	224
14. The Long Goodbye	243
Epilogue	258
Index	261

Illustrations follow page 199.

Acknowledgments

WE would like to thank Dee Brown, M. L. Carr, Bob Cousy, Charles Grantham, Mike Glenn, Ron Grinker, Gerald Henderson, Ken Hudson, K. C. Jones, Richard Lapchick, Spike Lee, Reggie Lewis, Cedric Maxwell, Bob McAdoo, Brian Shaw, Paul Silas, Jerome Stanley, Jo Jo White, and Robert Willens for their courage and honesty; David Stern for his courtesy; the Rev. Al Owens for his energy; and the English High School kids for their wise input.

Thanks to David Black for his persistence and guidance; to editors Tom Miller and Jim Hornfischer for their faith and insight; to Philip Nobile and Eric Nadler, who once fought to preserve this project; to Zelda Spoelstra for her assistance; to the *Daily News* strikers, who provided inspiration in the most difficult of times.

Finally, we thank our families for their support: Marilyn Araton; Beth, Ruth, and David Albert; Sharon Kushner; Randi Walsman; Ota, Stefan, Halley, and Larisa Bondy; Bianca Berger; and Eugene and Marna Hancock.

Introduction

THE Boston Celtics are a New England institution, a symbol of an American game. They are more than a fading basketball dynasty; they are a sacred establishment in fashionable parts of Boston and its suburbs, bestowed with fanatic loyalty, bedecked in sixteen championship banners that recall names like Cousy, Russell, Havlicek, Bird.

The Celtics also happen to be one of the most despised franchises in all of professional sports. To many, the white shamrock on a green background is a symbol of entrenched power, of imperiousness, of status quo. "To me," said black New York filmmaker Spike Lee, "the Celtics represent white supremacy."

The Celtics and their historical overlord, Red Auerbach, are ignored in much of Boston proper, hated in most other NBA cities, viewed with suspicion by a majority of players, owners, and agents. They did not earn this dishonor overnight, but in the course of thirty-eight winning basketball seasons since 1946. They did it with Auerbach's gloating victory cigar, with their powerful lobbying influence throughout the league, with bad-faith bargaining, and eventually with their insular corporate attitude. There is an underside to the guts and the glory, to the leprechauns, banners, and ghosts in the rafters.

In some ways, the Celtics are no different, no more guilty, than the vast majority of predatory professional sports organizations in America. While college teams are correctly scrutinized for their improprieties, pro clubs have been granted a large degree of immunity from criticism outside the limits of the playing field. Working under the aegis of perfectly legal profiteering, these franchise owners and officials can hardly be called criminals. And yet they are guilty of many things.

Across town from the Celtics, at Fenway Park, the Boston Red Sox have ignored the poor neighborhoods of Roxbury and Dorchester with a shoulder as cold and as elitist as that of the Celtics. There are few blacks on the roster—or in the stands. "Danny Ainge once took me to a Red Sox game," said Cedric Maxwell, the former Celtic forward. "I spent the whole game counting black faces in the crowd. I think I counted them on my two hands." The New York Knicks, owned by Madison Square Garden Corporation and Paramount Communications, enjoyed a questionable $100 million tax break from former mayor Ed Koch and struggling New York City. The Utah Jazz has relied on a disproportionate number of white players for years, presenting what it must believe is a palatable image to local fans. In Phoenix, where the bench traditionally has been balanced with token whites, the Suns' gorilla mascot has mocked the strut of black players.

The New York Yankees, under exiled owner George Steinbrenner, once threatened to move from the South Bronx unless the city tore down a piece of the surrounding community park and built a parking lot. New York City had renovated the stadium for more than $100 million and maintained its upkeep. That was not enough. Al Davis's Los Angeles Raiders have exacted seed money from a handful of California cities and toyed with the affections of Oakland, whence they came. Teams like the Brooklyn Dodgers, Atlanta Flames, and Baltimore Colts have broken the hearts of their cities' residents with lucrative betrayals of community·spirit. The NFL owners replaced their players during the 1987 strike, bringing an entire players' union to its knees while compromising the credibility of their sport. Not a single pro football franchise stood above the fray.

These teams are all in business to make money, to win games in the process of building revenues. In America, this is their free-market right. But because the Celtics are the Celtics—with their enormous national profit base and ruthless front office—they have seized every natural advantage. The Celtics have walked over players and pandered to their largely white audience with less regard for propriety than other franchises might be obliged to show. "Whether or not they're a white team, that perception is there," said Golden State Warriors vice president Al Attles. "The perception is what matters." They have danced winding sambas around contractual legalities, yanked strings when they have needed only a slight tugging. They are not gracious winners—in any arena.

There is always an applicable exception for the Celtics, it seems. There was a reason Larry Bird did not have to play in the 1991 All-Star Game in Charlotte, even though Charles Barkley did. There was a reason Robert Parish wasn't ejected from a crucial playoff game against the Detroit Pistons in 1987, when he knocked down Bill Laimbeer with a punch to the back of the head directly in front of an official. There was a reason Alan Cohen could negotiate for the purchase of the Celtics while he was running the New Jersey Nets. And there was a reason the Celtics could sign Brian Shaw to a contract that superseded the one he already had with an Italian League team. There was always somebody—a referee, an arbitrator, the NBA commissioner himself—saying it was all right.

There have been no watchdogs to bark at their ethical trespasses. The Celtics own the local TV and radio stations that broadcast their games. They hire the announcers, make their own rules. They do not own the local papers, but they have had a series of incestuous relationships with some of the most influential writers and columnists. Bob Ryan, a *Boston Globe* columnist, co-authored Larry Bird's autobiography and books by Bob Cousy and John Havlicek, and wrote a glowing picture history of the team in 1989 (foreword by Auerbach himself) during one of the club's bleakest seasons. *Boston Herald* columnist Joe Fitzgerald was the ghostwriter for Auerbach's last autobiography in 1985. It has always been this way, since the *Globe's* Jack Barry dispatched glowing pieces about the Celts dur-ing their formative years, and since the defunct *Boston Record-American* generated a disproportionate amount of obsequious coverage with writers like Dave Eagan and Sammy Cohen, Auerbach favorites.

The opinions of Auerbach, Alan Cohen, and Jan Volk have been championed boisterously throughout Boston, throughout NBA recorded history. They have been foisted on some who wanted to listen, on others who would have preferred to hear something else, but could not. The voices of dissent were largely ignored or quashed. Players ostracized by the Celtic front office, important names like Cedric Maxwell, Jo Jo White, Gerald Henderson, Sidney Wicks, and Bob McAdoo, were in turn abandoned by most mainstream sportswriters. Agents who had been tricked or disrespected by Auerbach, Volk, or Cohen were treated with great suspicion, often mocked by the media. Scott Lang was supposed to be a jerk, a sucker, for letting Henderson sign a contract without a no-trade clause. Jerome Stanley was a destructive brainwasher for implanting notions of better deals in the minds of Brian Shaw and Reggie Lewis. The accused were offered a brief rebuttal time, nothing more—a ten-second sound bite, a short paragraph in the middle of a twenty-five-inch story.

In this book, written by two New York sportswriters with no debts whatsoever to the Boston Celtics, the tables are turned. The rules are different here. As observers with access to both insiders and outsiders, we researched and wrote *The Selling of the Green* to balance the scales. This is not the world according to Celtic press releases and NBA video highlights. Auerbach, no genius or philanthropist, is demystified. The outsiders speak, they make charges, they are given their full say. The humiliated opponents, the alienated former Celtics, Boston's ignored black community are offered a leading voice, a forum. Events unfold from their perspective, not from Auerbach's or Volk's. Naturally, we have interviewed Celtic officials too. But this time, they are the ones on the defensive. Their version of history is not necessarily accepted as fact.

Finding the dissidents was not a problem. Jerome Stanley, the agent for current Celtic stars Shaw and Lewis, was in Los Angeles, glorying in his triumphs over Volk and Cohen. Once Lewis had signed his new contract and Shaw had finally agreed to play in Boston, Stanley wanted to set the record straight about his own disdain for much of the old-guard hierarchy. "Just don't make me sound bitter, because I'm not," Stanley said. "I won."

We went to Rome to speak with Il Messaggero officials, and found them extremely hospitable when they discovered the visiting reporters were from New York, not Boston. Former Syracuse Nationals players, now spread across the country, couldn't wait to discuss the arrogance of the Celtic organization. "Call me back in a few days," Dolph Schayes said, and this was typical. "I might think of something else." Paul Seymour said, "Let me have your number. I'll go into my closet and get back to you."

Henderson, Maxwell, White, and McAdoo, four black former Celtics, were all anxious to reveal the biased administrative and economic practices of the Celtics that damaged their careers and reputations. In Boston's black community, leaders, average citizens, and a former gang member explained how they felt detached from and abandoned by the Celtics. Even franchise insiders—like former owners Harry Mangurian and Irv Levin, coach Bill Fitch, and current vice president of community affairs Ken Hudson—had surprising things to say about the sometimes outlandish workings of their organization.

The result might be some sort of bible for Celtic haters everywhere, or *Satanic Verses* for the Boston Garden faithful. Neither is our intent. Our own basketball loyalties are balanced enough. One of the authors, Harvey Araton, was a Celtic fan from childhood. The other, Filip Bondy, cheered for the Syracuse Nationals. As reporters who have covered the NBA since 1979, we both fell in love with the sport long ago. We both wait anxiously for opening night each season at Madison Square Garden, for the Celtics' first visit to New York. We admire the Celtics' classic, selfless playing style; Bird's no-look pass and a pump fake from Robert Parish. We have always appreciated the depth of character displayed by the great, enduring Celtics stars, from Bob Cousy to Bill Russell to Dennis Johnson.

We still believe that the NBA, warts and all, is the most progressive and humanistic of the four major American professional sports leagues; that David Stern is the most open-minded commissioner of a closed-minded lot. There are no helmets obscuring the players in the NBA, no fences or Plexiglas between participant and fan. The players are some of the most spontaneous, open, and intelligent athletes in our country. From a reporter's vantage point, pro basketball is the most compelling competition of all. Sitting courtside, hearing the squeaks of sneaker soles on hardcourt and the dissing between rival players, a sportswriter experiences the event in a fashion that can never be realized in pro football. For us, eluding a player diving out of bounds for a loose ball is infinitely preferable to sipping Cokes and watching instant replays in the sterile environs of a glassed-in football press room.

Unfortunately, the NBA's runaway success in the eighties and nineties has brought with it a slow erosion of values—seen most clearly in the behavior of the league's original and showcase team, the Celtics. Since 1946, when owner Walter Brown first pieced together a last-place club with string and glue, this team has gone from $10,000 in operating expenses to more than $30 million in revenues. The Celtics were once members of an eight-team league with no member franchise more distant than St. Louis. Today, they are at cold war with Il Messaggero in Italy and they own international licensing rights in Japan.

As the Celtics exerted their manifest destiny, they often treated players as shop workers or turncoats. They molded their racial composition to whatever the market would bear. They did what they wanted, because there was nobody to stop them.

Our book ignores the championship banners and listens to those with untold stories to tell. In the process, we hope it demystifies the Celtic Mystique, and gets down to the business at hand: the Boston Celtics Limited Partnership.

Chapter 1

Romans and Vandals

FOR a few days in August 1990, it was all falling apart for the Boston Celtics. Red Auerbach figured it was a profiteering, international conspiracy; some secret, sinister alliance between an ambitious Italian team and an upstart African-American agent.

Il Messaggero, the Rome team that stole starting point guard Brian Shaw from Boston a year earlier, had just stolen Celtic draft pick Dino Radja, signing the nimble six-eleven Yugoslav forward to an outrageous $3 million per year contract. Shaw was still stubbornly dreaming about Italy, refusing to obey a court order and don the green uniform once worn by Bill Sharman and Bob Cousy. And incredibly, Reggie Lewis, the fourth-year swingman and first-year ingrate, was talking about leaving the Celtics if they did not demonstrate the proper contractual appreciation.

By now Auerbach had traced his problems—and half the problems of the world—to one mastermind: Jerome Stanley. Stanley was everything Auerbach mistrusted. He was young; he was an agent; he moved too easily in a hip, black world; he negotiated with rich Italians; and he didn't care a bit about Celtic Pride. This slick inner-city creation was suddenly the official representative of Reggie Lewis, an explosive scorer, and for Shaw, a well-rounded playmaker and rugged defender. There was paranoid talk, too, that Stanley might land the Celtics' first-round pick Dee Brown, the third young buck in Boston's projected three-guard rotation. "Here is a guy who has never done one contract," Auerbach protested to his favorite media outlet, Will McDonough of the *Boston Globe*. "I mean, what can this guy tell them, or promise them he can do compared to some of the top agents in the game? What does he have, a spell over these guys or something?"

What could be worse? Nothing. Nobody. Stanley was a nightmare for legendary president Auerbach, for owner Don Gaston, for new CEO Dave Gavitt, for general manager Jan Volk, for vice chairman Alan Cohen, for the Celtics' entire white hierarchy. Stanley thrived on the antagonism. The agent remembered every slight, every hand not shaken, every eye contact averted. There had been a Christmas dinner with the Boston brass in 1989, when Stanley was still an aide to agent Leonard Armato, a slick, handsome man with international connections. "It was like Cohen had a tough time eating at the same table with me," Stanley said. "He wouldn't shake hands with me. He couldn't relate. He's some pandering sixty-two-year-old Jewish, Gulf + Western tax attorney. I'm some LA-assed black dude smiling at him. I had a difficult time engaging with him."

To Stanley, Auerbach was just a distant figurehead, even more remote than Cohen. "He's white, he smokes cigars, he's supposed to represent some kind of intelligence." Stanley, this thirtyish graduate from USC law school, this escapee from south central Los Angeles, actually sat before the great Celtic heads of state in Boston, and with the posturing of Khruschev at the UN, said directly to them, "I will put you in the lottery." Stanley was all about the future, a crazy uncertain future, and the Celtics were not comfortable with that idea. Auerbach would not even speak with the man.

The Celtics had done their best to avoid this situation, to seize control of their own destiny in a most backhanded fashion. In late January 1990, Volk embarked on a hush-hush mission to Italy to steal Shaw from his Roman holiday, from paradise. Volk had told nobody in the media, almost nobody in Italy. He had not informed Il Messaggero of his itinerary. The Italian League team was midway through its regular season, starting its drive for the playoffs. This was a surging club, challenging perennial powers in Milan and Bologna. Shaw was its star, its most popular and valuable player. Teammate Danny Ferry, the cleancut Duke kid, was more renowned in the United States as a Final Four participant. But here in Rome, Shaw was emperor.

Originally, Shaw had problems adjusting. He complained of unfair pressure from the local media. He even argued that local statisticians were favoring teammate Ferry, not crediting Shaw with all his assists and rebounds. Shaw did not yet understand that statistics in Italy were a very inexact science and that few fans were sophisticated enough to care about anything beyond points and the final score.

Shaw averaged 25 points, 9.1 rebounds, 2.7 steals per game during his season in Italy. More important, he had flair, a dangerous waist-high dribble, and emotion. "He was more loved than Ferry," said Gianluca Luceri, the public relations director at Il Messaggero, a robust man whose tastes run to LaCoste shirts and form-fitting slacks. "The Roman public is 'hot.' Brian was more hot than Ferry. He understood the character of the Romans. Danny is well-educated, but he is more closed."

Slowly, Italy grew on Shaw. He lived luxuriously in a three-bedroom apartment on Piazza Barberini off Via Veneto, a few blocks from the flowing Spanish Steps. "The apartment building was very old on the outside, but great on the inside," said Shaw, no architectural historian. He had a $900,000 contract, maid service, a tutor in Italian, a BMW M3. There were only twenty of those cars in all of Europe, and Shaw would unknowingly, conspicuously drive his rare auto through forbidden roads past ancient ruins where Antony once praised Caesar. Police left Shaw alone. They mailed any speeding tickets directly to Il Messaggero. Everything was taken care of.

Shaw's twenty-one-year-old girlfriend, Lory Butler, an art student, had come to Europe with him and was enamored of the glories of Rome. On just her second day in Italy, she had charmed a
guard at the Galleria Borghese and had been invited to visit a floor
filled with art treasures normally closed to the public. The artistic
and athletic worlds were at the beck and call of this attractive
celebrity couple, even in a country as historically pigment conscious
and divided as Italy. Life was very nearly idyllic here for Shaw, and
certainly convenient. When he traveled to the Il Messaggero practice center, Shaw drove along suburban Via Salaria to Settebagni,
about thirteen miles from downtown. The verdant Centro Sportivo,
part of the Banco Roma Sports Club, included a modern basketball
court in an atrium setting. When Shaw first practiced there, the center had no weight equipment. Shaw and Ferry mentioned the problem, and suddenly there was a room dedicated just to this purpose.
Anything the young Americans wanted, they got.

There were one or two games per week, not three or four. The
team was truly a family, unlike most American pro sports clubs.
Instead of calling their team an "organization" or "franchise," players and officials in Italy use a word that means "society."

On a typical NBA road trip, a team's few white players might
head in one direction for some serious drinking. Some of the black
players might divide into groups of two or three and spend time at
the hotel bar. There are exceptions, odd couples like Chris Mullin
and Manute Bol. But even among relatively enlightened NBA player reps, there are often awkward barriers between races. At a 1986
player rep meeting in Maui, there was an ugly scene after the wife
of Golden State forward Purvis Short stumbled on a party attended
only by the white player reps and their families.

Relations on the Il Messaggero team were very different. The
players would mix, go out for dinner together on the road. During
home stands, they would bring their wives and girlfriends to club-
sponsored functions. Everybody watched out for Shaw and Ferry.
"We were in a different country, and we didn't have a clue," Shaw

said. "In the NBA, they'd just leave you on your own and say every-thing was your responsibility."

Shaw and Rome were becoming a better fit, but he was still an American. On some lonesome nights without a game in town, he longed to strut his evolving skills before friends and critics back in the States. Over Christmas, he had gone home with Butler and watched the Celtics beat the Clippers by a point at the Los Angeles Sports Arena. He'd wondered aloud what it would be like to play again for Boston. "Let's face it," he said at the time. "Throwing the ball inside to Marco Ricci isn't the same as throwing it in to Robert Parish or Kevin McHale." Shaw was ripe for a little seduction. The Celtics pounced on him, offered a three-year, $3.1 million pact. Armato suggested a meeting to discuss the contract, but Shaw pulled out of the deal, canceled the negotiating session.

An ugly intramural battle took place back in Los Angeles between Stanley and Armato, who believed his aide was "doing things to undermine my relationship with my clients." Stanley and Armato parted ways. Five days later, Shaw left Armato. Three law-suits would follow between these two agents before matters were settled in April 1991. "Armato hates me because Brian fired him," Stanley said. Clearly, Stanley already was wielding a good deal of influence over Shaw. He visited him in Italy, tried to make him understand his great marketability.

Shaw had reason to want more money from his dealings with the Celtics. He had received the league minimum, $75,000, his first sea-son, as the underrated twenty-fourth draft pick out of California–Santa Barbara. Armato had allowed the Celtics to pull the old salary cap trick. In this sleight-of-hand, Volk informs the agent that no salary slots are available. More militant representatives do not put up with this, insisting on a player transaction that will free a more lucrative slot.

Cohen phoned Shaw several times in Rome during the weeks leading up to Volk's trip, detailing terms of a five-year, $6.65 million offer that began with the playoffs at the end of the NBA's 1990 season and included a $450,000 signing bonus. This complex contract was laid out, long distance, into the innocent ear of a slightly homesick Shaw. "It was already agreed to when I went over there," Volk said.

Volk arrived in Rome, and proceeded to Shaw's apartment on the night of January 22, 1990. Shaw had no agent at the time, a brief window of opportunity that the Celtics realized would close shortly. Less than a month earlier, he had come to an informal agreement with Stanley that hadn't been finalized. Shaw was an unrepresented player, a throwback to the days when Auerbach could simply inform a player what he would be earning during the next season.

"Brian was twenty-three years old and thought he had a handle on business," Stanley said. "He didn't know the salary cap or anything like that." Among the things Shaw did not understand was this: If he stayed in Rome and finished his two-year contract with Il Messaggero, he would return to the NBA an unrestricted free agent. He could command a tremendous salary, perhaps as much as $2 million to $3 million per season. Shaw hadn't even finished the first season on his two-year deal with Il Messaggero. But Volk knew there was a loophole, an escape clause that would allow Shaw to break the Italian League contract between June 20 and July 20. The two men talked for three hours that January night, only a little bit of that time about the terms of the contract. Shaw was intoxicated by Volk's attention—and by the money. He was earning $900,000 with Il Messaggero, but this new offer was even bigger. In the back of Volk's rented limo, in the late-night hours of January 23, the two men spoke about how Shaw would revitalize the Celtics. Then Shaw signed the contract. The limo hurried to the U.S. Embassy so that Volk could have the document notarized before anybody's mind was changed. The deed, incredibly dirty by NBA standards, was done. Volk, emissary of Celtic management, secret agent, returned home to announce to Cohen his triumph over an unrepresented player. The point man had signed his point guard.

"Brian left $3 to $5 million on the table," said Armato, who remained convinced that Stanley advised Shaw to sign just to avoid paying the upcoming agent's commission on his Il Messaggero pact. "Brian didn't utilize or understand his leverage."

"It was no way to run a business," Stanley said. Normally in the NBA, there is a very different rhythm to this sort of negotiating dance. A player is signed only after months of squabbling between agent and team. Details like deferred payments and bonuses are hammered out by experts. When the signing takes place, a press conference is held and the happy player poses before the home team logo.

The rules were changed here. Even Volk agreed it was an unorthodox way to operate. He kept the contract a corporate secret for a month, fearing countermeasures by Il Messaggero. "I think some of the things that we're doing now are bizarre, without any comparisons," he said later. "I had to go to Drnis, Yugoslavia, to sign Stojan Vrankovic. It's frustrating [losing players to teams in Europe]. And yet the opportunity and the possibilities are there to the extent that it makes dealing with that frustration also worthwhile. You try to do things within the framework of the rules and laws as we understood them." Volk was understanding the laws better now, learning how to stretch them in the international theater.

For a few weeks, Shaw was quite pleased with his new contract. It would make him a rich man, and he would be playing again with the best athletes in the world. In a radio interview from Rome, Shaw said he was "relieved" at the signing, that it was "a load off my shoulders." Stanley, too, figured it was a done deal, and said nothing to Shaw about his own reservations, about the lost opportunity at free agency. Eventually, however, Shaw came to believe that he'd been had.

As the Italian League season reached its climax, Shaw's attachment to Rome and to Il Messaggero grew stronger. Butler coaxed him to stay. She wanted to live in Rome or move back to Los Angeles, where their families still resided. It would have to be one or the other if he wanted her to stay with him. He grew even closer to Dr.

Carlo Sama, charismatic president of Il Messaggero and an influential man in Gruppo Ferruzzi, the second most powerful corporate group in Italy behind Fiat. Shaw had an opportunity to join Ferruzzi in some capacity if he stayed, and soon Sama was talking about a renegotiated $2 million contract if he signed on for another season. Shaw's father, Charles, had become a close friend of Sama. He counseled his son to stay put. It would mean millions of dollars to him.

After Il Messaggero was eliminated in the quarterfinals of the playoffs by Scavolini-Pesaro, the future champions, Sama invited all the players and staff to his luxurious house for an informal ceremony. Sama gave special thanks to Shaw, who had scored 46 points in the finale, and offered his departing point guard a silver plaque in appreciation of his efforts. As Shaw spoke to the gathering, he began to cry. "I looked at Brian's eyes, and there was great commotion there," said Luceri. And that is when Shaw told everybody that he would be back. He did not know when, or how. But he would return to finish the job he'd started at Il Messaggero.

Shaw officially hired Stanley as his agent, told him he wanted to stay in Rome. Stanley sent a letter to the Celtics informing them of his client's intent. The letter was ignored. In early March, Shaw and Stanley headed to the NBA commissioner's office in New York for arbitration. They brought a limited wardrobe, planning a short stay. The Celtics postponed the hearing, an act of questionable ethics but unquestionable efficacy. Shaw headed back to Rome feeling even more alienated from the NBA team that held his rights. After a hearing on June 13–14 that Shaw did not attend, arbitrator Daniel Collins ordered the player to sever his ties with Il Messaggero.

When Shaw finally arrived in Boston that June, he panicked. "He had a total vision," Luceri said. "He saw that the team was rebuilding, that this was not a good enough team for what Boston demanded. There was none of the Celtic Pride. He wanted to come back to Il Messaggero." He did not want to be here in Boston. He decided he would not report to the team. Butler, as promised, did not want to go anywhere near here. She eventually moved to New York City and took her art studies to Pratt Institute. The Celtics were a mess on the court, were reorganizing the front office, and as yet showed no sign of their modest 1990–91 revival. Shaw feared reprisals from the fans for his decision to leave Boston a year earlier. Players were not supposed to say no to the Celtics, even if it meant losing millions of dollars. That tenet was enforced by Auerbach, by the media. In the *Globe* on June 22, Bob Ryan wrote, "I think he [Shaw] is not as tightly wrapped as we all once thought and am starting to think it's a good thing he won't be back. The Celtics never had this trouble with Sam Jones." Shaw missed Italy.

The Celtics, turning up the heat like it was an afternoon playoff game at Boston Garden, next went to a federal judge in Boston, U.S. District Judge A. David Mazzone. "A homer," Stanley would call him. Shaw filed a thirteen-page affidavit with the court, explaining how he'd been tricked into signing by Cohen and Volk. He wanted to return his $450,000 signing bonus and be finished with Boston. "I recognized that my naivete and weakened emotional state and lack of independent counsel or an agent caused me to sign the Celtic contract," he wrote in the affidavit. Mazzone didn't buy it, finding that "there is a written signature on that contract which is clean and unambiguous."

An appeals court, and basketball's international ruling body, FIBA, all ruled against Shaw. The NBA, always quick to back the Celtics in a pinch, threatened punitive action of its own. The contract with Il Messaggero had been signed in Virginia, and somehow this made it more vulnerable to U.S. law. Starting July 19, Mazzone began fining Shaw $5,000 for every day he did not break his contract with Il Messaggero and honor the deal he had signed with the Celtics half a year into his Il Messaggero pact. The dollar amount of the fine actually was suggested by Celtic attorney Neil Jacobs and was based on a formula that took Shaw's signing bonus and salary at Il Messaggero into account. It was a strange ruling, backing the legality of a second contract over a preceding one, but this was Boston, and Stanley understood the game. He wasn't flustered.

"The $5,000 fine was irrelevant," Stanley said. "Any idiot could figure where the deep pockets were." They were back in Italy, in the tailored pants of Sama and Il Messaggero. The club was more than willing to pay the fines as long as there was any hope of getting back its top player. The Italian Basketball Federation backed Il Messaggero, and Enzo DiChiara, counselor for the Ferruzzi Group, fought back for a while. "This is like a personal war of Mr. Cohen's to obligate a person to play for him," DiChiara said at the time. "The more Brian sees of what is going on, the more he is resolved not to go to Boston."

After a few weeks of hiding out on the pretext of a long-scheduled Alaskan fishing expedition, Shaw and Stanley met with the Italians and finally decided their mutual wish to remain together was fruitless. It had been ruined by the Celtics and the NBA. Commissioner David Stern and league counsel Gary Bettman weren't going to let them out of the Faustian pact with Volk. The league also wouldn't allow Stanley to talk trade with another NBA team. "Stern wanted to put this maverick Italian team in its place," Stanley said.

On July 26, Shaw gave up his dream. He severed his ties with Il Messaggero. But he still wasn't going to report to the Celtics. At a meeting in the Grand Hyatt in New York, with Celtics senior executive vice president Dave Gavitt and new head coach Chris Ford, Shaw and Stanley pulled another little surprise. "They [Gavitt and Ford] expected everything to go smooth and we told them, 'Trade us,'" Stanley said, not disguising his satisfaction. "They had kept insulting Brian's intelligence. They had guys talking to Brian, they had a black guy call that Brian likes. That's why this thing warms the cockles of my heart. They had such disdain for me. The attitude was, 'We're white, we're the Celtics. We're going to kick your ass.'"

While the Celtics were trying to steal beloved Brian Shaw, Il Messaggero was hatching a revenge plot against its powerful archrivals across the Atlantic. Appropriately, it had enlisted the aid of Marc Fleisher, son of the late Larry Fleisher, former Players Association head and an old Celtic nemesis. Decades earlier, Larry Fleisher had fought Auerbach for the basic right to represent NBA players as an agent. Now, in April 1990, Marc Fleisher had taken over as the agent for Dino Radja from a little-known rep from Baton Rouge, Louisiana, named Garth Ridge. Marc Fleisher met Radja at the International Championships and saw copies of two contracts he had signed with the Celtics. The first was a one-year deal Radja received as a second-round draft choice in 1989, worth $425,000. The second had come after the Celtics successfully pirated, warred, and finally bargained with another international rival, Jugoplastika of Yugoslavia, over the rights to Radja. The Celtics had added a second year to Radja's contract at $375,000 and a third year at $450,000.

Marc Fleisher, a quick learner trained by his ingenious father, recognized that this second contract negotiated by Ridge was illegal. It was not the first time the Celtics had erred or stretched the rules during forty-five years of contract maneuverings, but they would pay dearly for this move. The pact violated the Collective Bargaining Agreement provision from November 1988 that stated a contract could not be renegotiated during its first year. That provision, ironically, had been pushed by the owners to discourage hot, successful rookies from seeking immediate compensation. When Radja signed this second deal, league attorneys assured Volk that nobody would raise objections, so that the overseas transaction would be facilitated. The deal was accepted by Jugoplastika. But then Fleisher spotted an opening.

"I was down in the Orlando Classic and I saw Jan Volk, and I told him, 'You screwed up,'" Fleisher said. "He denied it. The Celtics were convinced they would win the case, so there was no settlement. The league had backed them up, and they were overconfident."

There was another reason for Volk's stubborn, foolhardy stance on Radja. Volk's career was at stake. Like many people in the Celtic "family," the ambitious Volk owed his professional standing entirely to Auerbach. Auerbach always wanted it this way, with his players and his underlings. It was like this with K.C. Jones, Satch Sanders, Chris Ford. The position of sole benefactor ensured Auerbach loyalty, gave him real power over people. Auerbach never enjoyed trading for a player who already had made his reputation elsewhere— Auerbach made just one major deal, Mel Counts for Bailey Howell, in the thirteen years that Bill Russell played in Boston—and he likewise tried to groom people from within the organization for top posts. Family friends were the most dependable loyalists of all.

Tod Rosensweig, vice president of marketing and communications, had family connections. Volk, the Celtic GM, was another classic example of patronage. He grew up in Newton, Massachusetts, and spent summers working at his father's summer camp in Marshfield. His dad, Jerry, gave Auerbach quite a deal on facilities for the Celtic rookie camp, which was held there for over twenty years. Jan Volk's brother, Mark, became a trainer with the Celtics. Jan earned a law degree from Columbia University in 1971, then accepted a proposal by Auerbach to work his way up through the Celtics organization, starting as director of ticket sales. Bright in a narrow business sense, persistent but not particularly imaginative, Volk was the perfect pupil for Auerbach. He would not overstep his expanding bounds. Volk was being groomed to assume power over all player personnel matters.

These plans started going awry in 1986 with the death of Len Bias, and then Volk proved very shortsighted in his dealings with the overseas market. He botched the Shaw matter in 1989, allowing the player to go to Il Messaggero. Back then, informed that Shaw was considering Italy as an alternative to Boston, Volk arrogantly told Armato, "Tell Brian to brush up on his Italian." A reasonable offer of $750,000 would have kept Shaw in Boston and avoided all the international intrigue. Instead, Volk and Cohen would not climb above $400,000. "It was a little error in judgment," said Armato, who retained amicable relations with the Celtic organization. "They misread things, but it was nothing personal. Everybody makes a mistake. Before, they were a bit paternalistic in view."

Now, in the summer of 1990, Shaw's intentions were still uncertain. Dave Gavitt, senior executive vice president, was assuming power in Boston, and Volk was embarrassed. Once a golden boy in the organization, Volk, as well as the Celtics, was in danger of losing another player, Radja. The Celtics weren't about to go down without a loud legal struggle.

They went down, nevertheless. Fleisher won the Radja arbitration before a special master on July 12, 1990. All contracts were voided. The Celtics merely retained Radja's draft rights. Fleisher met with Volk and Gavitt, an old family friend, to possibly work out a new contract. Both parties made sincere efforts, but the Celtics wouldn't budge above $900,000. The salary cap stood in the way. Meanwhile, Real Madrid and Barcelona of the Spanish League and Verona, Milan, and Il Messaggero of the Italian League started the international bidding at $1 million. Radja was gone soon enough, and the Celtics, a first-round playoff victim to the New York Knicks the previous April, were plummeting in August. "How could he turn down $3 million?" Volk said. "Were they getting even for Shaw? Probably."

Between hearing dates before Mazzone for Brian Shaw, Jerome Stanley was approached by Donna Harris, the fiancée of Reggie Lewis. Harris told Stanley that Lewis wanted to interview him, possibly to hire him as his representative. Lewis, a friend of Shaw's, was beginning the final, $400,000 season on his contract. He would become a restricted free agent in June 1991, meaning he could sign an offer sheet with another NBA team that the Celtics would have to match. He could also negotiate with a team in Italy, which the Celtics now had to respect as a legitimate threat. Harris wasn't sure that Lewis's current representative at ProServ, David Falk, was being firm enough, or that he was willing to use the overseas option as a strong trump card. Stanley flew out to Boston and met with the couple. He laid out a battle plan.

"I told them things are going to get hot. There's going to be ther-monuclear warfare," Stanley said. "When that happens, they could fire me, or stay strong, and we break the bank." Lewis and Harris were impressed. At the end of the Celtic summer league season, Lewis told ProServ and Falk—the fast-lane, mainstream representa-tive for both Michael Jordan and Patrick Ewing—that he had found a new agent. It was Stanley, the man of Auerbach's and Volk's night-mares.

"It comes over the fax machine in the Celtic office that I'm Reg-gie's agent, and they had diarrhea," Stanley said. "Gavitt's not there. They give the fax to Volk. It's like a kick in the stomach. Here's their other set of young legs, and this know-nothing shyster, me, I've got them both, Reggie and Brian."

Stanley called the *Globe* and informed a couple of sportswriters that he was now Lewis's agent and that there was really no such thing as a restricted free agent in the expansive global market of the nineties. Lewis, according to Stanley, was an unrestricted free agent in the international marketplace. He was going places. Italy, and Il Messaggero, was just a twelve-digit phone call away. The *Globe* reported this and did a balanced profile of Stanley that included analysis by friends and enemies. Auerbach, who would never meet or talk with Stanley during any negotiations for either Shaw or Lewis, launched a public relations offensive of his own. In Will McDonough's column, Auerbach charged that Stanley was luring players to Italy out of self-interest: "In the NBA, the most an agent can get out of a player's contract is 4 percent," Auerbach said. "Overseas, the agent can pick up 10 percent right off the top for himself…. You think these guys [players] would be smart enough to see through something like that." Auerbach was flirting with slander here, but he and the Celtics persisted. They threatened to file a decertification suit against Stanley, claiming that he encouraged a player, Shaw, to breach his contract. "Shaw and Lewis were the key to their decade, and they were desperate," Stanley said. "Guys like Volk and Auerbach were trying everything. But I really believe Gavitt had no control over the stick at this point."

It was extremely difficult for a qualified black agent like Stanley to enlist big-name sports clients, to gain the trust of black or white players. Black players were afraid that white club officials wouldn't respect a black representative. This fear was based on reality, not paranoia. Fred Slaughter, one of the very few well-established black agents, still bristles when he thinks about the patronizing treatment he received from Bob Ferry, former Washington Bullets GM and later an NBC commentator. "When I was negotiating a three-year deal for John Williams," Slaughter said, "he sat there and said, 'I don't think you understand. One plus two equals three, plus four equals seven.'" Slaughter didn't have such problems with the Celtics, and is quite proud of that fact. "My credentials and my size are such that some people won't fuck with me," Slaughter said. "I went to Columbia Law School, like Jan Volk. Now, Jerome Stanley, he's smaller, he's just getting into the business, and where'd he go to law school? USC?"

Stanley, drilling Lewis on what lay ahead, prepared his client for all the psychological minefields. He warned him that the Celtics would have one of his former college coaches and a black player call, both encouraging Lewis to sign quickly. Soon, the coach phoned. Then, M. L. Carr phoned. "Every time they pushed a button I had predicted, the bond between Reggie and me grew stronger," Stanley said. The Celtics were swinging wildly now, even phoning Il Messaggero to threaten a suit over Lewis. An attorney in Rome called Stanley to tell him about this, and they both had a good laugh. Lewis wasn't going anywhere. Lewis knew it. Stanley knew it. But the Celtics, burned by Shaw and Radja, were wary. Lewis sat tight in Baltimore for a week as the local media kept the issue alive. Gavitt, Volk, and Auerbach wondered what more could go wrong, what irreplaceable player would steal off next with Stanley to the hated Il Messaggero.

If this was war between the Boston Celtics and Il Messaggero, then nobody in Italy quite understood how it had begun. The Celtics, after all, were everybody's heroes, everybody's idea of big-time

American basketball at its very best. Names like Larry Bird and Kevin McHale were magical there, sprinkled generously about the pages of the national sports daily, *La Gazzetta dello Sport*. The country could not hear enough news about the NBA. In the past decade, the popularity of basketball in Italy had exceeded that of any sport except soccer. Each professional team was permitted two foreigners, usually Americans, and these imports were the focus of great expectation and attention. If the basketball refugees proved successful, as Bob McAdoo and Michael Ray Richardson had, they were rewarded with the stature of national heroes.

Richardson, banished by the NBA for drug use and eventually banished by Bologna for the same reason, had emerged by 1990 as the third most recognizable sports hero in Italy, behind only Argentinian soccer import Diego Maradona and World Cup hero Toto Schillaci. On the European TV sports channel, it was difficult to avoid seeing Richardson on almost a biweekly basis being hoisted onto the shoulders of his Bologna teammates after yet another buzzer-beating 3-point basket. The easy pace of the Italian League schedule and the lack of dominant, physical big men stretched the careers of many American players. Even Kareem Abdul-Jabbar seriously considered a last fling in Italy, but feared he would lose his luster fast if he failed to average 20 points and 10 rebounds a game.

Jabbar shouldn't have worried. If Romans eyed Neapolitans here with contempt, if light-skinned northerners sneered at dark-skinned southerners, they still respected the rich, successful American basketball hero of any color. This sport remained a novelty. Its graceful participants were a marvel. The same was not necessarily true for soccer players from other countries, even stars. Diego Maradona, the fireplug Argentine soccer star, was cruelly derided by fans outside his pro team's home of Naples, called "a monkey" and other slurs. During the 1990 World Cup, midway through a television variety special from Florence, a comedian wondered how Italy's national soccer hero Schillaci, a tanned Sicilian, might do in a possible match against Cameroon, the surprising African side. "Of course," the comedian joked, "he could play for either team." The racial joke was accepted, even applauded, by an appreciative audience. But again, this was soccer, not basketball. Black NBA stars were welcomed here, for the time being, with great hospitality. A few, like Bernard King, vacationed regularly in Italy even if they still played in America.

While all the Italian League teams chased foreign talent to fill their two openings, only Il Messaggero hunted for truly big game: young NBA players just starting their lucrative careers, seeking giant contractual options. Only Il Messaggero, a newspaper corporation with the backing of the Gruppo Ferruzzi, had that kind of money. When Armato first contacted Il Messaggero about Shaw in 1989, the Italian team simply assumed the Celtics were not very interested in the player. If they had been, certainly they would have offered Shaw a more reasonable contract. Then, as the negotiations with Il Messaggero became more serious and more tangled, Sama and other Ferruzzi officials became insulted. They realized that the Celtics were, in fact, very interested in Shaw. They also understood that the Celtics didn't view Il Messaggero as a serious competitor in the bidding. "Messaggero for the Celtics is the enemy, but only because they didn't think to find an enemy here," Gianluca Luceri said.

By the time they were negotiating with Marc Fleisher for Radja, Il Messaggero representatives were ready for a prolonged, expensive fight—one they still wished to avert, if possible. Sama asked Fleisher to set up a dinner meeting with Gavitt, a peace offering. But it never came about. "Their attitude wasn't 'Let's screw the Celtics twice,'" Fleisher said. "But at times, Messaggero officials were very anti-Celtic. Sama said to me, 'What the Celtics are doing is wrong.' Il Messaggero is a little brash, they're the new kid on the block. It bothered Gruppo Ferruzzi, one of the two most powerful companies in Italy, that the Celtics thought they were better than them."

Team officials took particular pride in the team's elite financial status, which placed Il Messaggero alone among Italian League clubs. They spoke often, with pride, about a new computerized scoreboard that was in the works for the arena, Il Paleur, in 1991. When Fleisher was talking contract with Il Messaggero officials, the first offer on the table was a nine-year deal. Fleisher said he'd accept fewer years. He said Radja even would be willing to sign a one-year contract, but that such a pact would necessarily require a great deal of money up front. Offhandedly, Fleisher commented that nobody, not even Il Messaggero, had enough money to complete such a contract. "It was like I really insulted them," Fleisher said. "All of them stood up together and said, 'Yes, we do.'"

To back up this claim, Sama immediately gave Fleisher a high-six-figure legal fund with which to wage judicial war against the Celtics. Weary of their skirmishes with Boston, Il Messaggero officials were not willing to throw themselves into the middle of another fray. They would not file any lawsuits or legal appeals. But they could throw money at the problem in America, tell Fleisher to take care of the dirty work. As it turned out, there really wasn't much need for it. Once the Celtics lost their arbitration over Radja's contract before the special master, much of the air went out of the franchise's bloated balloon. Gavitt, wisely, retrenched and focused on Stanley and the two wayward guards.

"I think the Celtics had a certain arrogance, and that bit 'em on the butt," Marc Fleisher said. "When the Celtics lost arbitration, that arrogance left, but it had been there for a long time. I remember my father was always going around saying what nonsense that attitude was."

That attitude had started with a cigar in the mouth of Red Auerbach, and was born in a building on Causeway Street.

Chapter 2

Seeing Red

T HERE always is something alluring about a trip to the old Boston Garden, with its sixteen championship banners dead-still overhead and its cracked parquet floor even deader below. The Garden was built to last in 1928, brick by brick and beam by beam, before anybody had heard of sky boxes or basketball in the middle of June.

Time, and change, were never welcome visitors here alongside the elevated tracks on Causeway Street. The colors inside this old movie set are still yellow, brown, and green—earth tones, with no pretentious purple or pastel frills. The early evening activities are ritual. Ron Harry stands on a wooden platform atop the promenade, bangs down on the aging Kimball organ to get the reluctant instrument started. "Got to get a new organ," Harry says. "I have to slam it to the floor just to get a note out." Harry will put up with this organ, with its sweet screeches, for as long as it takes.

In a catacomb of press rooms, the familiar media faces arrive with their notebooks, cameras, and computers. They are fed greasy food and NBA statistics. Courtside, officials and attendants scurry about. Led by the accommodating and energetic public relations director, Jeff Twiss, these aides serve deadline-weary beat reporters with great earnestness.

A few players are on the court shooting baskets two hours before the game. Larry Bird is out there taking erratic bounce passes from some wide-eyed ballboy. Licking his fingers, dodging the fault lines in the court, Bird is knocking down "jump shots" with his toes still touching the floor. He is signing a quick autograph on his way back to the locker room. The warmup suits are old-fashioned, loose-fitting. They have been laundered a few times too often. The fans are starting to arrive. They are checking their programs, and they are pointing down to where Red Auerbach and Ted Kennedy will sit in the loge.

It is a seductive scene, one that has entranced Celtic zealots, chroniclers, and mythmakers for decades. Celtic Pride. The Celtic Mystique. At six-thirty P.M. on a warm weekday night in Boston Garden, an hour before tipoff to a playoff game in June, these phrases seem like more than words and concepts. They are almost palpable in this aging furnace that abuts North Station and bustles with fans commuting from the entire hub region. This is basketball the way it ought to be. No cheerleaders. No searing rock and roll music from a booming public address system. No glitzy actors or actresses in front of pregame TV cameras.

But there is a seamy, claustrophobic backstage at the Garden, far less appealing. It is locker room number seven—the room without enough room. Here is a half-star accommodation for NBA stars, courtesy of Auerbach and the Celtics. Here is where visiting players gather, cram together, and stare at ... what?

"This room!" Detroit forward Dennis Rodman said as he elbowed open the door to room number seven during the 1991 Eastern Conference semifinals. "Oh, no, not this room!"

Yes, this room. Open the door. Take two steps into a short, narrow corridor. You will pass an old, metal fan sitting against the wall. If you look hard at the corroded grill, you can make out that this is probably a relic from the sixties. This is the beginning—and the end—of the air conditioning.

Turn left. There it is: a dimly lit, poorly ventilated, overheated, sparsely furnished cubicle with all the charm of a truckstop lavatory. Hooks and cubbyholes instead of dressing stalls. Splintered wooden benches. Peeling walls with electrical wires sprouting in many directions. A shabby floor. And for twelve tall, sweaty athletes who have just been bused here from a hotel, the Celtics offer two showers, two sinks, one toilet, and one urinal.

Go ahead. Play ball.

"There are guys doing twenty-five years who would refuse to come in here," Detroit assistant coach Brendan Malone said.

That has always been the idea, of course; the reason that Auerbach and the Boston owners would never refurbish room number seven, never bring it close to NBA standards for a few thousand dollars. The Celtics themselves have a relatively luxurious locker room at home, renovated in the early eighties, equipped with a private training room, wooden stalls, color television and cassette recorder, and stocked refrigerator. Mysteriously, the NBA never forced the Celtics to upgrade the visitors' locker room to be physically safe for fatigued opponents. Mobs of media crammed into this room, a sure fire hazard. Besides embarrassment over such facilities in these boom times, the Celtics and the NBA were one star's crushed foot or aging reporter's heart attack away from a major lawsuit.

Opponents file forlornly into room number seven, endure the awful conditions, then become so furious at Auerbach's arrogance that they lose their concentration along with their hydration. "The advantage is purely psychological," Auerbach insisted. "Our room isn't any cooler."

But it is stifling in room number seven. It is dangerous. Bernard King, star of the Washington Bullets, had an allergic reaction to the mold spores there and nearly died from heart palpitations on a particularly bad night in February 1991. Auerbach's mind game wasn't so funny then.

The Lakers wilted during the steamy finals of 1984. James Worthy remembered that the team had gone out and bought its own giant fans and set them up in the locker room at halftime. They didn't really help. "You saw all the guys huddled together in the middle of the room in front of the fans with wet towels on their heads," Worthy said.

"Sometimes, before a big game, everybody's nerves run a little high," Worthy said. "You've got twelve guys and a lot of coaches who feel a little queasy. And you've only got one toilet in there.

"We just kind of lined up."

Worthy was not blind to the charms of the Garden. In the regular season, he said, it was a setting very different from the big, sterile superstructures in places like Miami and Charlotte. "If you've played basketball for fifteen or twenty years," Worthy said, "you started in a little sweaty gym like Boston Garden. You should be used to this sort of thing. But once you get to the summertime, it's not someplace you want to be."

Former Los Angeles Lakers coach Pat Riley became a bitter man that spring of 1984, later admitting to some Red-induced paranoia. For his own peace of mind, Riley began to study up on the Celts. Not the Boston Celtics. The Celts from Hallstatt, Austria—looters of Rome in 390 B.C. and the first peoples in northern Europe to produce iron and manufacture weaponry. Having studied their culture and social tendencies, Riley decided the Celts "had a very insidious quality, and that they liked strange and hidden places." Places like room number seven.

Visiting teams often try to get practice dates at Boston Garden to learn the dead spots on the parquet—dead spots that Auerbach always insisted did not exist. It isn't easy. During their 1991 first-round playoff series, the Indiana Pacers came into Boston and asked for practice time on a Saturday between games. The floor was down, waiting. The Celtics said forget it. Seven years earlier, Indiana coach George Irvine was tossed off the court (after practice) by a Garden security guard who caught him shooting baskets. "I don't give a damn who you are," the guard had said. "Get off the court." It was all part of the Celtic attitude that started with Auerbach.

Auerbach felt the need to manipulate the sport, embarrass opponents. He could never stop himself. He needed to feel he was doing something clever, home or away, that nobody else could possibly have invented. When the Celtics played the Knicks at Madison Square Garden in the sixties and seventies, Auerbach, then general manager, always arrived with a plan. Visiting teams have the choice of which basket they want to shoot at first, so Auerbach told the Celtics to wait in the locker room and take the court after the Knicks. That way, in Auerbach's ever-whirring mind, he would be able to see which basket the Knick players preferred.

"Red would come out and blow off steam that he wanted to start on the basket that the home team was already shooting on," former Knick Walt Frazier said. "So now the home team had to take its balls and go to the other end of the floor.

"What we did," Frazier said, "was warm up on the basket we didn't want anyway. We did this all the time with them."

And it worked. Auerbach, supposed chessmaster, would order the Knicks to shoot at the very basket they preferred. The Knicks giggled to themselves on the way to two championships.

Long before the days of $45 tickets and major network contracts, the NBA had to cajole fans to enter its arenas at bargain-basement prices. One way the league did this, decades before Larry Bird, was with the Boston Celtics, its main attraction. Just as the Celtics helped to boost TV ratings in the eighties, they were used in the early days to lure fans as part of doubleheaders during the regular season. The Celtics had trouble drawing at home—they averaged just 6,852 in 1961–62, in the midst of their championship string—but they were a growing attraction on the road. And no matter which game they were scheduled to play, opener or nightcap, the Celtics were the marquee attraction.

In the fifties and sixties, every NBA team wanted a piece of the Celtics. Players were sick of Auerbach's victory cigar, tired of what many of them described as "the treatment." The Celtic organization oozed arrogance. Auerbach was perceived as the walking embodiment of the poor sportsman.

Outsiders conceded he had the best players. They argued any coach might have won with them. Yet it seemed Auerbach was obsessed even back then with gaining a psychological edge over his opponents, then humiliating them.

On their first road trip to San Francisco, after the Warriors had moved from Philadelphia to San Francisco, the Celtics were scheduled to practice on Lincoln's Birthday in the same arena where the Warriors trained. The Warriors showed up for their practice, which was to be an intense warmup for the hated Boston invaders. There, already, were the Celtics. They were supposed to be practicing. Instead, with Auerbach's blessing, the players were messing around, laughing and lounging.

"You know, Sam Jones and John Havlicek and a couple of guys were playing two-on-two down here," said Al Attles, former Golden State Warrior forward and later their vice president. "K. C. Jones was sitting around over there. Tommy Heinsohn was over there doing something else. You're playing them. You have to practice, and they're saying, 'We don't have to. We don't need what is considered a regular practice. You guys have to do the normal things.'"

Teams like the Warriors could hope to beat the Celtics once in a while, taking some satisfaction in an Auerbach defeat. But there were four or five patsies that could only dream about staying close with mighty Boston for a quarter or two. To these traditional losers, Auerbach was a particularly graceless winner. To the Cincinnati Royals, to the Detroit Pistons, the cigar in the mouth was a bimonthly kick in the pants. A trip to Boston meant certain defeat. It meant hot air blowing on you from the vent in the visitors' locker room, and maybe a physical beating, too, by one of Auerbach's toughs—perhaps Jim Loscutoff or Bob Harris. The NBA certainly didn't seem to care. The Boston fans were even more unruly then than they are today. "They'd come in with drink," Oscar Robertson said. "They were hurling every insult you ever heard."

There was little hope for revenge. Robertson's Royals won only nineteen games in 1960, only one against the Celtics in nine meetings. "We couldn't even say the Celtics were rivals," Robertson said. "When you win just nineteen games, nobody is your rival." One time, Royal officials decided they'd had enough of Auerbach and his act. When the Celtics came to Cincinnati, five thousand cigars were distributed to the crowd. Everybody waited, hoped for a victory and a good smoke. In the Celtic locker room before the game, Auerbach caught wind of the plans and became furious. He gave a pep talk from the heart. But he betrayed his priorities. "Hey, this is not one to lose,'" Auerbach said. "I don't want five thousand people yelling and screaming at me, and making me look bad." The talk worked, or more likely it was just the Celtics' enormously superior talent. "We waxed them pretty good," Auerbach said.

Auerbach's tirades were more visible when they were aimed at referees. Again, this bullying worked best at home, where several thousand voices backed him up. It was sheer intimidation. If Auerbach wasn't making up the rules as he went along, then he was eagerly helping officials interpret those that already existed. "He knew the rules better than the refs," veteran referee Earl Strom said. "It was always tough seeing Red sitting on the bench." If the rule worked for Auerbach, it was a wonderful rule worth enforcing. Auerbach, a pioneer in the ref-baiting business, never let up. He was always looking for an edge, obsessed with the idea of influencing the outcome of a game.

In October 1983, Auerbach actually ran from his box seat onto the court to scream at referee Ralph Lembo after Lembo had ejected both Larry Bird and Philadelphia 76ers forward Marc Iavaroni following a scuffle. Auerbach was quite a sight that night. He took a detour from Lembo to yell at hulking Moses Malone. "Go ahead, hit me," he told Malone, who understood exactly what would happen to him at Boston Garden if he accepted Auerbach's dare. Auerbach had words, too, with Philadelphia coach Billy Cunningham. This was only the preseason, but Auerbach wanted to set the powerful

76ers and the referees straight. They were not to come into his building without worrying about some lunatic antics.

"How could a GM—as much as I love the man—get involved in something like that?" Cunningham wondered later.

As recently as the 1986–87 finals, Auerbach again bolted from his long-time Garden station, loge one, row seven, seat one, to chase the now retired Earl Strom all the way to the locker room. Auerbach, nearly seventy years old, screamed curses like an eleven-year-old. "Arnold, you're showing me all the class I knew you had," Strom shouted back.

And still, in Syracuse, they probably would say Auerbach had mellowed from the maniac he once was.

Industrial Agers once called Syracuse Salt City because its factories refined and packaged so much of the simple chemical compound that saturated its mines and natural springs. Nothing fancy here. Five hundred factories, 643,000 people trying to get through some long winters by the Erie Canal, which used to flow right through downtown until they filled it in with dirt and clay during the thirties. Do not tell any of this mundane history to lovestruck Dolph Schayes, who has a deep affinity for the little city. Since he arrived there from New York City in 1948 to play NBA ball for the Nationals—a team named after the defunct National Basketball League it had outlasted—Schayes never really left. Dolph Schayes named his son, Danny, after Daniel Biasone, the Nats' generous, sometimes melancholy owner. Dolph raised his talented son there, watched him grow to six–eleven and play his college ball at Syracuse University. Dolph Schayes still lives near Syracuse, in the adjacent suburb of DeWitt, and is the city's greatest booster. "It's a nice place to live," said Schayes. "A nice golf course, a symphony orchestra, a cultural center."

Back when Schayes was starring as a six–eight forward for the Nationals, other teams did not particularly enjoy visiting Syracuse. It was viewed as a cold backwater outpost with a damned tough basketball team nearly unbeatable in its own arena. The first home for the Nationals, until 1951, was the State Fair Coliseum. The second, a bit smaller, was the eight-thousand-seat War Memorial arena downtown. Both buildings still stand, which makes Schayes smile. "Shows you how progressive we are here," he said. In 1954–55, when Schayes averaged 18.5 points to lead the club and when the Nats won their only championship, Syracuse's record was 25–7 at home, 10–16 on the road, 8–6 at neutral sites.

Nobody hated to play at Syracuse more than Red Auerbach and the Celtics, who treated the place more like a disease than a city. The crowd sat nearly on top of the players, and they taunted the Celtic bench unmercifully. Auerbach still remembers one fat fan who sat at the baseline and made Red's life miserable. For years, the two most influential teams in the NBA, Boston and New York, tried to bully the Nationals and their owner, Biasone, into moving the franchise to a bigger, more hospitable city. With the television industry taking off, with transcontinental travel financially feasible, the league was hoping to go big-time. It wanted to capture the largest markets and compete directly with the NFL and the NHL. The Nats would not move, and their players resented the condescending attitude of big-city visitors. The Celtics were the worst. "The whole city had sort of an inferiority complex," Schayes explained. "We were the underdog of the league. The Green Bay of the NBA."

The Nationals were also a weapon that Auerbach used against his own players. "We all hated Syracuse," Tom Sanders said. "It was too cold there. So Red would always say, 'If you guys don't win, we're spending New Year's Eve in Syracuse.' One year we did. He kept us there, right in his hotel room, drinking Pepsi and eating Chinese food." If anyone had a problem with that, Sanders said, Auerbach would tell them, "If you guys don't like the way I run things, go see the GM. I'll be there an hour after practice."

In 1959, an opportunistic young businessman from Minneapolis, Bob Short, bought the once-powerful Lakers and watched the team struggle to attract fans with only Elgin Baylor as a star attraction. Two years later, Short stole the team from its city and its ten-thousand-seat arena, Walter O'Malley-style, and moved it to Los Angeles. The nickname, alliterative but illogical, remained: the Los Angeles Lakers. At the time, the Celtics and the NBA tried to pressure Biasone to join the Lakers on the West Coast, to become the San Francisco Nationals. Biasone refused. He was a stubborn man, remembered by former Nat center Johnny Kerr as "a tough little Italian guy with a heart of gold." Biasone was a fixture in Syracuse, the owner of the Eastwood Sports Center, a bowling alley. He paid his players what he could, suffered with them when they lost. He wasn't going anywhere. Eventually, it was the Warriors who moved from Philadelphia to San Francisco instead.

The Celtics were forced to trudge into Syracuse for another year, until Irv Kosloff finally bought the Nats and moved them to Philadelphia in 1963, making Schayes the player-coach. Schayes quit the sport after the 1965–66 season, after a few frustrating seasons chasing the Celtics in Philadelphia. He enjoys talking more about those Syracuse clubs, and the most intense rivalry in the eight-team league. "For us, we just hated the Celtics," Schayes said. "They were the guys in the green shirts that nobody liked. If they were walking down the street, we'd walk down the other side. This was no Isiah Thomas and Magic Johnson thing. No hugging and kissing."

The rivalry still lives deep in the hearts of Schayes, Biasone, Johnny Kerr, Paul Seymour, Alex Hannum, and Al Bianchi. In the early years, pre–Bill Russell up to 1957, Syracuse took its lumps but dominated the scoreboard. Auerbach, the coach, used tough-guy enforcers to beat up on the technically superior Nationals. Auerbach couldn't keep up with the Nationals, so he elbowed them off their game. He stalled. He hounded and bumped Schayes. "He used cops like Beeb Brannum, Bob Harris, and Jungle Jim Loscutoff," Schayes said. "They pushed, punched you in the stomach. Your pants were pulled on when you jumped. Guys were sent in just to push players around. We'd constantly have incidents. We had Al Cervi, who never went to college, and Paul Seymour. We were the dead-end kids. Many of our games ended in fights. They played a certain brand of ball, and it was hard to ignore it." Once, Schayes was driving for the basket when Harris lifted him up and threw him over his shoulder. Schayes suffered a broken nose and wrist. He had a cut over his eyes stitched up in the locker room and tried to shoot his free throws anyway. He couldn't. "Naturally," said Seymour, the player-coach, "we had a riot after that."

Seymour is another of Syracuse's great boosters, and perhaps Auerbach's greatest detractor. He would bring his special brand of Celtic hatred to a true art form a few years later as coach of the St. Louis Hawks during the famous Egg Game of 1961. The details of that night change drastically with each telling and each storyteller. The way Seymour remembers the four-hour game, Auerbach orchestrated a massive egg barrage in retaliation for being hit by a yolk in St. Louis. "Everyone in the stands at Boston had a half-dozen eggs," Seymour said. "Then it starts getting physical, there's a little fight, and Red runs to the scorer's table, grabs the mike away from the announcer, and starts yelling and gesturing to everyone to throw the eggs." Seymour said he wrestled Red for the microphone that night at Boston Garden, screaming, "If they're gonna get me, they're gonna get you, too."

Seymour was player-coach of the Nationals for four years, until 1960. After a little more than a year in St. Louis, he returned to spend almost thirty years in Syracuse, working in liquor and real estate businesses. Seymour used to tell Schayes about the Celtics, "Every time one of those guys takes a shot at you, you go over and belt Red." If Schayes had only listened to him, Seymour said, "It would have put an end to that shit in a hurry." To this day, Seymour believes Auerbach and the Celtics are some of the biggest cowards on the face of the earth. He used to call the Boston coach "Red Draw-bach." "They had an arrogant air about them, and this was even before Russell came and they weren't winning a thing," Seymour said. "It came from Red, who was always trying to push someone around to suit himself. I always thought that Red would be the type of guy who, if he was standing on the street corner and some kid came up to him for an autograph, he'd say, 'Who asked you to come over here?'"

No item was too petty to argue about between the Celtics and Nationals. The two clubs once warred over beverages in the locker rooms. After games at Boston Garden, the Celtic trainer would charge the Nationals $20 for the soda and beer. Seymour decided he would do the same to the Celtics. When he did, Auerbach stormed into the Nationals' locker room, screaming that all this stuff was supposed to be free.

It would drive Seymour and the others crazy to know that Auerbach is still playing psychological games with the old Nationals, revising history. Ask the Celtic president about those furious confrontations of the fifties and sixties and he will not give an inch. He will claim that the Celtics were no more concerned about the Nationals than about any other NBA team. He will ignore the fact that from 1949 through 1958, the Nationals held a 52–50 edge over the Celtics in all-time regular season and playoff games, including two remarkable overtime showdowns. According to Auerbach, the hysteria was just a by-product of small-town hype. "They had to find somebody to have a rivalry with," Auerbach said. "What else could you do there? They had a hell of a ballclub, but the main rivalries, in my opinion, were Chamberlain-Russell and Boston–New York—one and two."

A man once paid to be impartial, former NBA referee Sid Borgia, remembers Syracuse-Boston a very different way than Auerbach. "It was the unequaled greatest sports rivalry in history," Borgia said. "The refs should have received combat pay for working these games.

"They wanted to eat me up many times in Syracuse. Once, [fellow ref] Johnny Nucatola and I had to have police protection to leave the court. We waited thirty minutes in the dressing room, but still had to have a car backed up to the exit door so we could leave the building. The fans wouldn't let us back in our hotel, so we had to take a train back to New York in the middle of the night."

After Russell came, the dynamics of Syracuse-Boston were different. The Nationals had nobody to match up against this extraordinary player. Kerr, the six-nine center, was agile enough but could not leap, rebound, or intimidate like Russell. The Celtics had quicker players to put on Schayes, like Frank Ramsey. There were seasons when Syracuse would lose the series, 10–2 or 10–3. This grated on players like Bianchi, who has never been one to give up on a good vendetta. "Oh, they were good," said Bianchi. "They were the best. But the way they went about doing things—crying to the refs, the show-off stuff, the victory cigar, Auerbach using all the little ploys like no heat in the locker room …"

During Bianchi's rookie season, in 1956–57, he was assigned to cover Cousy, who promptly dribbled behind his back and through the legs of Bianchi on the way to the basket. Bianchi was thoroughly humiliated. Seymour called a time-out, told Bianchi the next time Cousy pulled something like that, the Boston guard was to be knocked unceremoniously on his ass. Bianchi obliged, happily, as often as possible. "It got to the point that when we played them in Syracuse, nobody knew if Cousy would show up," Bianchi said proudly. "The gamblers from the North Side would be out there, saying, 'Ay, is the Cooz here?'" In the end, when Cousy was on his retirement tour in 1963, Syracuse threw a farewell night for the Celtic guard that matched any other. From out of the silence, a fan yelled, "We love ya, Cooz," and there were tears in the eyes of the two refs. It took nineteen more years before Boston fans would be as gracious, when they chanted for the Philadelphia 76ers to go on and "beat L.A." after a seven-game Eastern Conference final.

Bianchi suffered mightily at the hands of the Celtics for decades to come—as a reserve on the 76ers, as an assistant coach with the Phoenix Suns, and as a general manager with the Knicks. He was sitting on the end of the bench his final playing season, in 1965, when John Havlicek stole the inbounds pass to beat the 76ers in game seven. He was with Phoenix when the Suns lost that three-overtime classic to the Celtics in chaotic game five of the 1976 finals at Boston Garden. Bianchi blamed referee Richie Powers—and the Celtic intimidation factor—for that defeat, which gave the Celtics a commanding 3–2 series lead. He had a point. A replay of that game still shows that Garfield Heard's inbounds pass was picked off by the Celtics with the score tied, 95–95, and that Celtic forward Paul Silas very clearly signaled for an illegal time-out from the foul line with one second remaining. Powers, facing Silas, ignored the signal. If he had recognized it, the Celtics would have been assessed a technical foul. Then again, Powers had plenty of reasons to overlook the violation by the Celtics. He had received a death threat in the mail a week earlier. Minutes after his noncall, he was attacked and punched by a Boston fan for putting back two seconds on the clock at the end of an overtime period.

"There's always some kind of dark cloud at Boston Garden," Bianchi said. "When I was a player, somewhere in the back of your head you think something crazy is going to happen. When you have that thought process, that's not good." After the game, as an assistant coach, he chased Powers through the bowels of Boston Garden, screaming at him. Bianchi still wears a mock championship ring he had constructed for the occasion. It bears two inscriptions: "Phoenix Suns, 1975–76 NBA champions" and "Fuck you, Richie Powers."

In 1962–63, the Nationals' last season in upstate New York, Syracuse and Boston split their series, 6–6. After being dominated for years, this was a moral victory for Biasone, who took the losses to Boston the toughest of all. Auerbach had honed his cigar act by now, lighting up at every winning opportunity, blowing the smoke in what appeared to be ever-widening circles. "You've got to give it to them, because they were always so good," said Biasone, eighty-one years old in 1991. "But let's face it. In our day, when Auerbach would light up one of those victory cigars, you'd want to take that cigar and shove it right down his throat."

To Biasone, Auerbach is a lifelong manipulator, a guy who would take his basketball and go home if you didn't play by his stilted rules.

"You got the feeling Red wanted certain rules just because it would be better for him, and forget about the league," said Biasone. "I'd been screaming for three years that we had to have some kind of time clock, otherwise the game wasn't gonna go. I knew this from one game we played against the Celtics. They had Cousy, who was the best dribbler. They're beating us by 1 point with about eight minutes left. So Red gives the ball to Cousy, and they go into a stall. Would you believe that neither team took a shot for that whole last eight minutes?

"I said to Red right then, 'We gotta have a time clock.' But he was with the guys who didn't want it—because he had Cousy."

Biasone probably was talking about the Celtic 111–105, four-overtime playoff game on March 21, 1953. Cousy scored 50 points that night—30 of them free throws. Biasone was already steaming when Celtic henchman Bob Brannum picked a fight with Schayes and both were ejected. When Auerbach ordered Cousy into the stall, Biasone was beside himself. During a big playoff game, fans were walking out of the arena. There was nothing Biasone could do about it.

Once Russell came along, Auerbach had the rebounder he needed to set the fast break in motion. The Celtics were soon champions and suddenly it was as if they'd invented the running game—an up-tempo style already practiced by the Nationals, whenever they weren't playing the Celtics. The Celtics patented the fast break, publicized it in a major market, won titles with it. Biasone watched incredulously as Auerbach was credited in Boston with this evolution in the sport, the way fans and media in New York came to believe the champion 1970 Knicks under Red Holzman were the first practitioners of team "dee-fense."

Slighted, insulted, Biasone would see green whenever he was angry. He would retreat into his own obsession, forget the world outside the parquet floor. Kerr remembers flying home from Boston after a demoralizing loss to the Celtics and landing in a typical Syracuse snowstorm. "Here we are getting off the plane, climbing down the steps, and there's Danny, in the cold, hands in his pockets, face all red, snow all over him, and he says, 'Can't we beat anybody?'"

Kerr, humbled by Russell on too many nights, shouldered the brunt of the frustration. Long after his shots were being rejected by Russell, Kerr would go on to become an announcer for the Chicago Bulls. Even then, Kerr admitted he had a tough time calling Celtic games with any sense of objectivity. Some names, the ones connected with old Boston heroes, would stick in his throat. In 1990, Kerr attended the farewell retirement party for Earl Strom in Potsdam, Ohio. There was an auction of Strom's collectibles, and one of the items was a painting that Heinsohn once created of a Bermuda beach house. Kerr purchased the painting for $700. "I hung it over the fireplace," Kerr said. "Now I always know that when I start thinking about the old days, about how those SOBs ruined everything every year, if I just can't take it anymore, I'll just pull the painting off the wall and burn it."

Alex Hannum now lives far from Syracuse, in the small California town of Santa Maria. He is semi-retired, owns a small construction business. He called his three seasons as coach at Syracuse, beginning in 1960, the most fun he can ever remember. His team ran like crazy, captured the hearts and minds of Salt City. Hannum remembered Boston and Auerbach as the arrogant enemy, the same way that players like Schayes and Bianchi did. Hannum had first learned to hate the Celtics three years earlier as a player-coach for St. Louis. On April 13, 1957, in the seventh and decisive game of the finals at Boston Garden, the six-seven Hannum nearly prevented Russell and Auerbach from winning their first title. In the second overtime, the Hawks were trailing, 125–123, with one second left. Hannum put himself in for a trick inbounds play that he had helped originate in Rochester. Hannum threw the ball the length of the court, off the backboard, on purpose. Bob Pettit grabbed the rebound, got off a good shot, and the ball was on the rim when the game ended. In Hannum's mind, this very fortunate Celtic team was no dynasty, no unbeatable machine, regardless of what the Eastern press was spouting. When Russell went down with a sprained ankle the next season in the playoffs, St. Louis beat them in six games for the title. Celtic officials made it known they felt the Hawks won only because of Russell's injury. Hannum fumed, but he would have his revenge on Auerbach again nine seasons later in Philadelphia.

When the Nationals moved to Philly and became the 76ers, they remained the Celtics' chief rivals in the East for years. They were still too small to handle Russell—until January 13, 1965, when Wilt Chamberlain was acquired for Connie Dierking, Paul Neumann, Lee Shaffer, and $150,000. Hannum, exiled in San Francisco with the Warriors since the Nationals moved to Philly, was hired back by the 76ers in 1966 to succeed Schayes. Auerbach went to work again on Hannum's nerves, lighting more cigars than ever before. "That was Red's way of trying to get to you so he'd have an advantage," Hannum said. "Any way he could try to beat you, he would. I wasn't going to let the cigar stuff get to me, though. It wasn't like I had no success against him. Over the thirteen years, the only times he didn't win the title, I did, so I always felt like I was the thorn in his side."

The second championship that Hannum won came in 1967 with the 76er team of Chamberlain, Luke Jackson, Chet Walker, Hal Greer, Wally Jones, Billy Cunningham, Larry Costello, and Dave Gambee. There was still a lot of Syracuse left in that club, a lot of scrambling around. "We always said in Syracuse, 'Give us a big man, give us a Russell to match their Russell, and we'll see how great the Celtics are,'" Hannum said. "Well, that Sixer team was my old Syracuse National team, with Wilt and Luke Jackson. I look at it that way. And when we beat the Celtics in five games in the conference finals, we looked at that as the championship."

Through the media, Hannum continued to argue with Auerbach about which club was the greatest of all time. Hannum insists it was that 1966–67 Philadelphia club, a team of great depth and quirky foul-shooting techniques. Auerbach, who always put down Chamberlain more often than was necessary, scoffed at this. He said people just feel they have to say some other team than the Celtics was the greatest. But that Sixer team went 68–13 in pre-expansion days, winning forty-five of its first forty-nine games—a remarkable feat in the strong, ten-team NBA. If it was not the best ever, that team was very close to it. Whatever Auerbach said, on any subject, could not be taken as gospel, or as the words of an enlightened man.

Chapter 3

Pride and Prejudice

RED Auerbach, who by reputation helped pave the entryway for blacks in the NBA, once walked up to his starting forward, Cedric Maxwell, at a team Christmas party in 1978 and said, "You know, Maxwell, you remind me of that old movie guy, Stepin Fetchit." Maxwell, a black second-year player from Charlotte, North Carolina, had never heard the expression before. He smiled, said, "Thank you," and took it for a compliment until he repeated the exchange to a friend from back home in North Carolina. His friend did a double-take and said, "He called you *what?*"

"He couldn't believe that a Jewish man would say that to a black man," Maxwell said. "For a long time, I was waiting for him to say that to me again. I was going to say, 'Yez, suh, massuh.'"

Auerbach, in all probability, had intended this characterization as a compliment. Fetchit was a movie actor who portrayed shuffling, obedient, generally unmotivated black men. In his own unenlightened way, Auerbach was trying to tell Maxwell—a beacon of potential on one of the worst Celtic teams in franchise history—he was a likable kid and a coachable player. Auerbach just didn't understand the implications, the way Al Campanis didn't understand the impact when he said blacks "didn't have the necessities" to manage a base-ball team during his infamous "Nightline" undressing in 1987. Auer-bach didn't need to understand. He was used to operating in a world where his role was not so unlike that of a benevolent plantation fore-man. He owned all the players and made up all the rules. There was nothing wrong with this Stepin Fetchit comment if Auerbach believed there wasn't.

Explaining the dismissal of Tom Heinsohn as Celtics coach on January 3, 1978, Auerbach said, "I love the guy. I was hoping I could stretch the thing out as long as I could, because I was hoping and hoping these monkeys could turn it around." At the time, the Celtics were in the midst of a period when a majority of their players were black. Again, the insensitivity of his comment was lost on Auerbach. Hadn't he been talking about all of the Celtics? Why should his black players take offense?

Racial sensitivity was for others, not for Auerbach. Outsiders had to meet stiffer criteria. In his autobiography published several years later, he wrote that Bill Russell sensed racial bias when unsophisti-cated Boston sportswriters ignored his defensive contributions to focus on less relevant statistics like scoring. Auerbach wrote, italiciz-ing for emphasis, "Remember. It's not what you tell them, but what they hear." Many of the black Celtics in 1978 were new to racially polarized Boston and to the team. What they interpolated from Auerbach's vocabulary and attitude as far back as 1978, according to Maxwell, was an alarm. It told them: "If you're a black Celtic, as long as you're producing you're accepted. But if you're not, then you are just a black."

During his eight years in Boston, Maxwell said he never told the Stepin Fetchit story. He likely would have been committing profes-sional suicide—at least in Boston—to volunteer such blasphemy. In Boston, to speak negatively of Auerbach would be more than criti-cizing a legend; it would be the actual defacing of a public monu-ment. Indeed, a statue of Auerbach stands near Faneuil Hall in Quincy Market, facing northward toward Boston Garden. There is a rolled-up program in Auerbach's left hand and a cigar in the right. The cigar, of course, represents Auerbach's 885 regular-season and playoff victories as coach in Boston. The statue itself bespeaks sixteen Celtic championships, a source of immeasurable pride throughout New England.

Through the years, not even the biggest Celtic stars—including the greatest white hope of all, Larry Bird—have been as invulnerable as Auerbach in Boston. Nothing is. The shrine of Boston Garden finally has been declared obsolete. A new arena is scheduled to rise next door. The city itself has been routinely attacked from outside and from within as less accepting of black athletes than whites. These assaults and insults are tolerable. Think what you will of the city, but do not imply Celtic complicity—even when discussing their blatant whitening during the eighties. That might nudge Auerbach off his pedestal.

Four decades of New Englanders have been conditioned to view the face on the Celtic dynasty as one would recall a favorite old uncle. Or godfather. Auerbach, to them, is the boss of all professional basketball bosses. And like the fans, the Boston media learned its ABCs at the foot of this sharp, abrasive, opinionated Brooklynite. His word was accepted as gospel, whether or not he was blowing smoke. "He's a character, an original, and I like him very much," said Irv Levin, a Los Angeles movie producer who owned the Celtics from 1974 to 1978. "But Red knows how to maneuver, and he got into a situation up there where he could do no wrong. All through the years, the press and the public believed that, and it wasn't fair to a lot of people."

"The way it works up there," said John Y. Brown, the ex-governor of Kentucky, who succeeded Levin as Celtic co-owner for a year and whose term was as overwhelmingly unpopular as it was brief, "is that whatever goes right Red did. Whatever goes wrong, the owner did." The former owners can have their say now. Finally.

Brown was a freewheeler from his days as an American Basketball Association owner. He was hardly an innocent. But Brown did not truly find out about the Auerbach legend until late January 1979, when the Celtics traded Jo Jo White to the Golden State Warriors for a first-round draft pick. White, a ten-year backcourt star and member of two championship teams, was slowing with injuries. He also engaged in a bitter contract dispute with the front office— AKA Auerbach. When the deal was made, the press unloaded on Brown, the newcomer, the outsider, the man who didn't understand that someone of White's stature was not supposed to be sent away for some rookie to be named later. Two weeks later, however, Brown made a more stunning deal, this time without consulting Auerbach. He traded the first-round pick acquired from Golden State, plus two others the Celtics owned in the 1979 draft, for New York's high-scoring Bob McAdoo. Auerbach, of course, hit the roof, as did all of Boston, lambasting Brown for having sabotaged Auerbach's plan to revive the ailing Celtics with those three first-round picks.

"So on the one hand, everyone up there ripped me for trading Jo Jo White for a first-round draft pick," Brown said. "But when I used the pick to trade for McAdoo, they said, 'That jerk got rid of the draft picks Red got to rebuild the team with.'"

Brown left for the political arena soon. Auerbach had the last word again. He always had the final word; he simply outlasted everyone else. If he was questioned, he would dismiss the critic with a wave of his 885-victory cigar, as he would brush off criticism of the cigar itself. For years, he would light up before the end of the game, humiliating opponents. It was a self-aggrandizing gimmick even his own players hated. They were the ones exposed to the retaliatory elbow in the mouth. "You see, when you're winning, and you've been around as long as I was, more than any other coach, they're always looking for angles to get at you," Auerbach said. "Anything to put you down, say something derogatory about you. It's a form of jealousy, so I dismissed it."

Auerbach often used his pulpit to bully friends, foes, and impartial observers alike. Only a fool, however, would argue with his success or deny his immense contributions to what is arguably the world's most famous sports franchise. It is too easy t⟨

Robertson does, that the Celtic Mystique was creat⟨

Russell walked through the door. If nothing else, Au⟨⟩

good sense to listen to his college coach, Bill Reinhart, who'd spotted Russell as a sophomore at San Francisco. Reinhart convinced
Auerbach that Russell would be perfect for the Celtics, who maneu-
vered to obtain Russell's draft rights from the St. Louis Hawks.

When Russell was gone after eleven championships in thirteen
years, Auerbach found many of the same Russell-esque qualities in
the fiery eyes of Dave Cowens. And when Cowens was winding
down a decade later, Auerbach took the advice of his scout, John
Killilea, and waited one year for the prize of the 1978 draft, junior
eligible Larry Bird. This was a meager price for a future windfall.
Most of all, Auerbach understood that basketball in its purest form
was the melding of individuals into a team structure—but not to the
point where free-form expression and spontaneity were obstructed
by the coach's own ego, which in Auerbach's case was immense.

It was easier to forget the side of Auerbach that years later would
be described by Cedric Maxwell as "crude and obnoxious." It was
better to smile and remember Auerbach as the franchise glue, the
keeper of the Celtic flame, the occasionally pompous and often
ornery father figure. He was the lovable grouch who would tell
them, in a moment of pique, "You want to get traded to Cincinnati?
They're interested, you know." It was the era of the sports dictator.
Few were as good and dedicated to the cause as Auerbach, whose
control of the team was predicated on fear and respect, probably in
that order. "You know what BOSS spelled backwards is?" he was
fond of saying. "Double S-O-B."

"Red always articulated our roles up front," Tom Sanders said,
"and we attacked those roles with vigor. We were slotted, and there
was a lack of choice." There were designated scorers, like Heinsohn
and Sam Jones. Sanders's role was setting picks, playing defense,
and going to the boards.

K. C. Jones remembered Auerbach scowling at Sanders in huddles. "Why'd you take that shot?" Auerbach would say.

Sanders, throwing his hands up, would answer, "I only took one."

"We had six plays with two or three options off each, and half the time we wouldn't run anything if the break was running, which happened most of the time once we got the strength with Russell," Bob Cousy said. "He [Auerbach] just knew how to win with the least amount of wasted motion."

Auerbach was not alone in this knowledge, but he had the best players and he quickly consolidated his power within the organization. "Most people think Red was a basketball genius, an X and O guy, but he wasn't," Tom Heinsohn said. "His strength was in management, being in control." This allowed him to trade an established star like Ed Macauley for the rights to Russell, whose poor offensive skills were considered a risk. Years later, when he was persuaded Bird was worth waiting the year for, no one was going to talk him out of it. In New York, conversely, the corporate parent, Gulf + Western, refused then-coach Willis Reed's request to draft Bird, wanting an immediate dividend from the fourth pick of the draft.

The more championships the Celtics won during the Russell era, and the more numbers there were to retire, the easier it was for Auerbach to get his message across: Celtic Pride had created a Celtic Mystique. Being a Celtic meant being part of something great, something special. A player could even take Celtic Pride to the bank in the form of an NBA champion's playoff share.

By 1991, forty-one years after Auerbach's arrival in Boston, Celtic Pride and Celtic Mystique were the prototypical sports cliches—born of truth but repeated so often that they blurred the rush of events. While Auerbach was certainly the architect who shaped the house, historians have been presumptuous in crediting him with buying and arranging all the furniture. Whatever coup the Celtics pulled off, it was always easy to assume that "Red had done it again." Sometimes, particularly in the case of the Bird-era team, he simply hadn't.

Auerbach, in fact, had little to do with the acquisition of two

Celtics superstars, Robert Parish and Kevin McHale. Without them, Bird notwithstanding, the Celtics of the eighties would not have won a thing. After John Y. Brown bequeathed McAdoo to the Celtics and Auerbach in 1979, Boston signed Detroit Pistons free agent M. L. Carr. In those days, a team either voluntarily agreed on compensation for the signing of a free agent or submitted to an arbitrary award by the commissioner. No team could possibly prefer the latter, so the Celtics worked a deal with Detroit coach Dick Vitale— McAdoo for Carr, plus two Detroit first-round picks in the 1980 draft. Detroit promptly finished with the league's worst record, leaving the Celtics with the number one pick of the draft, which they traded to acquire Parish plus the draft position to take Kevin McHale. The following spring, Parish and McHale teamed with Bird and Maxwell on what was the league's most formidable front line. They were so good, the Celtics won the 1980–81 championship with two starting guards, Tiny Archibald and Chris Ford, who had been considered retreads two years earlier.

Fans, media, and officials from other teams were stunned by the quickness with which the Celtics had been rebuilt. Auerbach, sixty-three years old, again was widely hailed as a miracle worker. In a 1990 poll, NBA general managers voted the Parish-McHale deal as the most lopsided in history. "The master had struck yet again," according to the brief Auerbach bio in the 1990–91 Celtics media guide. There was not a single mention of Bill Fitch, then the Celtics coach, who did all the work.

For two weeks following the signing of Carr, Fitch had called Vitale every day, telling him McAdoo did not want to play for the Celtics, that they had to trade him. "You're getting Bob McAdoo," Fitch told Vitale. "He's your missing piece. Your first pick isn't going to be that high, anyway." Tragically for Detroit, Vitale finally agreed and Fitch was the proud owner of the first pick in the entire college pool. That season, Bird's first, the Celtics catapulted from last to first in the Atlantic Division, but were overpowered by Philadelphia's huge front line in the playoffs. Fitch remembers that at the

Olympic trials in Kentucky, everyone advised him to lead off the draft by taking Purdue seven-footer Joe Barry Carroll.

Fitch, however, had coached ten years earlier at the University of Minnesota, and his contacts there were telling him that the lesser-known McHale was far better than most scouts believed. McHale wasn't a seven-footer, but he was a gangly six-eleven with the kind of post-up offensive game that was the rage of the NBA. Fitch knew that the Golden State Warriors, who owned the third pick, desperately wanted Carroll. He knew that Utah, picking second, was after Louisville's Darrell Griffith.

Fitch told Golden State's general manager, Scotty Stirling, "We'll trade picks if you give us a player."

"Which player?" Stirling said.

"Well," Fitch said, "if you get Carroll, what are you going to do with Parish?"

The irony here was that Fitch viewed Parish merely as a backup to Cowens and possibly as a power forward. By reputation, Parish was an underachiever with potential. But when Cowens suddenly retired during training camp, Parish stepped in and blossomed into an All-League center. McHale immediately became the NBA's premier sixth man. Fitch had left an indelible, if hardly acknowledged, imprint on the Celtics. He left Boston in 1982, a bit tired of hearing about "Auerbach's genius." He respected Auerbach, thought of him as a good friend. But Fitch had his own ego, and it was being ignored. Worse, the media were regularly citing him for un-Celtic-like behavior. Fitch came to Boston an outsider and would always remain that way. Since Auerbach intended to reduce his own role in the organization, Fitch did not relish the idea of staying behind to be second-guessed and reminded of "how Red would've done things."

Another piece to the eighties puzzle arrived the following season when the Celtics lured Danny Ainge out of the Toronto Blue Jays organization. The Celtics had drafted Ainge, a Brigham Young All-America guard, in the second round of the 1981 draft, despite the fact that Ainge insisted he was sticking with baseball. A year later, trouble with curveballs and a .211 lifetime average had Ainge leaning in the direction of the NBA. The Celtics settled matters financially with Toronto and, once more, the basketball world believed Auerbach had made a player appear from a puff of smoke.

"No, no, I drafted Ainge, or I suggested we did, anyway," said Harry Mangurian, a Florida businessman who was John Y. Brown's partner and took sole ownership upon Brown's departure. "I wasn't a basketball guy, but I wanted to feel like I knew what was going on. So I did what had served me so well in the horse racing business for twenty years: I talked to as many people as I could.

"I used to spend hours with people like Angelo Drossos from San Antonio and Stan Kasten, who was Ted Turner's guy in Atlanta. I think it must have been Kasten who told me Ainge would never stick with baseball. I remember someone saying, 'He just can't hit.' So that draft, we had two second-round picks, and I said to Red, 'Let's take Danny Ainge.'

"Red said, 'Harry, the kid's playing baseball.'

"I said, 'Well, it's worth a shot. We can talk to him.' That's what we did."

Auerbach never credited Mangurian with that suggestion. He did not credit owners, or coaches, with personnel decisions. "If he took your idea, it was his idea," an anonymous Celtic front office official told the *Hartford Courant* in April 1991. Looking back, Auerbach said Mangurian was a likable guy but "too much of a businessman."

Mangurian's business acumen, however, bailed the Celtics out of a predicament after the 1983 season. Then the Celtics suspected Kevin McHale's agent, John Sandquist, was advising his client to sign a huge free agent offer sheet with the New York Knicks. It was money the Celtics would never volunteer, for it would betray the team's salary pecking order that unofficially mandated Larry Bird as highest paid. Mangurian sat down with the Knicks financial statement and noticed that three of their players—Marvin Webster, Sly

Williams, and Rory Sparrow—also had expired contracts. He called Auerbach and Jan Volk, the Celtic executive vice president and general manager, into his office.

"I want you to prepare offer sheets to all three of the Knick free agents and make sure they're attractive enough so that they can't turn them down," Mangurian said.

Auerbach and Volk looked at each other in disbelief. They thought they were rid of an owner masquerading as a general manager when John Y. Brown left town. Suddenly they had a guy telling them to sign a one-dimensional shotblocker, Webster; a head case, Williams; and a slow point guard, Sparrow.

"Harry, we don't need those guys," Auerbach said.

"Just do it," Mangurian said.

The offer sheets were announced at the league meetings in New York, stunning everyone, most of all the Knicks. For a while, they considered calling the Celtics' bluff by letting all three players go and then pursuing McHale. In the end, they feared the Celtics would match whatever offer they made on McHale and they would wind up with nothing. They matched the Celtic offers and dropped out on McHale. For weeks, Knicks GM Dave DeBusschere cursed Auerbach, believing, quite naturally, he'd been behind the scheme. DeBusschere sounded like most coaches and players who'd ever sat in the cramped, overheated Boston Garden visitors' locker room, furious at the thought of Auerbach in the boiler room, stoking the fires. It was an image that Auerbach loved, that he cultivated. The omnipresent, omnipotent Oz. Only a few saw past this provincial myth. Usually they were from out of town.

"Red's a smart guy, but he's no mastermind," said Dolph Schayes, who maintained his Syracuse cynicism through the decades. "It developed from him lighting all those cigars, and the legend just grows each year."

Arnold Jacob Auerbach, thirty-two-year-old son of a Russian immigrant tailor from Minsk, was officially introduced to the Boston media as the team's new coach by founder and owner Walter Brown on April 27, 1950. Two days earlier, the draft had taken place in Chicago. The Celtics were the buzz of the young NBA. People could not believe how they had passed over one player with their first pick, or had chosen another with their second.

With their first choice, the Celtics selected Bowling Green center Charlie Share. With their second, they took six-five forward Chuck Cooper out of Duquesne. Share was a controversial pick in Boston because he wasn't Bob Cousy, the local backcourt wizard from Holy Cross down the Mass Pike in Worcester. Cooper raised eyebrows across the country because he was black, the first black ever selected by an NBA team.

Cousy, like Auerbach a native New Yorker, was heartbroken that the Celtics hadn't drafted him. He was instead taken by the Tri-Cities Blackhawks and, somewhat bewildered, asked himself: "What's a Tri-Cities?" He began a quick study on the renowned cities of Moline and Rock Island, Illinois, and Davenport, Iowa. Auerbach, meanwhile, was quickly quizzed on why he'd passed on Cousy. He turned to owner Walter Brown and immediately demonstrated his knack for patience and understanding with his legendary complaint, "Walter, am I supposed to win or am I supposed to worry about the local yokels and please these guys?"

With Auerbach, as always, there is legend and there is fact. It is widely believed, not just in Boston, that Auerbach facilitated the major changes in the sport and drove it relentlessly into the modern era. This historical perspective says that the game would not have developed any commercial appeal in its early fifties lumbering, low-scoring form. So Auerbach got Cousy and transformed the Celtics into a fast-breaking harbinger of the high-voltage, 70 percent-plus black NBA of the future. More important, with the drafting of Cooper, Auerbach supposedly ushered in the era of the black player who would much later dominate the sport everyplace, it seemed, but Boston.

But when Auerbach finally did get Cousy, he cursed what he

thought was rotten luck. "Let's just say he didn't immediately see the value in a small man," Cousy said. Auerbach was no different from any other basketball coach who couldn't see the forest through the trees. Big was always beautiful—hence the selection of Charlie Share. To Auerbach, Cousy—generously listed at six-one—was little more than a flashy sideshow, a guy who belonged in a Globetrotter prelim. Given a second chance to obtain Cousy, Auerbach was just as vehemently opposed. During the summer, Cousy's rights had been passed along to the Chicago Stags, who folded in October. The league's commissioner, Maurice Podoloff, assumed the Celtics would now take Cousy, the natural territorial choice. Auerbach told Walter Brown, "No way." He wanted big Max Zaslofsky and his 16.4 points per game.

At a league meeting, the names of Chicago's three best players—Zaslofsky, Andy Phillip, and Cousy—went into Syracuse owner Danny Biasone's hat for a random drawing. New York picked out Zaslofsky, Philadelphia took Phillip, and the Celtics were stuck with the man Auerbach would one day call the "greatest playmaker who ever lived."

"Red was beside himself when he drew Cousy," said Zelda Spoelstra, who worked for the commissioner's office and was at the meeting.

The Celtics already had received six-eight, sweet-shooting Ed Macauley as a gift when the players of still another defunct team, the St. Louis Bombers, were dispersed. By pure good luck, by Celtic fortune, Auerbach had been handed the two players who would lead his team in almost every statistical category for half a decade. They would have to do until the new St. Louis Hawks miraculously (for Auerbach) appeared for the 1955–56 season and were willing to surrender the draft rights to Russell in 1956—only because they were so anxious to acquire hometown star Macauley to boost their gate.

Certainly without Macauley and Cousy, and probably just without Cousy, Auerbach's first couple of seasons in Boston would have been terrible trials. The Celtics would have been the same porous franchise they had been during their first four years of existence. Given the volatility of the sport in those days, it is entirely possible the Celtics would not have survived at all, or that Auerbach never would have lasted long enough in Boston to draft Russell, to win even one championship. Instead, Cousy transformed the Celtics overnight into an entertaining team, and together with Macauley and Bill Sharman into a competitive one. No Auerbach-coached Celtic team would ever have a losing record. Undoubtedly, the day Auerbach shook hands on a job with the Irishman Walter Brown was the luckiest in his life.

Walter Brown paid Red Auerbach $10,000 to coach the Celtics in 1950. The negotiating session began with that very offer and ended with Auerbach's acceptance. The way Auerbach described it, that was pretty much how it went for sixteen years.

"Walter Brown was the ultimate sportsman," said Auerbach, sitting outside the gym while the Celtics practiced for the start of the 1990–91 season at their Hellenic College training camp in Brookline. As always, the cigar was wedged between fingers on his right hand. Auerbach seldom made eye contact. He stared mostly at the ground and looked up only to exhale smoke into the brisk October air.

"Sure, he was concerned with money, but only from the standpoint of existing. If he had made millions, he would have given away millions. Everybody loved him. The players loved him. He never had any big money because he was always doing so many things for nothing. He was involved with the Bruins, the International Ice Hockey Federation, the Olympic Committee, the Boston Marathon, Ice Capades, whatever they would put in front of him, he was involved in.

"I used to call him the Perennial President because he was doing so many things. There was always somebody in his office. It used to drive me crazy. I'd say, 'Walter, can't we talk? The season's over, let's talk about next year.' He'd say, 'C'mon, we'll go in the toilet.' We'd get there, he'd say, 'What's on your mind?'

"I'd say, 'Walter, what about my contract for next year?'

"He'd say, 'What do you want?'

"I'd say, 'I need this much more,' or, 'Same as last year.'

"He'd say, 'You got it. What else?'"

"I'd say, 'That's it.'"

Then they'd zip up. By all accounts, Brown was a hockey guy who simply fell in love with this new game and the inner-city toughs who coached and played it. He developed friendships and loyalties with several of the players, to the point that when Macauley was to be traded, Brown called and told him: "Red wants to trade you and Cliff Hagen to St. Louis for Bill Russell. I don't want to make the deal. I can't imagine the Celtics without you." Macauley, it turned out, had a young son who was ill, and he wanted to go home to St. Louis. The largest piece to the dynasty's puzzle fit snugly into place.

Without much understanding of basketball, Brown was a fan who left everything, more or less, to Auerbach, except for an occasion when he'd storm into the locker room after a loss, scream for a few minutes, and spend the next couple of weeks apologizing. He had founded the Celtics and negotiated for the name in a transparent attempt to appeal to the city's large Irish population. It was one of his most effective brainstorms. He was determined to keep the Celtics afloat despite years when they had very little to do with green but were deeply in the red. His Boston Garden investors demanded he buy them out by 1950. Despite pleas from his wife, Marjorie, and friends, Brown actually remortgaged his home to pay the Celtic bills. From this must-win position, Brown looked to Auerbach to build him a team that would literally pay the rent.

Auerbach didn't recognize a basketball genius when he saw one in Cousy, but he and his coaching brethren would have been blind not to notice the untapped market of talented black players. The best of them, to this point, had been left to Abe Saperstein's Globetrotters. Saperstein had made it clear that if any NBA team invaded his market, he wouldn't play its arena. The Globetrotters were the biggest basketball draw around. "I told Walter that Cooper could help us," Auerbach said. "The rest was up to him."

At this point, Brown, obviously unafraid of chances, was ready to take the plunge. The story goes that when he announced the Celtics were selecting Cooper, another NBA owner said, "Walter, don't you know he's a colored boy?"

"I don't give a damn if he's striped or polka dot or plaid," Brown is supposed to have said. "Boston takes Charles Cooper of Duquesne."

Before his death several years ago, Cooper said, "I'm convinced that no NBA team would have made the move on blacks in 1950 if the Celtics hadn't drafted me. Seven rounds later, the Washington Caps took Earl Lloyd, and a couple of months later, the New York Knicks bought Sweetwater Clifton's contract from the Harlem Globetrotters. But it was a case of the Caps and Knicks following the Celtics' lead. Walter Brown was the man who put his neck on the line."

Whether it was more Brown than Auerbach, or the other way around, and whatever their motives were, the point is that it was done. Auerbach was willing to do anything to win. Years later, when Auerbach retired from the bench in 1966 and appointed Russell as the first black to coach or manage a major American professional sports team, the Celtic veterans all believed it had been for a simple reason: Auerbach knew Russell was tiring of the grind and was unlikely to respond to anyone new. What's been hailed as a profound example of enlightened thinking was more likely a by-product of Auerbach's passion to retain the edge.

"What the hell, everything is words, I guess it's fine to throw around these tributes today," Cousy said of Auerbach. The Hall of Fame point guard always called Auerbach "Arnold," not "Red." It demonstrated his fondness for Auerbach while setting himself apart from the Celtic party line. Cousy became a broadcaster following his retirement in 1963, and became as serious and entertaining a voice as he was a playmaker. He talked about racial issues as openly and nonchalantly as he did about someone's jumper.

"In those days, we were averaging four thousand people a game," Cousy said, "so the point is, talking about the box office, promotion or anything else, what was the risk with Cooper?

"To begin with, Walter Brown, despite being an Irishman—

unfortunately, a lot of my Irish-Catholic friends are the biggest big-ots I know—didn't have a bigoted bone in his body. And as for Arnold, I mean, he was certainly no leader of civil rights. But show him a polka-dotted seven-footer who can dunk and he'll put him on the team. He was completely pragmatic. He was a little bulldog out of the ghetto with a killer instinct. He was completely one-dimensional; his entire life was *win*."

Pragmatism shouldn't detract entirely from Auerbach's good deeds. He did not use Cooper and Russell's color as alibis. He did not avoid selecting them for positions that could have been filled by whites. That in itself was progressive. But at the same time, as Cousy suggested, Auerbach was not so much a visionary as he was a street-smart survivor. These were tough, losing times. Auerbach did what he thought he had to do to win, conscience be damned.

Still, Auerbach was not about to tear down all societal barriers. If he appeared ahead of his time on the acceptance of blacks, Auer-bach still sounded like a dumb jock on his attitudes toward women. Women did not win games for him. Women were obstacles to over-come, like Wilt Chamberlain or a hostile crowd. They were unnec-essary distractions from the roundball at hand. Auerbach's wife, Dorothy, and his two daughters lived in Washington while Auerbach maintained an apartment in Boston. While Celtic owners sat in their boxes with their wives, Auerbach was nearby, alone. The story accepted in Boston was that Dorothy Auerbach insisted on remain-ing in Washington to be close to family. Several old Celtics laugh and shake their heads. One said, "Maybe that was true for a few years." Cousy said he once kidded Dorothy Auerbach, "He's in Boston six or seven months, I take him overseas for six weeks, so basically you get him two and a half months. Can you put up with this guy for two and a half months?"

For years, Auerbach encouraged his players to leave their wives back home because they would just get in the way. He never would consider the promotional stunt of hiring Celtic cheerleaders. This might be interpreted as a tasteful choice on his part, but Auerbach's reasoning, explained in his autobiography, was laughable. "First, you've got enough problems, without having girls hanging around the gym," he wrote. "Before you know it, they're making eyes at some of the guys, and some of the guys are going to stray. It happens."

Presumably, these were not his adolescent thoughts when he banished then *Boston Globe* reporter Lesley Visser from the Celtic locker room after a loss. It was one of the few times a woman reporter had ever met such resistance in the NBA, which was significantly more cooperative along these lines than football and baseball. In all likelihood, Auerbach was frustrated by some basketball problems and looking for a convenient target. Nothing new.

In Bill Russell, Boston had found a commodity previously unseen, a gifted giant who dominated the game everywhere but in the scoring column, who selflessly embraced all the game's nonglorified subtleties. Auerbach adroitly surrounded him with compatible players, reducing the pressure on Russell to score. The acquisitions of Cousy, Macauley, and Russell may have required incredibly good fortune, but Auerbach proved he knew how to parlay a good hand into a jackpot.

Three of the eventual starters around Russell were black, which added to the legend and humanistic quality of Auerbach's Celtics. Upon closer inspection, however, the Celtics' overwhelming domination of the period and the ensuing marketing of the dynasty blurred some of the facts. When Russell joined the Celtics for the 1956–57 season, Cooper and the team's second black player, Don Barksdale, already were gone. Within the next three years, the team added Sam Jones, K. C. Jones, and Tom Sanders. By 1960–61, although the Celtics now had the nucleus of black players who would carry them through the dynastic sixties, four of the top six minute-getters were still white. And by this time, most of the league's other clubs also had a nucleus of blacks.

In Cincinnati, there were Oscar Robertson, Wayne Embry, and

Bob Boozer. Philadelphia had Wilt Chamberlain, Guy Rodgers, and Al Attles. Syracuse had Hal Greer, Dick Barnett, Joe Roberts, and Cal Ramsey. St. Louis, champions with an all-white team in 1957–58, now had Lenny Wilkens, Sihugo Green, and Woody Sauldsberry. The league was getting blacker all over, not just in Boston.

"We had just as many black players in the sixties," Schayes said, "but the Celtics' blacks were dominant. Our guys were subs, so they didn't get as much publicity."

In fact, the argument might be made that the Nationals were more racially progressive than the Celtics, that it was more honorable for teams to include blacks who weren't established stars. White players easily could have been signed and placed on the bench without a significant drop in the standings. The Celtics, meanwhile, were beginning a long-lived practice of balancing out their roster with whites whenever they had black players who were starters. Their number of blacks peaked at eight in 1968–69—Bill Russell's last year as coach. The following season, the balancing act began once more.

By the time Cousy retired, for the 1963–64 season, with K. C. Jones stepping in to give the Celtics four black starters and John Havlicek as the sixth man, most of the teams had as many, if not more, black players than Boston. In the West, the San Francisco Warriors had Chamberlain, Rodgers, Nate Thurmond, Al Attles, and Wayne Hightower. Forever furious at Auerbach for his refusal to acknowledge him as the equal of Russell, Chamberlain maintained that Auerbach had little to do with acquiring the black players on his team. "I don't like Auerbach," Chamberlain said. "He coached five blacks and he had insights about playing them. But he didn't have anything to do with getting them. Never did. That was done by the old owner, Walter Brown. Brown was the guy who said it was okay to have blacks on a team in Boston."

It has been written often, and generally accepted, that Auerbach campaigned harder than most for his black players, who faced segregation and contempt not only in areas of the South and Midwest,

but in their home city itself. According to the party line, black players were part of the family as long as they were wearing Celtic jer-
seys. They were to be treated like Celtics—or, more precisely, like
white men. Again, this is the view from the long look back.

Once, according to Ed Macauley, some of the Celtics were playing cards on the train home from New York, where Sweetwater
Clifton had had a big night in a Knick win. Bob Brannum, one of
Auerbach's beloved tough white guys, suddenly piped up, "Oh, that
black son of a bitch killed us tonight." Macauley recalled the tension
didn't break until Barksdale said, "Yeah, that big jig was really tough
tonight."

Ignorant whites may have taken Barksdale's response to mean it
was all right to include racial taunts in fraternity banter, that this was
the appropriate way of dealing with a frightening issue within the
team structure. But as Cousy said, "None of us knew what it was like
to be black. We thought we were doing enough just by including
them, but none of us was particularly sensitive to the situation as it
really was." One night after an exhibition game, Cousy left Charlotte, North Carolina, with Cooper while the team stayed on
because the hotel would not accept Cooper, his roommate. Cousy
said it was his idea to leave, despite a widespread belief that Auerbach took the entire team and stormed out of town. The two players
reached the train station and climbed to the platform. They came
upon a sign pointing blacks in the opposite direction from whites.
Cousy vividly remembered Cooper's stunned look as they stood
together freezing in the late-night cold. "I teared up," Cousy said. "I
mean, what do you say?"

Did Auerbach understand any more than Brannum? Years ago,
he is said to have made liberal use of the word *schvartzes*, the Yid-
dish word for "black," though its colloquial use is far closer to "nigger." One player from the Celtics' golden years insisted that Auerbach had a perverse vision of Russell's torment. According to this
player's reading, Auerbach would admit that the abuse Russell took
in Boston wasn't very nice, but he felt it made Russell a better play-

er and, therefore, the Celtics a better team. According to this thinking, because the majority of the opposing centers were white, Russell took his anger and frustrations out on them. Auerbach wrote in his last book, *On and Off the Court,* that Russell "never did much to alleviate the tension." Auerbach didn't say what Russell should have done, exactly, after coming home to find his home vandalized, with feces smeared across the walls and furniture. Russell grew bitter and aloof, which seems to be a very human reaction.

Russell may have been the most visible target, but he wasn't alone. When K. C. Jones bought a house in Framingham, a cross was burned on his front lawn. Don Nelson, who lived in the next-door town, Natick, was "appalled and shocked. In his own wisdom Red somehow turned that around into a positive," Nelson said. "He was arrogant enough to realize the problem and spit in the face of those people who felt prejudices." Nelson meant that by signing and playing blacks, Auerbach was making a statement. Cousy, however, said he believed it was not strong enough.

"All of us could have done a lot more, given our standing in the community," he said. "We used to go out together constantly within the group, parties at each other's homes. But we could've been more forceful about it. We could've talked to them about the situation, taken them to restaurants, to our country clubs to play golf.

"I was told by my lawyer, who years ago put me through at my club, that the only question they asked about me was, 'If we let him in, do you think he'd ever invite Russell up here?' So we might have been vaguely aware of their embarrassment and anger, but the point is, you just kind of look the other way, even though you know people may be suffering. That's hard to live with now. I've tried to make my little statements through the years. I joined the NAACP. I got involved with the Big Brother program, and I'd bring a black kid to my church, which had an activist priest who was preaching against integration, and I'd parade the kid down the center aisle. Or I'd take him to lunch at the Worcester Country Club and watch the president come over and say, 'Who's this nice little boy?'"

Old habits die hard. Only when the controversy over PGA tournament host Shoal Creek erupted during the summer of 1990 did Cousy realize his country club was still without a black member. In a conversation with Holy Cross basketball coach George Blaney, he discussed the need to "agitate" for change. Until Shoal Creek, country clubs everywhere had been a quiet, unchallenged refuge for whites and, in many cases, men. In the wake of the headlines, some of the clubs—Shoal Creek, for one—claimed they would actively seek minority members. Others undoubtedly were hoping the pressure would ease and they could continue as they were.

By the beginning of 1991, months after Shoal Creek brought the issue to the forefront, the Woodmont Country Club in Rockville, Maryland, still had never enrolled a black member. It did, however, have the man who drafted the first black player in the NBA.

Red Auerbach, whenever he could pull himself away from his basketball team, had been playing gin rummy at the exclusive, all-white club for years.

The blacks who played for Auerbach in the sixties—proud and loyal men such as Sanders, Russell, and K. C. Jones—were a different breed from those who would follow. The Celtics invited them to come out of the rain, and provided respect and at least partial shelter. The injustices of the world they entered are now easily overlooked, dismissed as petty ignorance or minor flaws. The bigger picture is always the team portrait from That Championship Season, any season.

"With a coach other than Red, I would have been the same player, but the question is whether the results would've been the same," said Russell, who refuses to discuss the racial issues that drove him far from Boston, to the Northwest. "It's a team game. I played with very intelligent players. I played with highly motivated players. I was a contributor. I don't think what was accomplished could have been accomplished without specific surroundings.

"So Auerbach's presence was necessary. Having players with talent is one thing, but how do you get the most out of them? How do you turn that into winning consistently? That's the difficult thing. I liked Red, in spite of him. Oh, yeah, he could be annoying. But I'd just look at him. When I look at people that way, they understand."

Auerbach needed Russell. The players thought they needed Auerbach. They were the Celtics. They won championships. They broke records. They shattered barriers. One of those walls came tumbling down in 1964—the year the Celtics, with the addition of Willie Naulls from the Knicks, became the first team to have five blacks on the floor at one time. Once that season, when Naulls was in the game with the four black starters, Auerbach substituted Frank Ramsey for Naulls. Ramsey quickly scored a couple of baskets, and time-out was called. Back in the huddle, Ramsey, out of Kentucky, drawled, "Well, Red, it looks like Ah'm the new white hope."

Auerbach and his players broke up into laughter. A true visionary might have recognized the irony of the moment and not found it so funny. For by the end of Russell's career, 1969, the NBA was at the dawn of economic upheaval and the Celtics were in the market for white saviors. To compete with the upstart ABA, Auerbach, the Celtics, and the rest of the NBA would have to dig deep into their pockets. It would soon be impossible to dictate to a player what he would be making. Tradition and promises of playoff riches lost some of their leverage.

The days of basketball as organic sport and small-time business were coming to an end. Filling the seats, which meant attracting the fans however one could, would be essential. In Boston, the local yokels were still out there, waiting to be pleased.

Chapter 4

Green and White

THE great Celtics start and finish in Boston. Forever Celtics. That's how the song goes, words and music by Arnold Auerbach. "Chances are, if you started with us and did what you were supposed to do, then you would finish your career with us, too," Auerbach said.

The very thought of Larry Bird ever leaving town is as unthinkable as Auerbach's statue by Quincy Market walking off by itself. Bill Russell concluded his pro basketball career right where it began, in Boston Garden. So did Sharman, Heinsohn, and Havlicek. The Joneses—K. C. and Sam—and Satch Sanders took their final bows on Causeway Street, where the T's Green Line rumbles to its last stop, North Station, a few steps from the aroma of stale beer, fresh popcorn, and America's urban past.

Cousy finished here, too—if you forget a seven-game publicity stunt when he donned a Kings uniform as player-coach of a team that couldn't decide between Kansas City and Omaha as its home. Cowens would have retired here, but chose a brief and ill-advised comeback in Milwaukee. The coach there was Don Nelson, a waiver list stray the Celtics took in and raised as their own until Nelson decided it was time to quit.

Once in a while, someone like Danny Ainge has been traded. It's a competitive business; these things happen. Besides, Ainge was not what you would call your Retired Number Celtic. But the truly great Celtics, those headed for eternal afterlife in the bannered Garden rafters, simply do not leave. They are not dumped. They are not embittered. Not the way Jo Jo White, number 10 in your Retired Number program, left after ten years in Celtic green.

It has been more than a dozen years since White was granted the request he reluctantly made—to be traded from the Boston Celtics—amid a storm of anger and recriminations. It wasn't simply John Y. Brown's blasphemous proclamations as much as it was White's decision that he'd had enough of Brown, Auerbach, the city, the legend, the myth, and the dual realities for white and black Celtics. Especially when it came to money.

White called it "the totem pole treatment."

"If you were a black player and you were drawing what management thought was a good salary, and you sprained an ankle, you were expected to hurry back before the injury was healed," White explained. "One of us got hurt, it was, 'Put some ice on it and be out there the next day.' If you said anything, it was, 'Hey, we pay you to do a job.' Then it comes out in the papers and you're the bad guy. But if, say, Havlicek sprained an ankle, he was told to go take a holiday."

Jo Jo White arrived in Boston for the 1969–70 season, year one of the post-Russell era. The Olympian out of Kansas was a gifted, diversified, and worthy successor to Sam Jones in the backcourt. When he left, the Celtics were in chaos. In between, he was a vital component to a second generation of Celtic champions, in 1973–74 and 1975–76. He was the Most Valuable Player in the 1976 NBA Finals, and there is the lasting image of White sitting down on the court, exhausted but unbowed, during a break in the third overtime of game five against Phoenix. White's fluid jumper saved the Celtics that game, that series. He thus came to understand what it meant to be a Celtic, to embrace the notion that no organization was its equal, to acknowledge Auerbach as the creator of this champion's universe.

Auerbach was never his coach, but Tom Heinsohn was Auerbach's guy, and so Red's influence on players was as great as ever. Like those before him, White developed affection and respect for Auerbach, tempered by a healthy dose of fear. White's decade in Boston also coincided with tremendous social and economic upheaval within the sport, to which Auerbach reacted without tolerance and vision. There were victims—almost always black—and White ultimately felt he was one of them.

Auerbach being the godfather, it was always easier to direct one's frustration elsewhere, usually in the direction of the owner-of-the-month. But twelve years of post-career Celtic watching helped White to shape a more realistic historical perspective. If he complained about management as a player, he made certain to say he didn't mean Auerbach. Later, he acknowledged that was like trying to disassociate George Bush from U.S. policy in the Middle East.

"Let me put it this way," White said. "Management is aware of the city. Red was always smart enough to understand [racism] is there. Red plays the hand that's dealt him. That's why Red's always tried to keep it even—six whites, six blacks, maybe seven to five. No matter what they'd say for the record, it was always assumed there had to be a certain amount of whites on the team. We could predict what the team was going to be before we even played an exhibition game. You'd start with the blacks you knew would make it and figure everyone else would be white."

White left the NBA in 1981, held tight to his basketball, even attempted a brief comeback a few years ago in the Continental Basketball Association. He moved to Rochester, New York, his wife's hometown, and has now refocused himself to finding jobs paying fair wages for minorities. White came to believe he experienced similar injustice during his prime years with the Celtics, albeit on a far higher pay scale than the people he works with today. He recalled a contract session years ago when Auerbach told him out-right, "As long as you are here, you will never make as much as Havlicek."

White responded, "Does that mean I will never be as good as John, no matter how good I get?"

Auerbach's policy, as a means of affixing a ceiling to his salary structure, designated a senior Celtic star as the player who would make the most money. It was a matter of principle. That much White could almost accept, though he objected to what he called "significant differences in pay." He also wondered why a similar scale was not adhered to in the case of himself and Dave Cowens, the team's other star who was Boston's first-round draft choice the year after White. In addition, White came to realize that exceptions to this long-standing policy and others could be forced on Auerbach if the player was white. A Havlicek, a Bird, or a McHale was born with leverage that a Jo Jo White could never have.

"Right before I had an operation on my foot in 1977–78, my con-tract was coming up," White said. "They already had an offer on the table. Since that was the case, I had to play it out, even though I was in pain and felt terrible that I couldn't play up to par. Now when they noticed I had a limp on the floor, they pulled the offer right off the table. Reneged. The team wasn't very good, and since I wasn't playing the way I had, in their minds, neither was I. Where was Celtic loyalty?

"Now let's take Larry Bird. He signed a $7 million contract extension while he was hurt, and after he signed, he decided he would have an operation on both his feet. Then the Celtics come out and make it sound like it was their decision. Are you kidding?

"Again, you have a guy like Cedric Maxwell, who got hurt and made some statements when they pressured him to play. He becomes the bad guy, and the next thing you know he's run out of town. That's how most of the black players go. Myself, Paul Silas. Charlie Scott, do you know how he found out he was traded? We were on the road, and he got a call in his hotel room from a secre-tary.

"See, with the white players, it never gets to the point where they have to say, 'Pay me or I'm going elsewhere.' It always seemed to go smoothly back then, and still does now. With the blacks, that always seems to be the story. Reggie Lewis, he was using the same tactics any other player in the league uses: Get a tough agent, make the threat of going someplace else. In Boston, though, he's an ingrate. Was Bird an ingrate when he said he might retire if he didn't get such and such a deal? McHale, when his agent started talking about taking him to the Knicks?

"That's the way it is up there. If you're white, you don't have to deal with it because of the color of your skin. Reggie Lewis has to *force* them to treat him with respect. Otherwise it's like he says. He can go elsewhere."

White sounded a lot like Jerome Stanley, or the late Larry Fleisher. This was the same man who ignored feelers from the ABA out of loyalty to the Celtics. He believed they would always reciprocate. They didn't. Now, White believes the whole equation had changed. "The power is now in the hands of the player. If you're black in Boston, there's really nothing else you can do about the situation, except to send in the agent, take advantage of the power."

In Red Auerbach's mind, when the athlete discovered the agent, it was tantamount to Bonnie hooking up with Clyde. Both relationships were wholly predicated on robbing banks. "It was much more fun in the old days when you didn't have to deal with these agents, nickel and diming you to death," Auerbach said. "When players played for their pay every year."

The idea of players educating themselves and fighting for their true worth was terrifying to Auerbach and to the men who had dictated negotiations for years. Many owners and general managers feared the agent simply for financial considerations. But Auerbach also believed his unparalleled success was based largely on airtight control. Agents were powerful men other than himself who had the ear of his players. They were educated but oily, aggressive but underhanded. Worst of all, they were indifferent to Celtic Pride.

Auerbach was determined not to let them get a foothold. He told his players, "Any of you bring agents in here, I don't talk to them." By the mid- to late sixties, several of the Celtics had associations with agents—particularly the Boston-based Bob Woolf—but almost all were afraid of the consequences if Auerbach found out. "Even when I got there in 1972, it was taboo to mention your agent was coming in," Paul Westphal said. "Everybody knew the last thing you wanted to do was go into Red's office by yourself. I had [Howard] Slusher, and I remember him telling me, 'Whatever you do, don't go in there with him.' I did once. Red told me, 'You don't sign for this, you'll be buried on the bench, you'll never get anywhere.'"

Paul Westphal recalled hearing how Larry Siegfried one year announced he was going into Auerbach's office to "kick some ass." Predictably, Auerbach blew off Siegfried, a reserve guard most of his career. Desperate to depart with something other than the figure Auerbach had tossed at him, Siegfried suddenly asked for a case of Coke. Auerbach said, "What? Oh yeah, sure, you got it." Mission accomplished.

Some of the early-day Celtics, like Cousy and Frank Ramsey, simply circumvented Auerbach and worked private deals with Walter Brown. Ramsey had such confidence in Brown's good nature, he would sign a blank contract and mail it to the owner. But Brown's death in 1964 began the parade of absentee owners and established Auerbach's autonomy. There was nowhere else for a player to go.

"How's that bad leg?" Auerbach would ask Tom Sanders. "You thirty-six or thirty-seven?"

"No, I'm thirty-two," Sanders would reluctantly reply, his advancing age skillfully placed on the table as a management chip.

The more Auerbach talked, the more K. C. Jones knew the price was going down. "You wanna go to another team?" Jones would say later, mimicking Auerbach in mid-negotiation. "You can't shoot, you're short. Where you gonna go?"

Nowhere, of course. The Celtic players liked it just fine where they were. Auerbach was right when he said there was no place like

Boston. Every franchise was struggling for survival in this still fledgling sport, and most pinched as many pennies as they could. But once Russell was aboard, the Celtics represented the NBA's pinnacle. It was inevitable that Auerbach's players would quickly develop a greater sense of purpose and self-esteem, begin to feel that they were more than warm bodies filling a uniform and that they deserved to be acknowledged at the bargaining table. They wanted to stay in Boston, but they wanted to earn decent wages. They were the best in their business. Was that too much to ask? It was not surprising, then, that the first call for an NBA players' union was made in Boston. Or that Bob Cousy made the call.

Even with the arrival of Russell, Cousy was the league's premier draw, a maverick stylist on the court apparently unafraid to assume that role off the court as well. The very basic issues that moved Cousy to push for the creation of the NBA Players Association in 1956 would be laughable by today's standards. But it was not what Cousy's primitive union wanted which startled the owners, as much as it was that the players had organized to ask.

Cousy realized he was in far better position than most to be up front and risk becoming the target of the owners' scorn. He encouraged the stars of the other teams to do the same. He drove to Manchester, New Hampshire, one winter day to consult with Birdie Tebbetts, one of the organizers of the baseball players. He enlisted his old Holy Cross pal, a baseball player turned attorney named Connie Hurley, free of charge. Another friend in Worcester, an insurance man named Joe Sharry, offered his office in the basement of his home. The NBA Players Association was in business.

Dues were $10 a year, collected with varying degrees of difficulty by the team's All-Star representative. A breakthrough of sorts came when the union successfully forced a raise in meal money, from $5 to $7 a day. "The guys were impressed," Cousy said.

Once a year, Cousy and Connie Hurley would make the drive from Worcester to New York, to the office of NBA commissioner Maurice Podoloff. Cousy learned right away that the most well-intentioned commissioner of any sport is merely a dutiful employee of its owners. Podoloff would have the two union men staring at his secretary for hours before allowing them to be ushered in for an audience. "We'd state our case, ask for the things we'd discussed at our meeting," Cousy said. "He'd nod and say, 'I'll see what I can do,' and we'd go back to Boston with our tails between our legs."

Cousy acknowledged that it wasn't until 1964 that the union flourished. By then, he had passed along his presidency to team-mate Tom Heinsohn, and Heinsohn had brought in a friend out of Harvard Law School named Larry Fleisher. It nonetheless annoyed Cousy for many years that Fleisher got all the credit, and few ever recalled the union's pre-Fleisher days. Most of all, Cousy resented Fleisher himself for the perceived slight. "We stuck our necks out and took a lot of crap," Cousy said. "It would've been nice if he'd acknowledged that, if only for the sake of historical accuracy."

Fleisher had developed friendships with several of the Celtics, especially Heinsohn, by preparing income tax returns. Listening to Heinsohn complain about Auerbach and the other NBA power bro-kers, Fleisher sensed not only that the players were tiring of the mandated conditions but that they were bright and committed enough to do something about it. He visualized a time when basket-ball players, being more visible and thus identifiable to fans than baseball and football players, could wield tremendous power within their sport. Fleisher was a Jewish liberal from New York, a man in tune with the social upheaval of the sixties. The growing number of blacks in the sport also was in concert with the times. Fleisher believed men such as Auerbach were condescending to the players in general and the blacks in particular; that these players were sup-posed to be grateful just for being accepted into the club.

Fleisher also recognized the possibility of recruiting an unwitting ally in network television. In October 1963, the union was sched-uled to meet with the league's Board of Governors, it believed, to finalize an agreement for a pension fund, as well as a number of lesser issues. Walter Kennedy, who had succeeded Podoloff as commissioner, asked Heinsohn, "Let me get my feet on the ground." The union reps had assembled in New York for the meeting and wound up spending the day in the lobby of the Commodore Hotel. The Cousy treatment. Insulted and enraged, they plotted a boycott of that season's All-Star Game, scheduled to be televised nationally out of Boston Garden by ABC.

The owners never believed the players would go through with this threat, but the union was adamant. A blizzard hit Boston the day of the game, so the players' meeting set for one P.M. was delayed. It wasn't until late that night that Heinsohn got the signatures of all the players, pledging not to play if their pension demands weren't met.

The day of the game, the owners were furious, none more than Walter Brown. The man who thrived on handshake agreements in the men's room was being embarrassed in his own building in front of the whole country. Worse, ABC was sure to walk away from the NBA for good if there was no game. The future of the league was likely at stake. Playing the corporate bully, Laker owner Bob Short recruited a police officer Heinsohn knew as "Chris the cop" to inform Elgin Baylor and Jerry West that they'd be fired unless they played. Led by Heinsohn and Oscar Robertson, the All-Stars—now half white, half black—remained firm. Michael Jordan, Patrick Ewing, and Larry Bird can trace their extraordinary wealth to the moment Baylor told Chris the cop, "Go tell Bob Short to fuck himself."

Panicked, the owners quickly surrendered on the pension issue. With competition in the form of the ABA about to appear, this was just the beginning of empowerment for Fleisher and the players. Groveling at the knee of Auerbach was a thing of the past. They finally had some leverage. The union would threaten to sit out the 1967 playoffs if it didn't get a comprehensive collective bargaining package. In 1970, the NBA wanted to merge with the ABA. They used NBA commissioner Larry O'Brien's long-standing political connections and attempted to pull an end run through Congress to obtain antitrust exemption. When Ted Kennedy mysteriously appeared as a sponsor of the owners' legislation, he asked an aide how he wound up opposing labor in an industry that was increasingly black. "Oh, I called up Red and he assured me the players are against this union," the aide told Kennedy.

Kennedy, O'Brien, and the other "progressive" forces could not stop progress. The smoke now was being blown right back in Auerbach's face. He would enter the modern age of pro basketball as much an anachronism as Boston Garden. But he was no idiot. He would take his self-serving principles only so far. The previous year, 1969, the ABA had reached out for John Havlicek to the tune of $1.2 million in cash for three years, fully guaranteed. Havlicek, after seven unrepresented seasons with the Celtics, six of them title seasons, was earning $85,000 annually. Bob Woolf, Havlicek's agent, wrote in his book *Friendly Persuasion* that ABA commissioner Jim Gardner was calling Woolf almost daily. Auerbach called once and said, "Do you think another $250 would help the situation?"

The fact that Auerbach was even willing to call and bargain at all with the likes of Bob Woolf was stunning. Less-leveraged Celtics were still forbidden to send in their agents, under threat of banishment. But Auerbach knew he could ill afford to let Havlicek walk away. Havlicek had led the Celtics the previous season in scoring, assists, and minutes. Russell and Sam Jones were at the end of their careers. Auerbach bent over backward, raising his final offer to Havlicek to $600,000 over three years. It was more than Russell ever made, but more significant, it had been achieved with the assistance of the dreaded agent and the threat of imminent departure. Unsure where the new league would lead him, understandably unenthused by the prospect of leaving Boston, Havlicek ultimately accepted Auerbach's offer to remain a Celtic.

What choice did Auerbach have but to give in? Being white, Havlicek was easily the Celtics' most popular player. He was an All-Star the fans could relate to. He was celebrated by New England in typical white-star, superior work-ethic fashion. There was no way Auerbach could have stood on higher moral ground or could have accused Havlicek of being an infidel the way he would years later with Brian Shaw and Reggie Lewis. There was no way he could wage war through his media mouthpieces. He couldn't let Hondo slip away, no matter what indignities he had to endure.

"Red was very polite about the whole thing," Woolf said.

When the contract ran out in 1972, it was the same story, same player, different agent. Auerbach was still trying to circumvent the agent and deal directly with the player, loyal Havlicek. Havlicek found himself hiding out on Old Silver Beach on Cape Cod, trying to avoid Auerbach at all costs while his new agent, Larry Fleisher, tried to negotiate a decent contract for him.

The situation was absurd and Havlicek realized it. The Celtics were holding training camp at the nearby Massachusetts Maritime Academy, by Buzzards Bay. Havlicek wouldn't sign the three-year contract Auerbach had offered him, referring all calls to the man Auerbach dreaded most in the pre–Jerome Stanley days. While Fleisher and Auerbach did their dance at the negotiating table, Havlicek went into seclusion with his family in a little cottage by Old Silver Beach. Nobody but Fleisher had Havlicek's telephone number. He was unavailable to the media and, most importantly, to Auerbach.

"I detested contract talks, I hated them," Havlicek said. "I'm an avid fisherman, so I had plenty to do at the cottage. I'd put in my fishing, then run up and down the road for my workouts." Havlicek had to be careful, because Auerbach was part-owner of the Seacrest Hotel on Old Silver Beach, just a mile from the cottage. Little did Red know ...

In the end, Fleisher believed that Havlicek settled for less than he could have had. "I never used my steal against Philadelphia or any of my big plays as a tool for bargaining, and it wouldn't have worked, anyway," Havlicek said. "The thing Red was least interested

in was stats of any kind. There was no way to fight him. He was protecting his job. I was protecting mine. I just didn't want to leave the
Celts, and they basically came up with my price."

That was the bottom line.

When Don Chaney received an offer from the ABA's St. Louis Spirits in 1975, Auerbach staked out his old negotiating stance: He came
up with a figure and said, "Take it or leave it."

Chaney was no Havlicek. He wasn't a star, but he had been a
starting guard for five of his seven seasons in Boston, including the
1973–74 season when the Celtics won their first championship without Bill Russell. The floor leader of the Elvin Hayes–University of
Houston teams, Duck Chaney was a bigger version of K. C. Jones.
He was a reliable and thoughtful role player who would eventually
become head coach of the Los Angeles Clippers and the Houston
Rockets. While averaging double figures in scoring, Chaney was a
tenacious defender and, at six-five, could be counted on for five or
six rebounds a night.

As a black player in Boston, Chaney didn't enjoy the inherent
popularity of a white role player like Don Nelson. He saw that
Boston presented its problems for black players, but he also loved
his teammates and enjoyed playing for the Celtics. He desperately
wanted Auerbach to reach out to him with just a little good-faith
bargaining, but he suspected trouble when he approached Auerbach with the St. Louis offer. Auerbach said he didn't know
Chaney's contract had expired.

"Whether they were going to give me the money or not wasn't
the point," said Chaney. "The point is, they wanted to squeeze me a
while, and if I'd had no other choice, I would've signed for whatever
they wanted to give me. Certainly I loved it up there and would've
stayed. They didn't lowball me, they just wouldn't negotiate. It was,
'This guy's worth this much amount of dollars and that's what we're
going to pay him.' When I finally committed to St. Louis, it was a
shock to them. They miscalculated and got caught up in my loyalty
for the team. They just underestimated me."

Chaney had Paul Silas to thank for his newfound courage. When Silas arrived in Boston in 1972 from Phoenix, he was surprised at how seldom, if ever, Celtic players spoke about what they were earning. He lobbied teammates and changed the thinking of at least one.

"Red would say, 'I'm giving you this, don't you tell anybody else,'" Chaney said. "No one talked, not until Silas arrived. He started going around asking guys, 'What are you making? What are you making?' Everyone started figuring out where they were in comparison to the rest of the league. It wasn't that good, considering the salary structure had jumped after the ABA had come around."

Silas not only opened Chaney's eyes, but saw red himself after obtaining, with Larry Fleisher's help, backlogged salary lists of all the NBA teams. "I found out that white players were getting higher salaries than blacks," he said. As a second-round draft pick in 1964, Silas compared his salary with that of Dick Snyder, a white shooting guard who was also a second-round pick the same season. Silas was paid $9,000, $10,000, and $11,000 his first three seasons. Snyder got $12,500 as a rookie.

One of the lists was for the 1968 Celtics, which again suggested unequal pay scales for blacks and whites. Silas recalled that Sam Jones, K.C. Jones, and Tom Sanders were making "almost nothing." Sanders, by then a starter and an eight-year veteran of seven championship teams, was "at about $31,000." Larry Siegfried had apparently found a few extra dollars wedged between his cans of Coke. The white backup guard, in his fifth season with the Celtics, was "up near $60,000," according to Silas.

"John Havlicek deserved a lot of money," Silas said. "[Siegfried] was different."

Like Havlicek, Chaney would have taken far less than what the ABA was offering to remain a Celtic. But unlike Havlicek, he was expected to renounce the rights the players had battled for and won. After the episode, Auerbach told the Boston media he was going to give Chaney the money, but the player hadn't given him a chance. "Wasn't true," Chaney said. Ironically, Chaney finished his playing career back in Boston in 1979–80, traded there by the Lakers. But he left town immediately to begin his coaching career as an assistant with the Detroit Pistons. It was much easier leaving Boston the second time around.

Paul Silas, at six-seven, 220, was a rugged, hard-working player who impacted on his team in a firm but quiet way. In 1972–73, Silas's first season with the Celtics, he averaged 13.3 points and grabbed 1,039 rebounds. His presence allowed Dave Cowens, a good jump shooter, to draw opposing centers away from the basket, opening up the lane for Havlicek and Jo Jo White. Cowens improved in every statistical category and, more important, took less pounding, a career-lengthening consideration for a six-eight center.

Silas might have been the sport's greatest tactical rebounder. He barely left his feet, concentrating on position. During his career, Silas's back was the launching site for many opposing leapers, who nearly always failed to land the rebound. Silas was especially good on the offensive boards, averaging more than four rebounds per game with the Celtics. He was one of the first to actually study the arc and spin of his teammates' shots, enabling him to make the best educated guess as to how the ball might come off the rim. He didn't care how many points he scored, or if all of them resulted from opportunities he created for himself. He just worked.

But as a seven-year veteran when he came to Boston, he wasn't a born-and-bred Celtic and had developed strong ideas about what made the basketball world go round. Significantly, he saw it as a business and correctly understood the short shelf life of an NBA player. To make sure his interests were protected, he hired the ubiquitous Fleisher as his agent. In conjunction with his standing as a consummate team player, Silas became a strong union man. When the right time came, he offered himself to Fleisher as a test case against the reserve clause restricting free player movement.

As evidence for their unending claims that Boston represented a better way of NBA life, Auerbach and other Celtic historians have made an example of Silas. Silas, Auerbach contended, was a Celtic skeptic upon his arrival. "But after a while," Auerbach said, "he said to me, 'I used to think all that Celtic Pride and Mystique was a lot of baloney. But there's a lot to it and I'm glad to be part of it.'"

Yet Silas, who went on to become head coach of the Clippers and an assistant with the Nets and Knicks after his playing days, never really swallowed the legend.

"I came to believe *some* of the things," Silas countered. He believed in the selfless style of play and the players' caring for one another most of all. But Silas felt the tradition of the Celtics, as storied as it was and as charming as it could be, was a weapon Auerbach used to keep his payroll down, especially that of his black players. "Guys had an undying loyalty to the team," he said, "but the reverse wasn't true."

Silas's experience with the Celtics only hardened his old union ties, made him more determined not to get cheated when his four-year contract expired with Boston. Auerbach could preach all day about Celtic green. Silas would only take Uncle Sam's. After the Celtics won another championship over Phoenix in 1975–76 led by Cowens, Silas, and Jo Jo White, Silas believed his negotiating leverage was strengthened. He asked for $1 million over four years, which would have placed him behind Havlicek, slightly ahead of Cowens, and far ahead of White. Auerbach offered $600,000 for three years and wouldn't budge.

The argument could have been made that Silas, not being flashy or a big scorer, didn't sell tickets. But Auerbach claimed he never used those arguments. "Over and over," Auerbach wrote in his book, "I'd tell my guys: 'Your salary is what I see with my two eyes.'" He meant that statistics couldn't measure a player's true worth. When Russell was a rookie, in fact, Auerbach promised him that they would never discuss statistics during contract negotiations.

"All year, Red was telling Silas, 'You're my man,'" White said. "Silas was one of those guys you just loved having on your team, one of the guys the Celtics were famous for having. He was a guy who did all the dirty work and never said a word. Red knew Silas's worth to the team. That's why he worked on his head all year. 'You're my man.' But when it came time for the dollars, they did the moon walk."

It was the Tom Sanders story all over again, only now Silas had more options. As the contract dispute dragged into training camp, the Celtics by league rule had to tender Silas an offer. They did so, for $125,000. But here, finally, the luck of the Celtics had run out. The insulting contract offer to Silas was sent unsigned by the Celtics. An error by the secretary—at least that was who was blamed—created the possibility of Silas becoming a free agent. Auerbach had two choices: Pay up or make a deal. So Silas went to Denver, then Seattle, where he played a similar role on another championship team. Typically Irv Levin, the owner, was blamed for letting Silas depart. Auerbach squirmed off the hook. "Hey," Levin said, "when you're an owner worried about money and your general manager says, 'The guy's not worth the money,' you say, 'Great.'"

There wasn't a Celtic who couldn't see what a sad mistake Auerbach had made. Cowens begged him to keep Silas. White spoke in his behalf. Auerbach wouldn't bend, not the way he had for Havlicek.

"If Silas were white," Jo Jo White said, "it would've never come down to that, believe me."

Chapter 5

Changing Faces

BILL Russell's Celtics were always a lousy draw at Boston Garden. People would say Boston was a hockey town, surrounded by New England hockey villages. They would say the local media didn't know how to cover the sport. They never said that Bostonians didn't want to watch black basketball superstars.

"All your writers in this area were assigned to baseball, football, and hockey," Red Auerbach said. "There was nobody of any substance left to cover basketball. They didn't know the game. We were at a loss. So we went out all over New England. We'd play an exhibition at night and give a clinic during the day."

Few seemed to care. Even a messiah as determined as Auerbach couldn't successfully preach color blindness. New England was obviously not ready to embrace black sportsmen. When Bob Cousy retired after the 1962–63 season, Celtic home attendance dropped by about thirteen hundred per game—at a time when they were still an exciting attraction on the road. Ken Hudson, now the team's vice president for community affairs, was a college student near Cincinnati then, and would drive into town whenever the Celtics visited Oscar Robertson's Royals. "The place would always be packed tight," Hudson said. "It wasn't just a following, it was as if they were gods. Russell, Sam Jones. Just the sight of them coming onto the court was exciting."

To Hudson, a black man from Pittsburgh who settled in Boston as an administrator for Gulf Oil in the sixties, the Celtics were champions, heroes. In Boston, they were second banana to the National Hockey League's Bruins, a consistently lousy team that routinely played before sellout Garden crowds. Even when the Celtics were stockpiling those eleven titles in thirteen seasons, they never averaged more than the 10,517 fans per game they attracted in Russell's first season, 1956–57. Mostly their attendance hovered around eight thousand, dipping below that level for five seasons. But that would change.

The 1970–71 season, Jan Volk's first with the Celtics, Auerbach put his friend's son in charge of season tickets. The previous year, the Celtics had sold eight hundred. Based on memory, Volk estimated there was an immediate jump to eleven hundred, then seventeen hundred, then thirty-four hundred. "We were doubling it every year," he said. "We just kept going." By this time, the Celtic stars were clearly Havlicek, Cowens, and White, though White didn't feel like one of the elite. Most of the local endorsements were going to Havlicek, Cowens, and Don Nelson. The media had long been married to Havlicek and now had fallen in love with Cowens, the brawny redhead in the pivot.

"No matter what I did—35 points, 10 assists, 5 or 6 boards—the media would come through the locker door, head past me, and go right over to John and Dave," White said. "You're young and everyone has an ego. You open the paper and want to see some press on yourself. But all you ever heard was 'Cowens and Havlicek, Cowens and Havlicek.'"

Why did Boston finally respond to the Celtics in the early to mid-seventies? There were different ways of saying it, but it all came down to the same unhealthy idea. In *Ever Green,* his 1990 chronology of the Celtics, *Boston Globe* columnist Dan Shaughnessy admitted that Cowens's being white couldn't have hurt, but concluded that it was his fiery style and uncomplicated persona that appealed to fans. The less-popular Russell was more complex. Tom Heinsohn said, "It wasn't so much that Russell was black, but he was an enigma to most people."

Yet less than a decade later, Bostonians flocked to the Garden in record numbers to welcome Larry Bird, who spent his senior year at Indiana State running full speed from anyone with a microphone and a notebook. Bird was basketball's Howard Hughes, but the white enigma apparently wasn't as puzzling or distasteful as the black one.

The truth is, Cowens's playing style wasn't that much different from Russell's. Being left-handed, both presented problems of unfamiliarity for opponents. Although Cowens was an undersized center at six-eight, Russell was generally thought to be smaller than his listed six-eleven. Like Cowens, Russell was always an underdog against such a physical marvel as Chamberlain. A fire burned deep within both players, and a less discriminatory society would have embraced Russell for the same reasons in the sixties as it did Cowens in the seventies.

"I know people today talk about Bird, but I think Cowens had as much to do with turning the city on to the Celtics as anyone," Ken Hudson said. "He was a guy the Boston working class could relate to." After the Celtics won the NBA title in 1973–74, Boston Garden attendance surged by more than 2,000 tickets per game, from 11,102 to 13,307, roughly 1,500 short of capacity. Finally, after almost three decades, after eleven championships, the Celtics were becoming a hot ticket in Boston.

Cowen's fire turned on the fans. Heinsohn and the other players would tell him he needed to be emotional and physical or he'd be just another white guy. Actually, he was the *only* white guy. After a generation dominated by Russell and Chamberlain, Cowens represented the first white center since George Mikan who could be included among the league's elite. With the exception of Jerry Lucas, the other white centers were, for the most part, an assortment of immobile goons and geeks. Chamberlain was still a force in Los Angeles, Willis Reed had become the heart of a two-time Knick championship team in New York. Nate Thurmond was the inner strength of the San Francisco Warriors. There were a host of other talented black centers, like Elvin Hayes in Houston, Wes Unseld in Baltimore, Bob Lanier in Detroit, Bob McAdoo in Buffalo, and Sam Lacey in Kansas City. In Milwaukee, however, Kareem Abdul-Jabbar stood alone, at seven-two, the wonder of the basketball universe.

If ever there was a polar opposite to what Cowens represented in Boston, it was Jabbar. Russell had been difficult for middle-class Boston to accept. But Jabbar might as well have been from outer space. At least Russell had demonstrated compliance by embracing the Celtics' self-sacrificing way of life. Playing for an expansion team that couldn't have won twenty-five games without him, Jabbar was viewed strictly as an individual. The other Milwaukee Bucks were tiny, lifeless moons orbiting Kareem. He was powerful and intelligent, but moody and aloof. As a Muslim who had renounced his family name, Lew Alcindor, he was further marked as part of a murky black power movement. White America related to him then much as it now relates to Georgetown basketball coach John Thompson.

Jabbar was inordinately graceful with his unstoppable creation, the sky hook, and his long, loping strides. At times, he appeared to dominate the game without even exerting himself. His placid expression almost never changed, and when he didn't play well or his team lost, he was often and unfairly judged not to care. The matchup of Kareem Abdul-Jabbar versus David Cowens for the 1973–74 NBA championship hooked right into classic racial stereotyping—the "tough, hungry" white against the "talented, lazy" black. Given his fame and notoriety at UCLA, now standing tall and unforgiving on his NBA pedestal, Jabbar was the perfect Boston Garden villain. By comparison, Cowens was six inches smaller, his muscular arms ever in motion, his face a mask of emotion. To white Boston, he was some red-cheeked Saskatchewan tough on skates, digging the puck out of the corner.

That the Celtics won in a magnificent seven-game struggle only made their return to the top that much sweeter. That the series included one of the league's most dramatic finishes to a championship-round game only made it more memorable. Jabbar's sky hook, deep on the right baseline with three seconds left in double overtime, gave the Bucks a 102–101 game six victory. This Friday night game achieved the highest NBA television rating to that point—evidence that all of America, not just Boston, had hooked into the Cowens-Jabbar showdown.

Jabbar's theatrical shot sent the series back to Milwaukee for the deciding seventh game. The Celtics won easily, 102–87, as Cowens outplayed Jabbar with 28 points and 14 rebounds. Cowens had immeasurable defensive assistance from Paul Silas. The plucky forward was usually right behind Jabbar in the event Cowens, fronting the Milwaukee center, was beaten on an entry pass to the pivot. As a result, Jabbar was held scoreless for an unthinkable eighteen-minute period as the Celtics built an insurmountable lead. While the city of Boston undoubtedly interpreted this as a triumph for the working man over the dilettante Jabbar, Cowens understood completely that it was more a demonstration of how well he and Silas worked together. It made Cowens appreciate Silas as the perfect complementary player to himself. The two became close friends, more soul mates than teammates.

But when Silas left town following their second championship together in the spring of 1976, Cowens suddenly lost his enthusiasm for the sport. Eight games into the 1976–77 season, he took an indefinite leave of absence from basketball. Sidney Wicks took this abdication as a direct slap. Wicks was Silas's replacement, but he was nothing like Silas. Though he could rebound and score, he was flashy, sensitive, high-strung. He was used to having the ball. Now everyone in Boston, Cowens most of all, wanted him to transform into hard-nosed, selfless Paul Silas.

Wicks had come in a deal from Portland before Silas's departure. For Silas, Auerbach brought in Curtis Rowe, Wicks's old UCLA running mate. Both were established NBA players, albeit on substandard teams. From the time they arrived in Boston, it was as if, according to Wicks, people were saying, "What the hell are you doing here?"

Cowens has long maintained he was burned out at the time, that his decision had to do with no one but himself. But the timing, Wicks believed, was at best a subconscious snub. It validated the city's suspicions that he and Rowe couldn't be good Celtics, as if the bloodlines weren't right.

"Cowens didn't know Curtis or myself," Wicks said. "He wanted the situation he had before. I felt he was making a negative statement. The media made it seem like we drove him off. They'd rip you and never look you in the eye. They'd only talk to Cowens, Havlicek, or the coach. It was like, the great Dave Cowens didn't want anything to do with these guys, why should we? It seemed to me up there the black players in Boston weren't people. We were like machines. If we worked out, fine. If not, treat 'em like shit."

Heinsohn, still head coach, believed Wicks was a solid player and pleaded with people not to compare him to Silas. Wicks, who moved back to Los Angeles later and suffered the agonies of a serious auto accident, always retained respect for his Celtic coach. "The only person who took me for myself and treated me like a human being in Boston was Tommy Heinsohn." But Heinsohn wasn't enough. Neither Wicks nor Rowe, predictably under the circumstances, maintained his previous level of play. Both careers crumbled in Boston, and the Celtics simultaneously descended into what is considered the franchise's nadir.

When the bottom dropped out in 1978–79, the Celtics quickly became your basic NBA ragtag operation. Coaching changes—Tom Sanders for Heinsohn, Cowens for Sanders—were made in desperation. Players came and went with the quickness of a back-door play.

The last champs: The 1985–86 Celtics, with eight whites and four blacks in a league that is 72 percent black, walked over the Houston Rockets in six games. (© *Steve Lipofsky*)

Celtics founder Walter Brown risked losing his home to keep the club afloat. (© *Dick Raphael*)

Dolph Schayes of the Syracuse Nationals shaking hands with the enemy, Bob Cousy. (*Basketball Hall of Fame*)

Chuck Cooper, with Coach Auerbach, broke the color barrier only because Walter Brown stood up to the league's owners. (*Basketball Hall of Fame*)

The great Bill Russell (*right*) was the victim of relentless racism in Boston, where many wondered why he was so aloof. (© *Dick Raphael*)

Paul Silas liked being a Celtic—except on payday. (© *Dick Raphael*)

Coach Tom Sanders offers some advice to Jo Jo White, the brilliant guard who left town with a bitter taste in his mouth. White has criticized the racial composition of the team. (© *Dick Raphael*)

Don Chaney was another black Celtic who wasn't exactly treated like family. (© *Dick Raphael*)

Curtis Rowe (*left*) and Sidney Wicks sat at the end of the bench, where the taunts were loudest. (© *Dick Raphael*)

In a classic matchup of two of the game's greatest white stars, John Havlicek slips a pass by Billy Cunningham of Philadelphia. (© *Dick Raphael*)

Bob McAdoo believes his brief, unhappy stay in Boston derailed his career. (© *Dick Raphael*)

Celtic coach Bill Fitch, engineer of the Robert Parish and Kevin McHale deals, got little credit for the team's successes—and lots of blame for its failures. (© *Dick Raphael*)

Owner Harry Mangurian re-
lieved Auerbach in tense negotiations and made Larry Bird
the highest-paid rookie ever.
(© *Dick Raphael*)

Julius Erving (*left*) was the
NBA's flagship superstar until
Larry Bird (and Magic John-
son) came along and drove the
league to unimagined heights.
(© *Dick Raphael*)

Cedric Maxwell's thanks for doing the dirty work around the basket was a one-way ticket out of town with no handshake. (© *Dick Raphael*)

Two great whites, Bill Walton and Dave Cowens, jump center. Walton came to Boston in 1986, sans pony-tail, and helped Boston to its six-teenth championship. (© *Dick Raphael*)

Gerald Henderson's classic steal against the Lakers in game two of the 1984 finals ranked with Havlicek's and Bird's. But Henderson's reward was exile to Seattle. (© *Dick Raphael*)

Unhappy fans: John Y. Brown with his wife, Phyllis George *(center)*, and Red Auerbach and Harry Mangurian *(top right)*. (© *Dick Raphael*)

Owner Irv Levin is jeered at John Havlicek's retirement party. But he grins and bears it. (© *Dick Raphael*)

The Celtics' all-white front office starting five through the 1980s: Red Auerbach, president; Jan Volk, general manager; Don Gaston, chairman of the board; Paul Dupee, vice chairman; and Alan Cohen, vice chairman. (© *Dick Raphael*)

After the steal: Dennis Johnson and Larry Bird celebrate DJ's winning layup in game five of the 1987 Eastern Conference finals. (© *Dick Raphael*)

Isiah Thomas still wishes he could erase one pass—and one postgame comment—he made at Boston Garden on a fateful day in 1987. (© *Dick Raphael*)

In Cedric Maxwell's opinion, even the great Magic Johnson, here going against Danny Ainge, would not have been the star Larry Bird is in Boston. (© *Dick Raphael*)

Inside Boston Garden's cozy, country club confines, where black fans seldom venture, Larry Bird fires another three-pointer. (© *Dick Raphael*)

K. C. Jones's departure as Celtic coach wasn't handled quite as graciously as his retirement from the backcourt. (© *Dick Raphael*)

The long arm of the Celtics reached across the Atlantic to Rome and forced Brian Shaw back to Boston. (© *Dick Raphael*)

Robert Parish at the 1989 Celtics Invitational Classic golf and tennis tournament. Commercially speaking, Boston didn't open its arms to the venerable center. *(Boys and Girls Clubs of Boston)*

Rookie sensation Dee Brown: From facedown on a Wellesley Street to soaring high above the crowd. *(© Dick Raphael)*

M. L. Carr reached out to the Boston community—black and white- on his own. Here he speaks at the Roxbury Boys and Girls Club. (*Boys and Girls Clubs of Boston*)

Dave Gavitt (*left*), the new Celtics CEO, was ushered in by Alan Cohen. (© *Steve Lipofsky*)

Agent Jerome Stanley *(left)* wages "thermonuclear warfare" against the Celtics with his biggest weapon, client Reggie Lewis. (© *Steve Lipofsky*)

Reggie Lewis became the spokesman for the Boys and Girls Clubs of Boston in 1990. (© *Steve Lipofsky*)

With his long arms and strides, Kevin McHale reached all-star status as a power forward and across racial barriers inside the Celtics locker room. (© *Dick Raphael*)

Kevin Gamble demonstrated that he could score everywhere but at the negotiating table, moving Robert Parish to complain in October 1991 that his friend was being "nickeled and dimed" by Celtics management. (© *Dick Raphael*)

Levin and John Y. Brown pulled their franchise swap and chose up sides like it was a schoolyard scrimmage.

Many of these new Celtics were black, no longer a minority on the team. Combined with the losing, this created an explosive setting, especially when Auerbach appointed the hard-nosed Cowens player-coach, replacing Tom Sanders, who might have gone on to a long and prosperous coaching career had Auerbach just let him hang on the remainder of the season for the arrival of Larry Bird. "Obviously it was unfair," Sanders said. "But that's part of the deal."

Cowens being named player-coach was the final straw for White. He was team captain, its senior player. He wasn't even consulted on the Cowens appointment. He was openly bitter, an easy target for frustrated fans.

Few would dwell on Auerbach's Silas blunder. Few would acknowledge that Cowens was not the same player sans Silas, or admit that Havlicek could no longer outwork opponents now that he'd lost a step. The focus shifted to Brown's meddling, White's intransigence, the un-Celtic-like personas of Wicks, Rowe, Billy Knight, Tiny Archibald, and Marvin Barnes.

Len Elmore, the former NBA center and Celtic opponent, remembered what it was like to visit Boston Garden during this Ice Age. "People would walk past the bench and say, 'Cowens, Havlicek, you're great, the rest of you guys ain't worth a damn,'" Elmore said.

It became a regular occurrence, White said. When some of the black players, himself included, left the Garden after a game late at night to walk in the darkness toward their cars, they heard from the distance, among other things, "You guys fucking suck." Sometimes eggs would be smashed against the cars. The players routinely checked to make sure their tires weren't slashed. On occasion, they were.

This intolerance and contempt was not limited to the street. K. C. Jones, brought in by Sanders as an assistant coach, said he "got a sniff of racism on that team." Archibald, an All-Star point guard in

Kansas City, said he felt there was a reluctance to play him and White together in the backcourt. Both wanted to be traded. At practice one day, a frustrated Cowens announced there was no market for either. This only further alienated White from the Celtics and his former roommate, Cowens. He and Archibald were convinced the club only wanted Ernie DiGregorio, a flashy white player from down the road in Providence, to win the job. He couldn't, so the Celtics traded for Chris Ford, another white, and handed him a job.

"They said Jo Jo and I couldn't play together because neither one of us was a true point guard," Archibald said. "To me, that sounded like what they used to tell a lot of black kids in college who wanted to play quarterback."

In the late seventies, Boston was not the only town that couldn't relate to the changing face of the NBA. The league, still considered an upstart by historic standards, was fighting for consideration as a major American sports league. Some of the smaller-market teams were rickety, and the big-market franchises such as New York and Chicago were simply not very good.

The 1976 merger with the ABA and its new breed of stars like Julius Erving, David Thompson, and George McGinnis had failed to capture mainstream America. Two years in a row, the Bullets from the Maryland suburbs of Washington battled the Seattle SuperSonics in the finals. Both were strong, well-coached teams, but major-market ratings were low. As the eighties approached, the NBA was in danger of losing its network television contract with CBS.

In 1980, when Magic Johnson led his Lakers to the title against Erving's Philadelphia 76ers, the game six clincher was shown by delayed tape in the East, ending early the next morning. Few prime-time fans saw the six-nine rookie point guard play offensive center for the Lakers and score 42 points in place of the injured Kareem Abdul-Jabbar. CBS would not preempt "Dallas" for a league whose regular-season Sunday afternoon games were outrated by whatever programming other networks threw at them—bowling and trash-sport Superstars among the bunch. Without powerful, racially balanced teams like the Celtics and the New York Knicks of the early seventies, there was little promotion or exposure.

The consensus perception of the NBA was that its players made too much money, that they didn't play hard until the last two minutes of a game, or during the playoffs. The game was thought to be an undisciplined street-brand version of its former, purer self, another way of saying the league was too black to please the viewing public. A story published by the San Diego edition of the *Los Angeles Times* reported that up to 75 percent of its players were said to have used drugs. The league, by now, just happened to be roughly 75 percent black.

It was universally agreed that these NBA players were more talented than their predecessors. Teams routinely were making 50 percent of their shots, up from the 30s and 40s of the old days. But they were also considered less intelligent and motivated. The Auerbachs of the world believed they had been corrupted by money.

"It is a fact that white people in general look disfavorably upon blacks who are making astronomical amounts of money if it appears they are not working hard for that money," Paul Silas, then president of the Players Association, was quoted in a February 26, 1979, *Sports Illustrated* article entitled "There's an Ill Wind Blowing for the NBA." "Our players have become so good that it appears they're doing things too easily, that they don't have the intensity they once had."

Bob McAdoo a former Boston center now playing professionally in Italy, sensed that he was exactly the kind of player Paul Silas was talking about. It all looked too easy for him. His offense was a study in rhythm and grace, the opposite of his intradivisional rival, Dave Cowens. The largely white paying public viewed him as a man with some freakish magnetic shooting touch, not as a top-caliber basketball player. Players his size were not supposed to be roaming the perimeter, firing away from eighteen feet. No big man ever shot the jumper like McAdoo, a revolutionary player whose height would not necessarily determine his position on the floor.

After two years of junior college ball, then one season for Dean

Smith at North Carolina, McAdoo quickly became one of the top scorers in the NBA and an All-Star center with the Buffalo Braves. He was six-ten, 225, but his body and mindset really weren't built for traditional low-post chores. He was a classic face-the-basket scorer. Critics, unable to see he was out of position at center, labeled him a selfish gunner who cared only about points, not about winning. Although he was advertised as a franchise player at the box office, especially after his trade to New York, he never pretended to be anything of the kind.

"He wasn't a center, though you could play him there to create a matchup problem," said Willis Reed, who'd brought him to New York. "He was a guy who'd go out and shoot the guards for money and beat them. People didn't understand him, 'cause he didn't say a lot, but Bobby was a fierce competitor. If he was playing today in the NBA, you'd see him used at big forward, small forward, center, maybe even the shooting guard. He'd be the perfect complementary player for a guy like Patrick Ewing."

He would, in other words, be Karl Malone. In McAdoo's last full season with the Knicks, as a center, he averaged 26.6 points and 13 rebounds. He made 52 percent of his shots, especially impressive for a jump shooter. It was said he never gave the ball up, and he no doubt viewed the pass as a second or third option. But he also averaged 4 assists. Seasons like that one at Madison Square Garden earned him a listing in the NBA Register's section honoring the league's "All-Time Greats."

With Reed gone, with Red Holzman back in November 1978, McAdoo would soon be the fall guy for an impatient, unstable Madison Square Garden hierarchy. One Monday morning in February, McAdoo was asleep with his wife in his northern New Jersey home when the doorbell rang. It was not yet six A.M. McAdoo went to the window, looked down, and saw his friend and former Knick teammate Micheal Ray Richardson frantically pushing the bell.

"Mac, Mac, you been traded, you been traded," Richardson yelled to him.

"Get outta here, man, I'm tired," McAdoo told him.

"No, Mac, I heard it on the radio."

McAdoo told Richardson to bring the *New York Times* up from the driveway. Sure enough, there it was on the front sports page: MCADOO TO THE CELTICS FOR THREE NO. 1 DRAFT PICKS. Two nights before, as the Knicks and Celtics played in Madison Square Garden, John Y. Brown and Sonny Werblin had made the deal, under the influence of cocktails and, it was said in NBA circles, Brown's wife, Phyllis George, the former Miss America. George was a McAdoo fan. News of the deal broke late that Sunday night. Contacted at his home for a comment by a reporter, Auerbach yelled into the phone, "Call John Y., he made the fucking deal."

Boston turned out to be the worst place Bob McAdoo could ever go. He was the radical, new wave, black player, in the lair of basketball's old-line conservatives. Here, at Boston Garden, McAdoo was looked at as some hideous creature polluting a sacred shrine. This place, McAdoo would say later, was somewhere black players "try to avoid like the plague."

From the beginning, the deal had been wrong. K. C. Jones recalled picking McAdoo up at the airport in San Antonio after the trade to the Celtics and said that McAdoo seemed "very sad." It turned out McAdoo had good reason to be.

"Dave Cowens, who was the coach then, he and Red Auerbach really didn't want me," McAdoo said. "I even heard Chris Ford say, 'Oh, all this guy wants to do is shoot the ball.' You know, I'd been a winner all my life, and I was proud of what I had done. I'd always done my job, and that's what basketball's all about. But if you can't score, then shut up, sit down, let me do my job, don't come up to me with this Celtic crap. Everybody is an individual trying to do their job, the pressure's on you to take care of your family. All that other crap they talk about up there, they're just trying to manipulate you like you don't matter.

"I went up there and Cowens tried to play me seven minutes, ten minutes, tried to put me in chains. Tried to embarrass me, totally insult me. I wasn't going to accept that. He of all people should've been the first one to say, 'McAdoo is playing forty minutes,' the way I destroyed him on the court. Go back and look, I probably had some of my greatest games against Boston.

"He probably didn't think I was a true Celtic, or whatever. But the fact is, they just weren't going to accept my talent up there. They just don't accept black talent. Black talent in Boston fits in. White talent runs the show. It's unspoken in the league—but all the players know it, the black players. I don't care what a player tells you for the political purposes of staying in the league. I've heard this over and over from guys in the league over the years, and I've been asked about it by players, too. Blacks don't want to get traded up there and they don't want to get drafted. They just don't, because black players wind up getting kicked out of town. And after you finish with Boston, not only are you out of town, your reputation is destroyed. It's like, 'He couldn't play for the Celtics. He was bad.'"

Going to Boston began a two-and-a-half-year detour from which McAdoo's NBA career never fully recovered. He was never again considered one of the league's elite stars, though he did resurface to win two championships with Magic Johnson's and Kareem Abdul-Jabbar's Lakers. He continued banging home jumpers in Italy through the 1990–91 season, months before his fortieth birthday.

Anywhere but Boston. Those were McAdoo's watchwords, always. During the summer of 1980, just before the Celtics traded him to Detroit, McAdoo got a call from a reporter at his home in New Jersey. The reporter told him the Celtics had signed Larry Bird. The era of Dave Cowens was now officially over; the next white star was in the fold. The reporter asked McAdoo an ignorant question. Did McAdoo think he could play with Bird, or did he think he would be traded to one of the teams that badly needed his box-office appeal, such as the lowly New Jersey Nets? McAdoo, typically, was honest.

"Are you kidding?" McAdoo told the reporter. "The Celtics got their white superstar. They ain't going to let me anywhere near him."

Chapter 6

Bird Watching

O N THE DAY of the 1979 NCAA basketball semifinals, March 24, Jud Heathcote sat in the stands of the Salt Palace in Salt Lake City, watching an extraordinary player named Larry Bird hit ten straight shots in the first half against Ray Meyer and DePaul. Bird was supposed to have been playing with a bad thumb on his right hand. DePaul, with Mark Aguirre, Clyde Bradshaw, and Gary Garland, was supposed to have too many blue-chip players for Bird and Indiana State. In the aristocratic world of big-time college sports, Sycamores from Terre Haute, Indiana, were not supposed to go around beating Blue Demons from Chicago.

Bird's team won anyway, 76–74. "That's not a Bird, that's a whole flock," Jud Heathcote said.

The coach of the Michigan State Spartans, who would be Bird's next target in the championship game two days later, thus retired to his hotel room with Bird on his brain. He would have one day of practice to prepare for this blond, gawky sensation who, for all of that season, had treated the media and opposing defenses with equal disdain.

Over dinner, Heathcote thought about Bird, from soup to salad, right on through dessert. He studied films late into the night. He watched Bird, number 33 in the powder-blue ISU uniform, confound just about every kind of defense. At six-nine, Bird could take big defenders away from the basket and torture them with his quick-release, flick-of-the-wrists, feet-barely-off-the-ground jump shot. He was strong and clever enough to be a force around the basket. But what worried Heathcote most was Bird's sheer canniness, his ability to pass, to create, the hard evidence that anyone who stepped on the court as a teammate was immediately a better player. How could one player—a noncenter, at that—so dramatically affect the fate of such inferior talent around him?

That night, the answer came to Heathcote. It occurred to him that Larry Bird wasn't such a stranger after all. Making exception for style, he realized he'd been watching the same player all season—at six-nine the same size, give or take a fraction. Wearing number 33, same number. The color of the skin was different, the personality antithetical, but Heathcote's own star, Earvin "Magic" Johnson, was Larry Bird in his approach to the game. And Heathcote, by the end of the night, knew how he could prepare to win the national title.

The next day, Heathcote gathered his players for a prepractice meeting. He put his arm around Johnson, his nineteen-year-old sophomore, and told him for this practice he was being moved from the starting team to the scouting team. Johnson looked at his coach in disbelief. "Gentlemen," Heathcote said, "meet Larry Bird." He put four of his starters into a matchup zone defense. One player was assigned to Magic/Bird. The plan went this way: Whenever Magic/Bird would touch the ball, whichever player was closest in the zone would double-team with his hands up. The idea was not only to take away Bird's shot, but to force him away from the middle of the floor, reduce his passing options.

Heathcote turned back to Johnson. He handed him the ball. He said, "You be Bird."

"It was a light kind of practice," Heathcote said. "Magic was throwing passes every which way. He took shots from every crazy angle he could think of. He went into the corner and hit a damned hook shot. By the end of the day, there was nothing Bird could possibly show us that we hadn't already seen." By the end of the day, Magic Johnson had been Larry Bird and then some. He knew what Bird would face the following night. Bird was not only an opponent anymore, he was a soul mate.

"For me, that practice was mostly fun," Johnson said. "That was college, where you played a more controlled game. Maybe Larry had more freedom because he was so much better than anyone else on his team. But, for me, it was just fun getting the green light to do anything I could think of. Shoot it, drive it, kick it. I was Larry. I guess that was a beginning."

They had met before, played with each other for a U.S. All-Star team at an international tournament during the summer of 1978. For three games, with Kentucky's Joe B. Hall coaching, Magic and Bird played with the second unit behind more experienced players such as Jack Givens, Rick Robey, Darrell Griffith, and Joe Barry Carroll.

"I remember us always killing the first team in practice," Magic said.

"All I remember is that Magic wouldn't pass me the ball," Bird said.

They were just names and faces to each other then. Now, at the Salt Palace, at the NCAA championship game, they were standing together on the threshold of a rich, new world they would profoundly shape. They would enter the slumping National Basketball Association together, a prepackaged phenomenon. Magic being Bird on the day before he would win the national title was just the beginning. For the next decade, probably forever, Magic and Bird would be innocent actors on a transcontinental basketball stage that was ready to explode with big bucks and big names. Johnson would be a Laker. Bird would be a Celtic. Bird would get more attention, more acclaim as the greatest ever, but fewer titles. But before the pros could exploit their abilities and their pigmentation, college basketball was going to get its shot. The Celtics, who already owned Bird's draft rights, were watching with no sense of urgency.

✳ ✳ ✳

Even as Larry Bird was leading the Sycamore charge up Magic mountain, the Celtics really had no idea about what sort of prize they had. "I didn't know Bird was that great," Auerbach said. "If I said I did, I'd be lying. I knew he could shoot, he could pass. I didn't know he could rebound that well, I didn't know he had that tremendous competitive drive, how strongly he was self-motivated. I didn't know his leadership capabilities."

Auerbach didn't know much about Bird, because he hadn't bothered to find out. He was never a particularly avid follower of the college game. He didn't hire an assistant coach to scout opponents or colleges until 1971, when John Killilea came aboard straight out of coaching high school basketball in Quincy, Massachusetts. Even then, it was catch-as-catch-can. Killilea would only be permitted to scout a college game if it coincided with an NBA contest in the same city, or if it was along a linear flight route.

The first time Killilea saw Bird play was his sophomore season at an Indiana State–St. Louis University game in St. Louis. Killilea, a quick study, typically was in town only long enough to switch jets. Under strict instructions from Auerbach to head back to Boston as fast as possible and save a few bucks in expenses, Killilea was forced to leave the game at halftime. "I remember thinking this guy is so marvelous," Killilea said. "But I didn't see much of him."

Auerbach's scouting team at the time consisted of himself, Killilea, and Tommy Heinsohn. Auerbach would catch a few games at Madison Square Garden, melding into the crowd so that he'd be left alone by some of his least favorite fans. He would scout a few games in Washington, a few in Boston. That was it. He was strictly a Northeast corridor presence. Heinsohn would sneak a few peeks at college talent here and there, but he really didn't have the time. This left an energetic Killilea to do the bulk of the work, between a hundred other duties, for the grand salary of $25,000 per year.

As might be expected with this sort of disorganization and lack of commitment, there were some terrible drafting gaffes during the pre-Bird years by Auerbach and his overworked, underpaid staff.

The most ridiculous scenario, however, was saved for 1973. Then, Heinsohn, Killilea, and Auerbach all got it in their heads to draft different players, none of them particularly distinguished. Killilea championed Phil Hankinson from Penn, a six-eight forward who eventually was taken in the second round by Boston. Killilea saw him as "a Havlicek-type runner," but Hankinson averaged only 3.9 points per game after ripping up his knees. Heinsohn loved Swen Nater of UCLA, who was picked by the Milwaukee Bucks right before the Celtics had their choice. Nater would go on to become a classic journeyman center for seven ABA and NBA teams. Auerbach had decided on somebody else, though: Steve Downing of Indiana.

Through the years, for reasons known only to NBA general managers, loutish Indiana coach Bobby Knight has wielded a great deal of influence on draft day. Knight has never been known to be a particularly good judge of talent. Though he won the gold medal in the Soviet-boycotted 1984 Olympics with Patrick Ewing and Michael Jordan, he is infamous for cutting Charles Barkley and Karl Malone from that team while including the forgettable Jeff Turner, Steve Alford, and marginal centers Joe Kleine and Jon Koncak. He allowed Larry Bird to slip through his fingers.

Knight has won at Indiana University in part because of his organizational prowess and tactical skills, but largely because of the enormous pool of homegrown Indiana talent that walks onto his campus and begs for scholarships. Yet somehow, every draft, he is suddenly viewed as a great sage by men like Auerbach and former Knicks GM Eddie Donovan, who are impressed by his stature. In 1984, the Nets drafted Turner ahead of Vern Fleming and Jerome Kersey because Knight recommended him. Back in 1973, Knight had prepared a twenty-minute highlight film of his forward, Downing. This was about all Auerbach had seen or heard of this kid. Killilea couldn't remember ever scouting him. But Knight said he could play big, and that was good enough. Auerbach took Downing, outbid the ABA Pacers for him. Downing averaged 2.7 points his first season, 0.0 points his second. That was it.

Having learned a lesson of sorts, Auerbach allowed Killilea a bit more freedom to travel around and get a feel for the college talent. Still, this was rudimentary stuff. There was no ESPN broadcasting games from all over the country, no computer analyses or serious NBA scouting network. There were no spring or summer meat markets, as the NBA now sponsors in Orlando and Chicago, to sort through the marginal talent. A few schools provided videotapes upon request, but that was all. Even for scouting upcoming NBA opponents, the technology was Stone Age. There was no Kodak Analyzer—a favorite videotape splicer later pioneered by Celtic coach Jimmy Rodgers. Killilea would chart the plays of Philadelphia or Los Angeles, then go to the local newspaper office to send his scouting sheet back to the Celtics via a forerunner of the fax machine.

Killilea caught up with Bird again one night in Cincinnati during his sophomore year, in a tournament game at Cincinnati against Arkansas and Sidney Moncrief. This time, Killilea was truly awestruck by both players. "It was this great two-point game that they both completely dominated," Killilea said. "Both players revolutionized the game in their own way, changed the way we looked at their positions. They were two of the greatest in the decade."

Killilea brought this news back to Auerbach, who listened. But when it came time to draft Bird as a junior eligible in 1978, Killilea was no longer around to get the credit. Killilea had gotten an offer from former Celtic Don Nelson in Milwaukee. "I was making $25,000, and Nelson offered me about $40,000," Killilea said. "All of a sudden, Red was this great guy taking me to his grandchild's apartment, going out to dinner, seeing his apartment redone. We were suddenly family."

But the paycheck, $25,000, was still going to stay the same. Killilea moved on—first to Milwaukee, then to New Jersey, then to Houston. Auerbach remembered enough about this kid Bird to give him a shot. "Red was looking for a new 'hope,'" Jo Jo White said. "As soon as Cowens slowed down, we all knew that.'

❖ ❖ ❖

Everybody knew about Earvin Johnson. He was old news. Already Magic as a high school teen in East Lansing, he was an urban black kid with an engaging smile and infectious enthusiasm. From the day he walked into Jenison Fieldhouse on the sprawling Michigan State campus, Heathcote and others felt this glow about him, a sense he was going places, with the ball and with his life.

Bird, though, was different. Virtually unheard of before his twenty-first birthday, he was a pale white kid from the Indiana sticks who couldn't conform to Knight, the legend at Icon U., and dropped out to work on a garbage truck. He moved on to flourish as a diamond in the NCAA Division I rough at an unheralded Missouri Valley Conference school in the drab Illinois border town of Terre Haute. "Earvin was one of these kids college coaches knew about from the time he was fourteen, fifteen," Heathcote said. "Before the end of his junior year at Indiana State, who really knew anything about Larry Bird?"

Even then, who really knew? "I had friends in Denver, which is where I transferred from," Bob Heaton, a Bird teammate, said. "I went back for a visit once and they'd all heard of Larry, the guy scoring all the points. They were just shocked when they found out he wasn't black."

Now, on the day before the biggest game of their lives, Heathcote had come to the realization years before others would: Johnson and Bird together were about to take the game back from the runners, the dunkers, and the giants who dominated the sport and made it predictable from within five feet of the basket. It didn't matter where you put these two on the court. The offense would work around them. They were revolutionary players of the eighties, players for any position, all roles, converging on Salt Lake City from different corners of the basketball universe.

By all rights, in any other year, the joyous Magic Johnson should have owned Salt Lake City. Instead he had to share it with this shy, white curiosity. Those close to Bird couldn't decide if he was afraid or unimpressed by this national showcase. The year before, on the night of the 1978 title game between Kentucky and Duke, Bird found himself at a table in a Terre Haute restaurant with Heaton, his roommate, and an Indiana State recruit. Heaton looked up at the game on a television screen near the bar. He said to his two companions, "Imagine playing in a game like that, with the whole country watching." Bird looked up at the TV for a moment. "Yeah," he said. Nothing more. He quickly returned his attention to his beer and food.

Through its 33–0 run to the title game in Salt Lake City, Indiana State was besieged with requests for interviews with the mysterious Larry Bird. Local Indiana writers, national publications, and papers from all over the country asked for his time. But no group pursued Bird more than the Boston writers, who did everything but set up bureaus in Terre Haute. The downtrodden Celtics were anxiously anticipating the end of the tournament and the beginning of contract negotiations with the white star they'd been awaiting for a full year. They had gambled that Bird would be another Heinsohn or Havlicek, that he would revitalize the team and the attendance figures. All season, Ed McKee, the sports information director at ISU, tried to fend off the Boston writers.

"Larry just didn't care," McKee said. "The Boston writers all wanted to talk about 'Celtic Pride,' and, to tell you the truth, Larry didn't follow the NBA, didn't know or care much about it."

Bird claimed he refused to talk to the media all season for the sake of the team. He said that all the attention focused on him wasn't fair to his teammates. Very likely that was an excuse. "Larry was the most shy and introverted guy I'd ever been around in my life," said Bill Hodges, the Indiana State coach. Finally, in Salt Lake City, concerned NCAA officials pressured Indiana State to get their showcase player to attend press conferences. Bird immediately demonstrated he was in no mindset, or mood, to fill anyone's notebook.

"Don't make me no difference," he said, when asked how important the championship game was to him. "I'm gonna get my money, win or lose."

He might have come off as a crude hayseed, but he was forgiven by a forgiving media that would not have overlooked such jive talk from a differently colored star. The psychological barriers remained airtight. Bird's life had not been easy. His family was poor. His mother, Georgia, worked long hours to help support six children. His father, Joe, was a wood finisher in a local piano and organ company, who seldom saw his five athletic sons play ball. By reputation, Joe Bird had a difficult time staying out of the bars. He committed suicide when Larry was nineteen, calling his wife on the phone and then shooting himself with a shotgun. This was shortly after Larry dropped out of Indiana University to marry and find work with the sanitation department back home in French Lick. By the time Larry Bird reached Salt Lake City, he was already divorced after fathering a daughter.

Where Bird frowned in Salt Lake, Magic smiled. Where Bird pushed the media away, Magic drew it like a magnet. Johnson's family life didn't appear all that different from Bird's, on the surface. Like Joe Bird, Earvin Sr. was a factory worker who earned a modest living. There were seven children. But Earvin Sr. and Jr. were always as close as father and son could be. They spent hours in front of a television screen, sharing a love for basketball. There was always a joy about Earvin Jr. The kid was out in the schoolyard by seven-thirty in the morning, shooting baskets and waving as the neighbors passed on their way to work. He was the blue-collar ethic personified, a characterization always attributed to white players.

"I'm loving every minute of this," Magic said at a press conference after Michigan State rolled into Salt Lake. "It's like a kid going to a birthday party." Asked the meaning of being in Salt Lake, he said, "You'll be in next year's program. You'll be in the 1990 program. You'll be in the 2010 program. You'll always be there. They'll never forget you."

Both players were exactly right about what was happening at the foot of the Great Salt Lake. The showdown of Magic Johnson and Larry Bird was all about history and money. Never had the NCAA had this kind of drawing power. College basketball had already begun to generate momentum with the emergence of two UCLA centers, Lew Alcindor and Bill Walton. The Final Four had had its share of memorable teams and players through the seventies: David Thompson and North Carolina State in 1974. John Wooden finishing his career with a champion in 1976. The unbeaten Indiana team of Bob Knight in 1976. Al McGuire's tearful farewell as national champion with Marquette in 1977. Now, however, it was reaching true March Madness frenzy.

"The college game may have already been on the launching pad," Al McGuire said. "But if it was, it wasn't until Bird and Magic came along and pushed the button that it took off."

They turned the game into an event, brought it to a new level in the American consciousness, Bird's churlishness versus Magic's charm. Their unselfish styles, their ability to make the pass, attracted basketball purists. But the underlying and more powerful magnetic appeal was the emergence of a white superstar at a time when the sport had clearly given way to the dominance of blacks. With the racial sideshow, this 1979 final would fare as well in Peoria as it did in the heart of Watts.

NBC televised the game, with McGuire and Billy Packer doing point/counterpoint commentary to Dick Enberg's play-by-play. The network had stepped into a bonanza telecast, even if a few at NBC didn't understand the powerful dynamics at work. A production assistant prepared an opening piece on Bob King, whose poor health had forced him to surrender the ISU coaching job prior to the season to his assistant, Hodges, a former insurance salesman. King and Hodges, instead of Johnson and Bird? When Don Ohlmeyer, the producer, found out, he nearly went through the Salt Palace roof. "Damn it," Ohlmeyer said. "This is a story about Bird and Johnson."

"Here was a guy, Ohlmeyer, who didn't really know anything about basketball," Packer said, "but he certainly had a feeling for the American public. He knew what they wanted."

The game drew a rating of 24.1, by far the highest in the history of the event. It came close several times in the eighties, but the NCAA final never scored that high again. More important, it established the NCAA Monday night final as an exclusive network prize. NBC in the mid-seventies had paid less than a third of the $48 million CBS shelled out for the rights to the tournament in March 1981. By 1985, the figure was $96 million over three years, and then $166 million over three years by 1988, and $1 billion over seven years by 1990, all doled out by CBS. Big business had linked up with Bird and Johnson, by way of the sound truck and satellite dish. Soon all three networks were showing regular-season and conference tournament games, while the growing all-sports cable network ESPN was contracting its own deals and broadcasting games from every nook and cranny of the country. The regional sports networks followed ESPN's lead. Between late November and Final Four time in the first week of April, the game was inescapable on the dial. The Big East, with commissioner Dave Gavitt brokering the deals, went from an original television income of roughly $350,000 for all nine schools to $9 million. And, as Gavitt put it, the money was "pushing upwards."

The college game was hot, and so was anyone under its umbrella, merely by association. Once praised as a slower, headier alternative to the pinballish NBA, it had been a game where a nonscholarship walk-on with minimal talent could step on the court and make a difference. Middle America liked to believe in the sixties and seventies that white student-athletes were still impact players. Play was boring, coach-oriented, well-intentioned.

Now, everything was different. Recruiting and scouting were viciously aggressive. The college game was up-tempo for the sake of its stars and, by extension, its television ratings. It featured a forty-five-second shot clock and a modified, closer version of pro ball's 3-point line. It had turned into college athletics' disco inferno, replete with deep-throated, high-profile deejays like Al McGuire and Dick Vitale. It was a black sport, marketed by whites for whites. Just like the professionals.

Sitting back and nodding in approval were the lords of the NBA. The college game already had been a decent farm system that didn't cost the league a penny. With this new visibility and popularity, it was a public relations agency marketing the future NBA talent pool via televised network and cable games.

"I had a warm smile the first time I heard Dick Vitale say about some kid, 'He's a definite lottery player,'" NBA commissioner David Stern said. "I knew it was happening. All of a sudden, they were being defined in their greatness by whether they were going to be in the NBA draft lottery.

"Fifteen years ago, you take a kid like Gary Payton, put him at Oregon, and he'd just be a name people may have heard. Now, by the time he graduates, he's been on every network, people have seen highlights of him on all those half-hour sports shows and maybe he's been on the cover of *Sports Illustrated*."

With this sort of wide-angle exposure, welcomed and supported by teams like the Celtics, came distorted pressure on the athlete. In the old days a player had the opportunity to develop his game until the age of twenty-one or twenty-two before he was judged by the viewing public. Now, in the Bird-Johnson era, he was being critiqued and discarded as an eighteen-year-old freshman. The major universities, which easily could have put a stop to this, were operating strictly out of self-interest. The growing figures were hypnotic. The possibility of a tournament windfall only intensified recruiting wars for coaches as well as players, and increased the temptation to cheat. The idea was simple—and cutthroat: Get a good high school player into your school any way you can and make sure he passes enough courses to remain eligible to play.

The smell of money turned would-be educators into de facto professional sports barons, calculating their revenues and maximizing their profits. The head coach became little more than a fast-talking mercenary, a Mr. Quick Fix, available year to year to the highest bidder. Media darlings like Rick Pitino and Larry Brown slinked in and out of contracts, leaving their recruits behind to fulfill letters of intent and scholarship commitments. This was deemed justifiable, somehow, because the coaches were climbing to a better job. Even those more honorable men who made long-term commitments to their programs weren't missing out on the windfall. Sneaker companies annexed the college basketball territory, with huge payments to coaches.

This wasn't a crime as much as it was a sad reality. Capitalism didn't legislate against bad taste. TV money was talking and schools were taking. Back in 1970, the NCAA basketball tournament was essentially providing money for uniforms and equipment. That was all. A first-round appearance that year was worth $8,263 to the school, a run to the Final Four $39,189. By 1979, merely qualifying for the tournament earned a school $39,189. Johnson and Bird helped their schools net $235,103 windfalls for reaching Salt Lake. A decade later—when single-season NCAA TV revenue had jumped from $8 million to $66 million—schools received more than that just for making the saturated sixty-four-team tournament field. In the eighties, participation in a single game on the road to Seattle for the final Final Four was worth $250,200. Seattle itself was a lottery for the four participants to the tune of $1.251 million per school, and some valued it at over $10 million when fresh endowments from alumni were factored into the equation.

Laden by such temptation, the eighties concluded with scandal at venerable basketball cathedrals Kentucky and Kansas. Kansas, a fairy-tale champion under Larry Brown in 1988, was put on probation for recruiting violations and became the first school not allowed to defend its title. Brown was long gone by then, to San Antonio of the NBA. "I would have stayed if I had known there would be violations," Brown said years later. Kentucky, meanwhile, was reaching into the pros for New York Knick coach Pitino to save its crooked, staggering program. Pitino, upon signing for millions, immediately denied money was the determining factor. Within a year and a half, Kentucky was a power again. Pitino was the most popular man in Lexington, a cottage industry with television and radio shows, three major endorsements, camps, clinics, and his New York–style Italian restuarant, the immodestly named Bravo Pitino, three blocks from Rupp Arena.

Other headliners made equal fortunes, but did not fare as well in the public relations department. Jim Valvano was driven from North Carolina State, his program ruined by neglect, as he busily raked in money from related interests. UNLV won its first national title in 1990 while its coach, Jerry Tarkanian, kept one eye on NCAA officials determined to turn the lights out on his program for violations dating back more than a decade. The consequences for a coach as successful as Tarkanian probably would be nothing worse than a mad dash to another university or a move into the TV booth. Valvano left Raleigh discredited. He was soon seen and heard nationally on ABC and ESPN, praised in many quarters for his insightful commentary. He was certain to get a call, sooner or later, to come fix someone's program. It would soon be forgotten that Valvano, a fast-talking New Yorker, recruited poor and, in many cases, unprepared black kids; that he exploited them to benefit himself and the university; and that he gave them little more in return than equipment, a half-court offense, and the occasional locker room motivational speech.

So corrupted was NCAA basketball that even a cigar-chomping, contract-crunching general manager from the NBA could stand on higher moral ground and speak disparagingly about college commitment. "I remember a college player who was All-America two years, was drafted high in the NBA and didn't make it," said Red Auerbach. "I was talking to his college coach and I said, 'Whatever happened to that guy?' He said he didn't know. I said, 'What the hell you mean you don't know? Here's a kid who helped to make you. He was All-America for two years, you had a helluva record, and you don't know where he is? You don't help him get a job or you don't hire him yourself?'

"That's college, where they should do more," Auerbach said. "Here we're pros, and we care more than a lot of college coaches except guys like a Bobby Knight, a John Thompson, a Dean Smith. I've been very close to a lot of the players—Havlicek, Heinsohn, Nelson. I still like to keep in contact with all of them."

Of course, Auerbach did not keep in touch with Gerald Henderson, Cedric Maxwell, or Jo Jo White. He did not offer a job to Dennis Johnson. He didn't mind helping former Celtics like Sam Jones and Wayne Embry find work, although notably it wasn't in his organization. But that is another story, another chapter. He was certainly correct about the sorry state of the NCAA coaching and administrative fraternity. College basketball had become, in large part, a process in which white men controlled athletic departments that were getting rich on black talent. The Black Coaches Association estimated in 1990 that there were 200 assistant coaching jobs held by blacks out of 5,000. Only 1 percent of athletic directors' jobs were held by blacks, and less than that by assistant athletic directors. "We're still looking at a college world where athletic departments have less than 2 percent of their staffs black," said Richard Lapchick, the director of the Center for the Study of Sport in Society at Northeastern University in Boston. "It's an old-boy network hiring and rehiring people who they know. And white society doesn't know black society."

It was naive to believe that white society had a legitimate interest in educating black youth. Too often commitment was defined by the athlete's willingness to take the charge or press full-court for forty minutes. Too often the focus had been on the failings of the so-called student-athlete, not on the shortcomings of the university. At the 1990 Final Four in Denver, a large gathering of writers and college basketball coaches and officials was moved to a long standing ovation by the story of Donald Taylor, a senior at a Brooklyn, New York, high school who commuted by subway to school, basketball practice, and games—more than an hour each way—from the upper Manhattan tenement where his family was crowded into one room of a homeless shelter. At the same time, many of these people believed John Thompson was wrong in his aggressive campaign against the NCAA's Proposition 42—a rules change that would have denied a scholarship to any student unable to score 700 on his SAT, according to many black leaders and educators a standardized and racist predictor of college preparedness. When he stepped forward to receive his award in Denver, Donald Taylor was a B student on course to graduate, but had yet to clear the SAT hurdle. Given the conditions of his home life, he might never have qualified for an education or a scholarship under Prop 42. Taylor recognized this hypocrisy and confided as much to a friend. Fortunately, Thompson was successful in his campaign against the proposition. Taylor enrolled at the University of Maine in the fall of 1990, working toward a degree as well as basketball eligibility.

The campus role of the student-athlete plunges deep into the heart of a multifaceted, multibillion-dollar issue. Too many have been blinded by vast sums of money and the roars of reverential crowds packing campus fieldhouses. Some well-intentioned observers have said and written that college athletes in football and basketball should be paid because it is the honest thing to do. While this solution might eliminate some under-the-table cheating, it would continue to reward the network of good old boys. Programs would still churn out uneducated twenty-two-year-olds. The only interests served, again, would be those of the athletic directors and coaches.

Indeed, as the nineties dawned, stories abounded of universities that actually allowed their athletic departments to spend far more than they earned. A study in the financial journal *Capital Ideas* found that the old university model, in which athletic departments reinvested basketball profits in education areas, was largely a myth. Several major programs were actually believed to be operating at large deficits. In a February 4, 1991, editorial, the *New York Times* urged the U.S. Department of Education to comply quickly with the Student Right-to-Know Act of 1990. Under this legislation, a study would determine whether athletic programs should be required to furnish detailed financial reports. It was difficult to comprehend fully the hypocrisy and greed of big-time college sports merely by studying the bottom line. One had to be there to see for oneself.

The eighties officially ended, aptly, at a Final Four in Seattle won by a Michigan team whose head coach had deserted the school for a million-dollar offer from Arizona State on the eve of the tournament. There at the Kingdome, all that Bird and Johnson had wrought ten years earlier was on display: the 50,000 fans; an imported Seton Hall star, Andrew Gaze, from Australia, on loan to coach P. J. Carlesimo for a single season; a media caravan on a Super Bowl–like holiday, eager to get through the mass press conferences designed to shelter the players and the issues, and looking forward to the next banquet courtesy of the NCAA and its hospitable sponsors.

All that urgency and hype were embodied in Seattle by Bill Frieder, the Michigan coach who had jumped ship on the eve of the tournament with the pathetic explanation that Arizona State had given him twenty minutes to make up his mind. Frieder hung out in the lobby of the Wolverine hotel, clinging for dear life to the dear old black and gold. He would tell anybody interested in listening— reporters, coaches, bellmen—that Michigan was still his team. That Glen Rice and Rumeal Robinson were still his main men.

"They couldn't disown me, even if they wanted," Frieder said. "I recruited the players, I hired the whole staff. I even hired the secretaries."

Frieder staked his claims in vain. In the end, it was Steve Fisher, Frieder's understudy, a man who relied on a friend's psychic powers to determine his lineup in the championship game, who would be canonized. Fisher's ascension to Bob Knight-hood was very nearly a divine act, beyond the mortal influence of jump shot or jump shooter.

Back in 1979 at the Salt Palace, nobody could have foreseen the gold rush that would lure Frieder, or the cult of coaches that would embrace him. Nobody bothered to look beyond the explosion of Michigan State's fast breaks and the brilliance of Magic Johnson's championship smile. This was still a players' game. Two players.

It was the beginning of a lasting rivalry and an inspirational friendship. Larry Bird and Magic Johnson would stalk each other suspiciouly, from a distance, for several years. But they would discover their common ground during the filming of a commercial at Bird's home in French Lick. Speaking more as Earvin than Magic, Johnson would say, "I realized that Larry and I have a lot of the same values." By the mid-eighties, they were good freiends, rooting hard to meet up each year in the finals, Johnson's Lakers against Bird's Celtics.

Johnson once went as far as saying he would like to retire the same year as Bird because "it just seems that's the way it should be." It would not happen that way at all. On November 7, 1991, just weeks after Bird appeared to have made a successful return from serious back surgery. Johnson stunned the country, even the world, by annuncing his retirement after testing positive for the virus that causes AIDS.

Bird was brokenhearted. Just that summer, Johnson had talked him into accepting an invitation to play for the 1992 U. S. Olympic team in Barcelona. It would be their only chance, Johnson told him, and they belonged on that global stage together.

It wasn't easy to become Bird's friend, to gain his trust. But once one did, it was unshakable. "I'm out of it," Bird told reporters the day after Johnson's announcement. "I can't believe what happened." He stumbled through practice and the next couple of games. He compared the loss of Johnson as a competitor, and the likelihood that his close friend was facing a death sentence, to the death of his own father. Meanwhile, there was no tribute to Magic Johnson that failed to revisit prominently a more innocent time, that 1979 night in Salt Lake City.

The final itself, while not a runaway, fell somewhat short of expectations, and certainly wasn't a classic in the style of North Carolina–Georgetown, NC State–Houston, or Michigan–Seton Hall. Bird was in trouble from the start, harassed by the quickness of the Michigan State double teams and outplayed on this day by Johnson. Heathcote's team had too many stars: Magic and willowy forward Greg Kelser, both first-round NBA draft picks; Jay Vincent, then a freshman; and a six-eight center named Ron Charles, who would later have a lengthy career in Europe. The Spartans were defensively well-prepared by Heathcote, by Johnson's impersonation of Bird. Bird was forced either to settle for questionable shots or to give up the ball too far on the perimeter, where his teammates were forced to create for themselves. Bird, the great white hope, had his limitations. He couldn't penetrate, not without some screens and options. The ISU offense became far more egalitarian than it could afford.

Magic and Kelser took control, building a 37–28 halftime lead. Bird became frustrated, calling for the ball, even running toward teammates with his hands outstretched. After averaging 28.6 points and almost 6 assists during the regular season, Bird missed 14 of his 21 shots, scored 19 points, and had only 2 assists. Even Magic sympathized, remembering, "Two guys on you and everyone else in the passing lanes. What could you do?" Johnson, the MVP, had 24 points, 7 rebounds, and 5 assists. He had risen to the occasion, but he would not be given credit for a K.O. over Bird. He had too much help, everyone said. Kelser, whose bright pro career would be ruined by a severe knee injury, had 19 points and 8 rebounds. And a six-two left-handed shooting guard from Creve Cove, Missouri, Terry Donnelly, spotted up for four long jump shots early in the second half to put the Sycamores away.

"I think early in the game maybe we saw a few things that told us we weren't going to be able to beat this team, that maybe we'd run out of miracles," said Heaton, later a Terre Haute insurance salesman, whose buzzer shot had beaten Arkansas in the regionals. "I remember sitting on the bench, and Michigan State took the ball off the boards in the first couple of minutes, and just exploded on the break. It was, like, 'Uh oh, what have we here?'" The end of a dream was what they had—and a revealing glimpse inside Larry Bird. He had demonstrated that, yes, it had meant something whether he won or lost. It was basketball, all he knew. It meant everything.

While the Michigan State celebration was unfolding on the court, Bird sat motionless on the bench, his face buried in a towel. A teammate, starting forward Alex Gilbert, ran over to see if Bird was all right. Only when Gilbert was standing over Bird could he hear the sobs. The sight stunned Gilbert, who would go on to become a correctional officer after playing several years abroad. He was raised in the rough, blighted river town, East St. Louis, Illinois. The year of the Sycamore title run, his older brother was murdered in the streets. He'd thought of leaving school. Bird, he said, would see him sitting off by himself, depressed and angry, and would slide next to Gilbert.

"He wasn't really good with words, but he tried to help in his own way," Gilbert said. "He'd try to cheer me up, or give me someone to take it out on." Once, Gilbert did. He looked up at Bird and said, "It's easier for you, Larry. You've got it all ahead of you. I wish I was in your shoes." The warmth left Bird's face. It was true he was going to be rich, but it was not as if he hadn't struggled to get there. If there was one memory of his dead father he'd put above all the rest, it was the night Joe Bird's feet were so swollen he'd needed help from his boys in getting his boots off. The next morning, the boots were on again and he was back to work. "Hey," Bird told Gilbert, "nobody's handing me or you anything. You gotta work for it, whatever it is."

Now, on March 24, 1979, in Bird's hour of defeat before millions, Gilbert found himself wanting very much to return a favor. Over the crowd noise and the Michigan State band, he yelled, "Get your head up, man! You got nothing to be ashamed of."

Bird didn't move. Gilbert tried a softer approach.

"Please, Larry Bird, get your head up."

Bird still did not move. Gilbert patted his shoulder.

"We're proud of you, Larry Bird," he said. "Everyone's proud. You'll see. You'll get another chance to beat that guy."

Bird always would have a lot of trouble beating that guy, staying with his rival, the genius playmaker, Magic. But the Celtics would give him that chance, and make a mint on the deal. Now, it was their turn.

Chapter 7

Selling Out

THERE was a moment in June 1978 when the destiny of the NBA hung delicately in the balance. In a Los Angeles hotel room sat Celtics owner Irv Levin, his Buffalo compatriots John Y. Brown and Harry Mangurian, and their high-powered attorneys. On the table was a proposed exchange of entire franchises. The Celtics would be dealt even up for the Braves, who were to be moved immediately by Levin to San Diego.

Part of the deal was to be an exchange of players. Levin wanted three—Freeman Williams, Kevin Kunnert, and Kermit Washington. Brown was partial to Tiny Archibald, Billy Knight, and Marvin Barnes. The men agreed to swap these players and leave the rest of the rosters intact, but there was one last order of business. Who was going to take the draft rights to this college kid Larry Bird, on whom the Celtics had just spent their first-round draft pick?

Brown and Mangurian didn't seem especially enthused. Bird was staying in school another season anyway, and there would only be a window of two months to sign him or he'd return to the draft pool. Levin knew Red Auerbach was hot for Bird, but who knew how good he really was, and who knew how much Auerbach knew? Four of the five years Levin was with the Celtics, Auerbach couldn't pick a basketball off a rack. In a four-year run, the Celtics' number one picks were Steve Downing, Glenn McDonald, Tom Boswell, and Norm Cook.

"You want this Bird?" Levin asked Brown. Brown acted like it didn't matter. Some college kid he knew nothing of was not going to be a deal breaker. Levin only knew what Auerbach knew from John Killilea. But he didn't really want the headache of having to sign a player within a short period of time. Levin decided that, in a small market like San Diego, he didn't need an agent putting a gun to his head over an untested rookie. He told Brown to take Bird. It would make Auerbach happy and get them off to a friendly start.

"I could've had him," Levin said, "and changed NBA history."

The crowd of about three hundred pushed into the Riverside Chapel on Amsterdam and Seventy-sixth, breaking the residential calm of Manhattan's Upper West Side. Neighboring streets were lined with double-parked cars. The cops on morning patrol rode by and pretended not to notice, a courtesy for the mourning.

Inside, the crowd was ushered to the second floor, where it nearly filled the pews of the large chapel. On January 24, 1991, the rabbi prayed for Nat "Feets" Broudy and soon introduced David Stern. Who better to eulogize a basketball life for a basketball crowd than the commissioner of the NBA?

Stern looked up from his notes, at Feets Broudy's family and the familiar faces who had come to say goodbye to the most famous timekeeper there ever was, the man who had been the heartbeat of Madison Square Garden for thirty-two years. "Other places around the country, who the hell even knew who the timekeeper was?" Stern quoted from an old newspaper column. Stern smiled out of fond remembrance and attributed the line to that "poet laureate, Red Holzman." In the back of the chapel, Holzman, the grizzled old Knicks coach whose emotional displays were almost always reserved for stone-faced referees, shifted in his seat and raised a finger to his eye. One row behind Holzman, sitting in the corner against the wall, no less a basketball god than Earl Monroe wept openly. Across the aisle, tough guy Dave DeBusschere stared at the floor with reddened eyes. Stern read a telegram from one of their old teammates, the senator from New Jersey, Bill Bradley. It was Bradley who developed the good-luck ritual of tossing Feets Broudy a towel minutes before the start of a game at Madison Square Garden during the late sixties and early seventies, when the Knicks owned New York.

Somehow, it would have been difficult to imagine the commissioner of football or baseball eulogizing the old-timer and timekeeper. The other major professional sports long ago surrendered their simplicity, their sense of family, but the NBA held on longer. There was still a chunk of it that was as quaint and warm as when it was little more than a basement social club. But those days, following a spectacular decade of growth, were disappearing as quickly as it took Magic Johnson and the Lakers to blow downcourt on a three-on-one fast break. In the place of the old mom-and-pop franchises were emerging the slick money machine of Stern, and an aggressively marketed collage of matchups and post-ups firmly rooted in America's sports consciousness, with tentacles reaching abroad.

"We're victims of our own success," NBA commissioner David Stern said one afternoon at the start of the 1990–91 season. His large, smartly furnished Fifth Avenue office, with stunning fifteenth-floor views of Madison Avenue and midtown Manhattan, reflected the phenomenal climb from the dark days of the late seventies for the league and himself. The kid who would sneak out of his parents' midtown delicatessen and into the old Eighth Avenue Madison Square Garden to watch the Knicks was now as rich as any man who ever played the game. The league's Board of Governors in 1990, with the urging of Boston Celtics owners and Stern allies Alan Cohen and Don Gaston, rewarded Stern for his remarkable empire-building with a five-year contract that few teams could fit into their salary cap: $3.5 million annually, plus $10 million in assorted bonuses. Since his previous salary was $1 million, this represented a raise of roughly $4 million per year. It didn't hurt that the National Football League was searching for Pete Rozelle's successor at the time, and Stern was a logical target. Not surprisingly, none of the owners was heard grumbling about the threat of the commissioner's unrestricted free agency.

With all of Manhattan's power-lunch establishments available, Stern had chosen instead a tuna fish sandwich embellished by a kosher pickle, a can of Coke, and the quiet comfort of his office. The nature of the man is to be available but not visible. A writer from any NBA city can pick up the phone and ask the public relations person or secretary for "David." None of this "Mr. Commissioner" for Stern, an unimposing but strong-willed man with wire-rimmed glasses who appears to be smiling even when he's not. One didn't expect oratory from Stern in the manner of the late baseball commissioner Bart Giamatti. He appeared to go out of his way to play the straight man, his public presentation at such televised NBA functions as the draft lottery hopelessly bland, almost sheepish. Inside Stern beat the heart of a forty-eight-year-old tax attorney, but his active and inventive mind had worked tirelessly to market the NBA, and the league had become a rocket to the moon. Even in 1991 recession times, with network ratings dwindling and executives reexamining the boom-time priorities that moved them to pay exorbitant sums of money for sports programming, the NBA appeared immune.

"In times like these, what you hope for is to just not lose any ground," Stern said. But while CBS was taking a financial beating with baseball, the NBA, now with NBC, continued to grow and prosper. Playoff ratings for the 1991 championship series increased substantially from the previous season as the league again struck gold with a matchup between Magic Johnson's Lakers and Michael Jordan's Chicago Bulls. The finals, as the event was colloquially called, wasn't yet strong enough to stand on its own merit, like the

Super Bowl or the World Series. A series between Portland and Detroit, as in 1990, failed to capture the nation's consciousness. "We're getting there," Stern said. This was debatable, but Stern's league was undoubtedly bigger than ever and so was he, deified as the sports commissioner of his time and perhaps of all time in a lengthy *Sports Illustrated* profile on the eve of the 1991 Finals.

In the seven years since he had succeeded the late Larry O'Brien, while brokering deals such as the four-year, $600 million television contract with NBC and while presiding over the league's exciting global expansion, Stern worked hard to be perceived as a regular guy. As with most of his work, he largely succeeded. But there were rumblings at the start of the nineties, mostly from the print medium he courted so successfully his first five years on the job.

Sportswriters accustomed to the NBA's less rigid infrastructure inevitably began to see the league bending backward for television, in the prepackaged style of the NFL. Every league event, including the draft and the All-Star Saturday amusement package, was moved into prime time. This was death for newspaper deadlines, but what Stern justifiably viewed as part of the evolutionary process for both media. By the same process, his league was not as down-home as it once was, not as accessible. The incredible shrinking press row was a particular sore point as more teams ringed courtside with their rich and celebrity clientele, moving more reporters up and out of the prime seats, a practice begun at Laker games in Los Angeles but spreading elsewhere. The idea of working from the loge was sacrilege to journalists, who had romanced the intimacy of the game for their readers. Access for print journalists to eminently marketable superstars like Larry Bird, Magic Johnson, and Michael Jordan had helped create a public relations bonanza. "The guy who really started it was Julius Erving, who was a public relations genius," Stern said.

Reporters covering the league appreciated its down-home flavor, as opposed to the restrictive Pentagon-like approach of the NFL. They felt a certain kinship to it, and unusually insightful writing helped bring the league and its players to life, especially in competitive newspaper towns like New York, Boston, Philadelphia, Seattle, and Los Angeles. From his long-time station at the *New York Post* and then *USA Today*, Peter Vecsey wrote a scurrilous but entertaining NBA notes column three times weekly—a curious mix of reporting, commentary, and personal attacks on anyone and anything remotely connected to the league. Struggling Knicks general manager Al Bianchi became so infuriated after being referred to as "Al Batross" by Vecsey, he went on national TV to vent his spleen. During halftime of a playoff game, while his staid corporate MSG bosses nearly fell out of their chairs, Bianchi vowed to take revenge, to go for Vecsey's throat.

Most NBA people complained about Vecsey, but they all read him, and their obsession with his column was an unconscious acknowledgment of its appeal. By the start of the 1990–91 season, even Vecsey had seen the future. The ultimate fly on the wall could be seen live, in front of an NBC camera, snarling out the halftime report. Vecsey's courtside seat was assured for life. Others still in the newspapering business were not so fortunate. Success had bred sellouts, of arenas and values. "Teams want to make money when it's available to them," Stern said with a sigh. "I should address it, I know." The sigh suggested he probably wouldn't. At this point, the NBA was in a position to ignore the veterans, some of whom could remember the NBA teams they covered being so solicitous as to pick up their travel expenses. The ink now ran a distant second to the sound bite. Fast pitches and quick takes were helping, as Stern said, "maintain what you have."

What the NBA had was an expanding farm of cash cows. With the exception of a few franchises in perpetual substandard shape, the NBA was well into an era of overall good fortune and karma, home and abroad. This, most league people, Stern included, believed grew largely out of the landmark 1983 Collective Bargaining Agreement. Larry Fleisher's Players Association, facing another potential showdown with the owners, was contemplating a playoff strike. The owners in turn decided that if the players struck, they would shut down, sacrifice the following season as well, until things were resolved to their satisfaction.

"I think both sides were hesitant," Stern said, "because you don't play with atom bombs"—not when detonation could elicit more apathy than anything else. In 1983, the Magic-Bird rivalry was only just beginning to pay league-wide dividends. The league, so afraid back in the player uprising of 1964 that networks would walk away and doom the league, was fearful again. Players were making big money. Fleisher knew it was in their best interest to work hard with the owners for a stronger, more publicly respected league. Eventually the union agreed to radical financial restructuring, a salary cap for each team in exchange for a 50-plus percent guarantee of gross revenues. Intelligent, forthright player reps like Bob Lanier and Junior Bridgeman also led a player movement toward drug regulation. They agreed to a comprehensive plan that allowed a player two penalty-free opportunities for voluntary treatment and imposed expulsion if the player was caught a third time by the authorities, NBA, or law enforcement.

"I think our players got high marks from the fans for that," Stern said. "Plus it helped that Larry Fleisher was much more of a pragmatist than, say, Marvin Miller in baseball. Miller was an ideologue, still fighting the steelworker battles of another generation. His view was that if the owners suggest it, then it's bad for the players. He almost doesn't admit something that might be win-win. It doesn't mean we always had this peachy-keen relationship. There were plenty of battles."

By 1988, Fleisher realized he'd won his quarter-century war. His signature fresh on a new six-year Collective Bargaining Agreement, he was looking for new challenges. He'd grown weary of political battles within the union, and the escalation of salaries had made it increasingly difficult to convince the young millionaires entering the league of the union's merits. To many of them, collective bargaining meant the player and his agent versus the general manager. Fleisher joked that perhaps the union had done too well for its own good.

For those twenty-five years, Fleisher had visualized the future of the NBA and was arguably the central figure in shaping it. It was not surprising that he would recognize Europe as the next frontier, taking a vice presidency with the International Management Group, in charge of worldwide basketball operations. On May 4, 1989, Fleisher was deep into negotiations with the Soviet and Yugoslav federations when he died suddenly at age fifty-eight of a heart attack following a workout at his Manhattan club. Two days after his death, his sons Eric and Marc signed Yugoslav Vlade Divac, and soon a couple of Soviet Olympic gold medalists, Sharunas Marciulionis and Alexandr Volkov, were on their way to the increasingly multinational NBA. Fleisher, elected into basketball's Hall of Fame in early 1991, had made one last indelible mark.

Europe now presented the NBA with a new source of white talent, though according to Stern, race had ceased being a factor years before. "I think what happened is that adults in the sixties and seventies were looking at a sport that they had known as a white sport turn into a black sport. Then we were the first sport to have these megasalaries, then the drug issue, then certain ownership undercapitalized. It created an image of a sport under siege, which we were. We took care of those problems. The race issue began to dissipate by the reality of the fact that this was a league that was going to be predominantly black, and that was it."

In an abstract sense, Stern was correct. Practically speaking, he was not. The entry for many into the emerging NBA of the eighties was the natural, ready-made marketing campaign of Magic versus Bird. Black versus white. The NBA could not have wished for better. Trends in the country were moving west to east, and out of Hollywood came the hip, young, black Showtime Lakers. Out of New England came the defenders of tradition, a formidable response to the wave of black domination. Larry Bird was the white hope. His Celtics were the white alternative. Together, they sold big.

❖   ❖   ❖

Would the NBA have soared as high without Bird in Boston, with Bird a neighbor to Magic Johnson in San Diego or with the Los Angeles Clippers? Bird in Boston was the perfect fit, like a brand-new baseball in the pocket of a timeworn leather glove. He looked like a player out of the old NBA, from Boston's glorious past. He dressed like the average guy on a barstool in Charlestown. When he went to Boston to meet Red Auerbach for the first time and take in a Celtic game, Bird blended into a crowd of 7,831. Attired in a tan sports shirt described by his agent, Bob Woolf, as "hideous," Bird sat at the Garden and watched the Celtics lose their seventh straight game.

Bird was the consummate no-frills common man. After several desultory seasons of street-smart, angry black dudes like Sidney Wicks and Marvin Barnes, everyone loved this concept—at least until Bird signed up with Bob Woolf, and the "pernicious" agent made his opening bid at $1 million per year. At this point, Auerbach excused himself from the parade and resumed his beloved agent-bashing position, initiating a media campaign against Woolf. He left Bird out of it, of course. As a result of Auerbach's tirades against Woolf, the Boston-based agent's kids were castigated in school. Auerbach's arguments, he claimed, were based on pure basketball logic, which he, naturally, had more of than anyone. "It's been proven," Auerbach said. "A cornerman can't dominate the game. A big man, occasionally even a guard. But one man playing a corner can't turn a franchise around."

Auerbach apparently hadn't watched Bird closely enough in college, where he was the original point forward. Nor had he grasped the decline of the NBA center's domination. The days when a Bill Russell could average 25 rebounds a game, as he did in 1963–64, were as dead as the wooden backboard. Vastly improved shooting was a part of this, but players were becoming more multiskilled and bigger at every position. Men six-ten, six-eleven, who years before automatically would have been centers, were now playing power forward. Small forwards, once the size of six-five players like John

Havlicek and Bill Bradley, were now guards. Around the basket, centers had more competition for the ball than ever, and it reflected most in rebounding stats. By the mid-eighties, only a handful of players would take in 1,000 rebounds in a season, roughly 12 per game, and among them were forwards like Charles Barkley, who is merely six-four, Karl Malone, and Buck Williams. The Detroit Pistons would dominate the late eighties using a flawed, high-post center, Bill Laimbeer, who was the fourth or fifth best player on his team.

All of this was lost on Boston. If Red Auerbach said Woolf was ludicrously overpricing Bird, that was good enough for the *Boston Globe*, which promptly paid its respects to the godfather by declaring the thought of such a deal financial suicide. Pro basketball, the *Globe* editorialized, had "achieved the ultimate, and the ultimate appears to have limited appeal." Luckily for the Celtics, owner Mangurian relieved Auerbach at the bargaining table just as tensions were reaching the boiling point. The goofy-looking kid from Indiana State signed for $650,000 a year, becoming the highest-paid rookie in history. With Bird's great success, it soon became clear that the *Globe*'s unquestioning support of Auerbach was a case of severe tunnel vision.

"We were playing on a Wednesday night against the Utah Jazz, and we were playing head-to-head with the World Series," Jan Volk said. "The Jazz had just moved from New Orleans, and they had no distinguishing players. People did not know who the Utah Jazz were. It was a revelation. It had nothing to do with the opponent. We were selling out the Boston Celtics." Larry Bird's Celtics.

Bird was an unproven, uncharismatic rookie joining a twenty-nine-win team that had sold out just one home game the previous season. These somber facts sobered no one. The hype was in The Hope. Attendance surged early, and when it was soon clear Bird was worth the money on the court as well, that the Celtics were winners again, every game was sold out. They would keep selling out right through the spring of 1991 and beyond. Celtic sellouts in Boston Garden would become as ritualistic as Bird bending down, fingering the bottom of his sneakers. But back in 1979–80, it was a startling turn of events, an increase of more than four thousand fans per game to an all-time high of 14,490. By comparison, the Lakers with Magic Johnson, eventual champions that season, played before an average of more than four thousand empty seats at the Los Angeles Forum. The Julius Erving–led Philadelphia 76ers, who eliminated the Celtics in the Eastern Conference finals, averaged 11,701 at the 18,276-seat Spectrum. On April 19, 1980, Easter Sunday, the Sixers played game seven of their Eastern Conference semifinal against the Milwaukee Bucks before a half-empty arena. The Sixers were a crazy, exciting club. But they were also a black team in another city that didn't always support such an attraction. "I honestly can't say it wasn't racial," Erving said.

America was certainly buying the Celtics. In addition to Bird, the team had noticeably reversed a league-wide trend, with seven whites (including Pete Maravich for the final twenty-six games and playoffs) and five blacks on their roster. Twenty-seven of the Celtics' forty-one road games that season were sellouts. Seldom in sports does a phenomenon develop that quickly. But Bird and the Celtics, on their way to a sixty-one-win season, suddenly were the Beatles on their first American tour.

"I wonder sometimes," said Cedric Maxwell. "Supposing it had been Magic, not Larry, who had come to Boston. Would there have been that excitement? Would there have been the same infusion of support right from the start?

"Magic would've had the new clothes, the Rolls Royce, a big house. Larry couldn't go out and buy a mansion, a flashy car. He drove a truck. He wore these ugly clothes that looked like handouts. Magic wouldn't have fit the hard-nosed mentality. I doubt anyone else, not even Magic, could have brought that kind of energy to Boston. And when I say *even* Magic, it's tough to swallow, because he's at least as great as Larry, maybe even greater."

When Bird joined the Celtics, Maxwell wasn't impressed. The coach, Bill Fitch, noticed their rivalry. "Maxwell made up his mind he was going to beat out Bird for that spot," Fitch said. Like Maxwell, Fitch didn't think that was going to be too hard. "For two weeks with Bird, it was like that Peggy Lee song: 'Is that all there is?'" Fitch said. "I was thinking, 'He's not very fast. He's big, but not fast.' Then he got the feel of it. You could see a little bit of it. He'd slip off a lefty pass." Maxwell took note of everything. The previous season, his second in the league, he'd led the last-place Celtics in scoring, shooting percentage, rebounding, and steals. His reward was being called Stepin Fetchit by Red Auerbach at the team Christmas party. Now all anyone could talk about was Larry Bird. It got on his nerves. "I had some of the racist attitudes like everyone else," Maxwell said. "I was thinking, 'Here comes this white punk kid—he can't play.' Didn't take long to realize that he could."

So could Maxwell, though not at Bird's spectacularly diversified level. Maxwell, at six-eight, 215, was strictly an inside player. Like Paul Silas, Maxwell was an excellent rebounder, even though he didn't jump high. He wasn't as big or strong as Silas, but was more of an offensive threat with his long arms and unusual instincts for the ball. Maxwell complemented Bird, as Silas had Cowens. Offensively, he was an excellent inside-out player. He drew crowds around the basket and was adept at making the pass to Bird, or anyone else, out on the wing. Defensively, he spared the slow-footed Bird embarrassing matchups by playing scoring forwards like Julius Erving and Bernard King.

Benefiting from a new presence, Maxwell averaged 17 points and made 60 percent of his shots during Bird's rookie season. Only Wilt Chamberlain and Kareem Abdul-Jabbar had ever reached those levels concurrently. The following season, 1980–81, when Bird's Celtics claimed their first NBA title in a six-game series with Houston, Maxwell was named MVP by the media covering the series. He traveled to New York with his Cincinnati-based agent, Ron Grinker, expecting to receive the customary sports car from *Sport* magazine.

At the press conference, he was instead handed a wristwatch.

"He's looking around and he's looking around," Grinker said. "Finally, he whispers to me, 'Where's my car?' Well, we were told they'd just decided they weren't doing the car anymore. So Max says, 'That sums up the luck of a black Celtic. You don't even get any respect in New York.'" Maxwell's candor and wit were a delightful staple of the Celtic locker room, for teammates and media alike. The man known as "Cornbread" dubbed Robert Parish "The Chief" (after the character from *One Flew Over the Cuckoo's Nest*) when the stoic seven-footer was acquired from Golden State. Kevin McHale simply loved Maxwell's intrepid attitude. He wasn't afraid to take a chance. When the Celtics ran into a scorching Bernard King in a 1983–84 playoff series with the Knicks, Maxwell vowed that King would not score his standard forty points against him.

"I'm gonna stop the bitch," Maxwell crowed.

With double-team help, he did, for two games in Boston. But when the series returned to New York, King ran wild. The writers couldn't wait to confront Maxwell, who was, as always, right where they wanted him. "The bitch," a smiling but unrepentant Maxwell said, borrowing from the rock world, "is back."

By the time Bird's Celtics won their second title in 1983–84, Maxwell's production had declined. McHale was becoming the league's preeminent power forward. The Celtics justifiably wanted McHale to have Maxwell's starting position, mirroring the Gerald Henderson–Danny Ainge situation. In 1984–85, the year he signed a four-year contract worth $3.5 million, Maxwell suffered a knee injury that limited him to fifty-seven games. Despite the fact that in the previous six seasons Maxwell had missed a total of only fourteen games, Auerbach insisted that Maxwell was not working hard enough to rehabilitate the knee. As always, the media bought into it. "He let his teammates down by not getting ready to perform," Bob Ryan wrote in the *Globe*.

That summer, Auerbach ordered Maxwell to the Celtics' Marshfield rookie camp. Grinker knew that Maxwell, like many other

NBA players, would not touch a basketball during the summer. This was not laziness, just the belief that there were simply too many games between October and June. There had to be time to recharge. But Grinker had also represented enough Celtics to recognize a pattern.

"What happened with Max would've never been said to a McHale, a Bird, or for that matter, a Brad Lohaus or Jeff Judkins," Grinker said. "Only to a Jim Ard, a Cedric Maxwell, a Kevin Gamble." Reading between the lines of Auerbach's demands, Grinker called Maxwell and said, "If you don't go, consider your Celtic career over." Maxwell wasn't budging from Charlotte, his home. Auerbach, he believed, was now trying to *treat* him like a Stepin Fetchit. Maxwell was the team court jester. Auerbach refused to see beyond this veneer, which he was able to do with another fun-loving Celtic, Kevin McHale. Auerbach wanted McHale in, Maxwell and his heavy contract out. He would do whatever it took. Even if it meant tarnishing the reputation of a well-liked Celtic, a two-time champion.

"Eight years, part of two championship teams, MVP of the playoffs, and they treated me like I had to go to their camp and prove I could still play," Maxwell said. "They forgot I was playing in pain for two years. I just wasn't going to go to their boys' camp and run around on concrete." Auerbach eventually traded Maxwell to the L.A. Clippers for Bill Walton. The irony of trading the man Auerbach had accused of malingering for one of the most often injured players in history was lost on everyone but Maxwell. When he was introduced at a Clipper press conference by coach Don Chaney, he said, "I'm just taking Bill Walton's spot. Don's already told me I don't have to practice."

For Auerbach and his mouthpieces, this was another coup—a complaining reserve forward for the greatest white center in history. "Phantasmagorical," wrote Bob Ryan. As for Maxwell, Ryan decided, "He traded himself." A predictable farewell. Maxwell recalled it being written in Boston that he would be an $800,000 backup forward. Why, he wondered, had it been okay that McHale was making $1 million a year coming off the bench as the league's premier sixth man?

It all turned out well for the Celtics when they won another title, Bird's third, in 1985–86. Auerbach had written a new chapter in Celtic history while revising an old one. He removed all references to Maxwell from the book he was finishing at the time with *Boston Herald* columnist Joe Fitzgerald. In a statement reported in the press, Auerbach implied that Maxwell betrayed his teammates by falling out of playing shape. The Celtic players did not necessarily agree. "With Cedric, that locker room stuff was an act. That freak was always ready to play," said Danny Ainge. "The Celtics just wanted to give Kevin more minutes. I was upset with the excuses they used. You want to trade him, fine. But let him leave with dignity."

Maxwell believed he left that way anyway, despite what was said and written. "No matter what Auerbach tried, he can't erase me from Celtic history," Maxwell said. "I wasn't surprised I left the way I did. If it happened once or twice, you'd shrug your shoulders. But it happened time after time, black players leaving under a negative cloud, riding the rails.

"Sometimes I spoke out on the racial divisions in Boston. It wasn't a secret. It was obvious. You look at the endorsements up there. In all the years I played, I never got one offer. The year I won the playoff MVP, nothing. You had white players who barely played in commercials. Rick Robey had this great deal with this Mercedes dealer in New Hampshire. Danny Ainge was everywhere. Now, I love Danny to death, but you can't compare what he's been to the Celtics to what Robert Parish is. Robert has never gotten his share, and he's probably the greatest Celtic center behind Russell. Excuse me, Dave Cowens.

"I'm not saying no black guy could be happy in Boston. Look at M. L. [Carr]. If you conformed your personality, if you became less threatening, you could be embraced as one of the family. But if you maintained your blackness, if you spoke out on an issue not relating to basketball, they got uneasy. Isn't it ironic? The Celtics were at the forefront of bringing blacks into the league, but now they are a team built through bias. They were selling to a particular audience, no question."

During the eighties, when nearly three of four players league-wide were black, the Celtics suited up twenty-four blacks and twenty-two whites. By comparision, the Lakers' corresponding numbers were forty-five blacks and fifteen whites, slightly above the league average. With the exception of Artis Gilmore for forty-seven games in 1988, the Celtics' backup center position to Robert Parish was virtually a closed white union shop, passed down from Rick Robey to Eric Fernsten to Greg Kite to Bill Walton to Mark Acres to Brad Lohaus to Joe Kleine. If a fading white veteran such as Walton, Pete Maravich, Scott Wedman, or Jim Paxson was available, the Celtics could be counted on to make room. For all but the end of the decade, the Celtics were guaranteed three whites on their roster, with frontliners Bird, McHale, and Ainge. The racial balance was maintained with the likes of Fernsten, Rick Carlisle, Wayne Kreklow, and Conner Henry. White reserves had staying power. Kite, who shot 40 percent from the field and 42 percent from the free-throw line, lasted four-plus seasons as a spot enforcer. This still left him almost four years shy of a record for undeserving players. Journeyman forward Steve Kuberski camped out on the Celtic bench for an inexplicable eight seasons during the seventies.

In Boston, all this seemed perfectly natural. "We happen to have been in a position to get some great white players," said legendary announcer Johnny Most, who happened to be a Celtic employee. "Then we happened to be drafting down low to get some more. To say the Celtics are prejudicial is a left-handed way of thinking."

In 1989, from out of left field, the Celtics picked slow-footed white forward Michael Smith, their third Brigham Young player of the decade, and bypassed Tim Hardaway of Texas–El Paso, an explosive point guard and precisely the player they needed. In less than two seasons, Hardaway was an All-Star and Smith had already blown two spoon-fed opportunities to be a starter. Smith was only

the Celtics' third white player of ten selected in the first round during the eighties. Three lower-round picks made the team, however,
and an unusual number of free agents unwanted elsewhere passed
through their summer rookie camp. "I think we recognize that to
have some balance on the team, in terms of race, has some possible
value," said Celtic part-owner Alan Cohen, who in New York years
ago with the Knicks was known as Bottom Line.

In other words, this discriminatory practice was just business,
demographics, the way a teen magazine or a running shoe might
target an audience. If it makes dollars, then it makes sense. "You're
talking about identification. That's life," said K. C. Jones.

"It's an Irish town," Ron Grinker said. "If they could have five
guys named O'Reilly, they'd be in great shape."

"Depending on the marketplace, I'm sure they will be sitting
around and they'll say, Okay, cut the shit, we're talking about this
white guy who is six-five and that black guy who is six-five,'" Bob
Cousy said. "And if they're absolutely even, or close to even, then,
yeah, maybe they'll keep the white guy."

Most discouraging, the owners seem to be correct on this issue of
tokenism—economically, not morally. A study in 1988 by Eleanor
Brown of Pomona College, Diane Keenan of Claremont Graduate
School, and Richard Spiro of First Boston Corporation found that
white fans didn't care if white players were given playing time.
Attendance was unaffected by minutes. However, these white fans
did seem to require white players in uniform, however meaningless
their role. "Apparently," the study concluded, "biased fans are pla-
cated by white players on the bench."

This would not be shocking news to players anywhere around the
league. The NBA is completely dominated by blacks, who have
comprised more than 72 percent of the players, on the average,
since 1980. An analysis of NBA rosters at the All-Star break in 1991
showed that 72.4 percent of players in the league (249 of 344) were
black, 27.6 percent (95) were white. Nine of the top scorers in the
league were black. Nine of the top ten rebounders were black. Nine

of the top ten assists leaders were black. Nine of the top ten steals leaders were black. A projected super-duper All-Star Olympic team, featured on the cover of *Sports Illustrated,* included Patrick Ewing, Charles Barkley, Karl Malone, Magic Johnson, and Michael Jordan—all black.

And yet at the end of the NBA bench—specifically, the three players on each team averaging the fewest points—the story was dramatically different. Here, in cheerleader land, forty-three of eighty-one players were white (52.6 percent) and only thirty-eight were black (47.4 percent). In other words, forty-three of the ninety-five white players in the league (45.3 percent) could be classified as token players. These numbers were not only dramatic, they represented an alarming trend. Just three seasons earlier, a similar analysis showed that 73.2 percent of NBA players were black, and that a somewhat more equitable 44.9 percent of players in the last three slots at the end of the bench were white. Thirty-one white players were classified as tokens then, out of eighty-three in the league.

While the number of quality white players in the NBA held steady at fifty-two from 1988 to 1991, the number of token white players increased rapidly, from thirty-one to forty-three. Black players in the league called this "stealing," as in stealing roster spots, stealing the means of earning a living wage.

This phenomenon was most striking with the four expansion teams, where two discriminatory factors were at work: Established teams left marginal players unprotected in the original expansion pools, so a high percentage of players available in the draft were token whites. In addition, the expansion franchises came from cities with relatively few black paying fans, and might have been marketing themselves with that in mind. The result was that Charlotte, Miami, Orlando, and Minnesota became repositories for white stiffs. In 1991, their collective rosters included nineteen whites (36.5 percent) out of fifty-two players, and eight whites (67 percent) out of twelve at the end of the bench.

"The general consensus is that the white player is going to get the nod for a marginal position unless the black player is a lot better," said Mike Glenn, a former guard with the New York Knicks and Atlanta Hawks. When he was coaching college kids, San Antonio Spurs coach Larry Brown would lecture his black players about white tokenism in the NBA. Brown, no radical, wouldn't call this practice by its name. But he recognized its existence. "The players are better off knowing it ahead of time," Brown said. "That way, they're motivated to work harder. They have to be a little bit better than the white guys in order to make the pros."

The Celtics' pattern is painfully obvious: Whenever they have had enough strength among their top eight players to contend for a championship, they have stacked the back end of their roster with token whites. When they've struggled, when their depth chart is paper thin, they have brought in some black reserves to take a look at them in more active roles. From 1958 to 1965, the Celtics had only one black who might be classified as a little-used reserve: John Thompson. As times got tougher in the late sixties and seventies, this changed. From 1984 through 1987, at the peak of the Bird years and leading up to the stock sale and overall expansion plans, Carlisle and Kite, both white, received free glory rides to two championships from the end of the bench. At one historic juncture in 1986, ten of fourteen players on the Celtic roster were white. "Why do they have whites at the end of the bench? I don't know," Glenn said. "It's different if they had to have them. But they have all the other guys already, the good whites who can flat-out play."

By 1988, their talent depleted by age, injuries, and trades, the Celtics went hunting again for legitimate contributors. The result was a sudden, desperate surge in the number of black reserves. Players like Artis Gilmore, Dirk Minniefield, and Otis Birdsong were brought in and tested with some quality time before basically flunking out. Fortune swung the other way one more time, in 1990–91, with the development of Brian Shaw, Dee Brown, Reggie Lewis, and Kevin Gamble. At the All-Star break, the Celtics were leading the Eastern Conference and had the luxury once again of padding their roster with valueless white players. The three players with the least amount of minutes played—Michael Smith, Stojko Vrankovic, and Dave Popson—were all white. Four of the five players on the team with the lowest scoring averages were white.

Cohen, however, insisted the quality of the team and the conscience of the organization has never been compromised. "I gotta say I don't think we really go out of our way. Red above all," he said. Auerbach, claiming it's "a no-win question," waved it off, as if the Celtic reputation as a white team did not exist. He has support for this attitude in Boston, some of it well-intentioned and well-researched. Racial groundbreaking seems to be on his side.

"In Boston, I think it's pretty easy to characterize the Red Sox [as racist]," said Richard Lapchick, the author of books and studies on the subject of racism in sports. "The confusion comes with the Celtics. It is at least a counterbalancing thing for the Celtics in that they've had three black head coaches. I don't think it's as important to the average white person in Boston or anywhere else how many black players there are if a black man is in charge. It would take a lot to convince me that they made a conscious decision that by having eight whites, they were going to sell better stock. They still had K. C. Jones, a black head coach, as the most visible person next to Red."

But one important reason Jones was hired in 1983 was *because* he struck a much lower profile than his predecessor, Fitch. A Celtic outsider, Fitch had quickly tired of hearing about how "Red does things," and tried to keep Auerbach at arm's length. Jones was an Auerbach loyalist. Auerbach didn't bother telling Jones he had the job, or asking him if he wanted it. Jones had attended a workout with the team in Chicago and was getting ready to fly to New York. A flight attendant informed him of the news, showing him a report in the newspaper. Jones went to Auerbach, who confirmed the report.

"Come in tomorrow," Auerbach said, "and don't bring an agent."

"Why should I get an agent?" Jones thought, leaving his fate in the hands of Auerbach out of habit. "There's a line of three hundred people out there who could coach the Celtics, and every one would take the job for 50 cents." This was precisely the sort of attitude that Auerbach had counted on. Five years, two NBA titles, and four trips to the finals later, it turned out that, based strictly on winning percentage, regular season (.751) and playoffs (.637), no one had ever coached the Celtics as well as K. C. Jones. Not even the man Jones says he "owes his life to," Red Auerbach.

Chapter 8

From the Sidelines

T HE night after returning to Boston Garden as a head coach for the first time since leaving the Celtics, K. C. Jones decided the thrashing his young Seattle SuperSonics had taken probably did them good. It couldn't hurt to learn from the best. It was early December 1990, but as far as Jones could tell, there was little wear showing on Larry Bird, Robert Parish, and Kevin McHale. The Celtics, with an infusion of backcourt speed, were even more formidable than they had been when they were taken from him in the spring of 1988.

"See that?" he recalled telling his Seattle players on the bench as the ball moved Celtic-to-Celtic, as if it had a mind of its own. "There's no N-E-G-A-T-I-V-E." Sitting now in his hotel suite on the nineteenth floor of the Meadowlands Sheraton, waiting to take the Sonics across a grotesque intersection of roadway to play the New Jersey Nets, Jones distinguished his beloved Celtics from this new band of wannabes. He made his point with a riddle designed to offend no one. "Our guys play hard, but do they play smart?" Jones said. "They come up and say they want to renegotiate. I say, 'Renegotiate? You did that yesterday.'"

Jones's stand against narcissism was an extension of the selfless, defensive style he displayed as the catalyst and point guard of the Russell Celtics. He lasted nine years, averaging 7.4 points while making 38 percent of his shots. Without attracting much attention, he was always very much a presence and a winner. He played for eight championship teams in those nine years. In his first coaching job with the Capital Bullets, he averaged fifty-one wins over three seasons. In 1975, his team eliminated the defending champion Celtics from the playoffs and lost in the finals to Golden State. But when Jones was fired in 1976, his phone didn't ring.

As in baseball and football, white, established coaches like Dick Motta, Kevin Loughery, Cotton Fitzsimmons, Gene Shue, and Bill Fitch wandered from one job to another. Jones didn't get his next chance for seven years, when he won sixty-two games and a championship in Boston. Nobody hailed him as a coaching genius. The sportswriters didn't vote him Coach of the Year. All Jones had done, it seemed, was hand the ball to Larry Bird. How difficult could that have been? "Everybody thinks it's a no-brainer coaching great players, but you have to get them to respond," Danny Ainge said. "People saw him as this nice, quiet guy, but he's so intense, so competitive."

He was a nice guy benefiting from great talent. Out west, however, people didn't see the Lakers' Pat Riley as the man who held a "no-brainer" position. Despite occasional implications that Magic Johnson would have made anyone look brilliant, Riley became a *GQ* matinee idol and author of a successful book called *Showtime*, borrowing a title from Magic and his teammates. Riley became the most sought-after motivational speaker from the professional sports world, earning as much as $20,000 a night to fire up the corporate masses.

With no previous head coaching experience, right out of the Laker broadcasting booth, Riley was handed the reins of the 1979–80 champions in 1982. Fueled by Magic's brilliance, his Lakers won four championships. Rival coaches, however, were eminently impressed with Riley. They praised his harnessing of the Lakers' talent. "Let me tell you something, that guy is a great coach," Hubie Brown said one day when he was coaching the Knicks. "He comes prepared."

Although sportswriters usually vote for coaches who turned around bad teams, Riley was named Coach of the Year for 1989–90, the season he chose to walk away from the bench and into the NBC television booth. The Knicks soon went after Riley for their vacant head coaching position with a fury, signing him to a five-year deal for $6 million plus incentives, despite the rumblings that had preceded Riley's departure from Los Angeles. Unlike Jones's exit from Boston, hardly anyone was sorry to see Riley go—from general manager Jerry West down to the last player on the bench. Riley, they said, was all ego now and not enough id. He wanted total control of the operation, to the point of assigning players' hotel rooms on the road.

Perhaps Riley's closest ally in Los Angeles was Magic Johnson. But even he admitted the Lakers had turned a deaf ear to Riley's set of goals and impassioned locker room speeches. "After nine years of Pat trying anything to motivate us, what else was there to say?" Magic said.

Riley, Magic said, was firm in his belief that he was as important to the Lakers' on-court success and their esthetic appeal as any player. The Knicks' eagerness to make him the league's highest-paid coach proved that Riley wasn't alone in this perception. His New York salary would at least quadruple the $300,000 K. C. Jones was making in Seattle for 1990–91. Despite years of success with the Bullets and his phenomenal success with the Celtics, Jones's salary was bettered by first-year coach Mike Dunleavy ($400,000) in a big market, Los Angeles, and equaled by second-year coach Bob Hill ($300,000) in a small market, Indianapolis. Five of the six black NBA coaches starting the 1990–91 season, in fact, ranked in the lower third of the salary scale, including Charlotte's Gene Littles, dead last at $175,000.

While Red Auerbach got credit in Boston at the expense of Bill Fitch and K. C. Jones, Riley somehow had become the motivating genius behind the Lakers—this despite the success the players enjoyed under Paul Westhead, pre-Riley, and Mike Dunleavy, post-Riley. There was also hard evidence, largely ignored, that general manager Jerry West was at the top of his class. West confounded opponents throughout the eighties and into the nineties by manipulating the complex salary cap and overcoming low draft position to add important players such as Bob McAdoo, Mychal Thompson, Vlade Divac, and Sam Perkins.

Riley, by almost all accounts, was indeed an excellent, hardworking coach. But he proved that being white, handsome, suave, and marketable could translate into millions of dollars and all the right jobs. He used his NBC weekend playoff forum to flirt with the Knicks, campaign for the job, and provide limited news updates. Thrilled with the attention, NBC allowed Riley this self-serving forum. Back in Los Angeles, Magic smiled knowingly at how Riley had managed to force his way onto the NBA stage, even as his former team was making yet another run for a title without him.

"That's Pat," Magic said. "He's got the arrogance and the confidence. That's the way he looks at himself. As a star."

Jones, meanwhile, continued coaching, getting no attention and not caring a bit. He had no media-pleasing, well-rehearsed monologue. He didn't lecture anyone. His coaching philosophy was, appropriately, an uncharismatic version of Auerbach's. He understood the first tenet of pro coaching was the ability to relinquish control so as not to stifle the creativity of the players. Sometimes, it seemed, only former players understood this.

"When I was coaching at Kansas City, I used to tell Tiny [Archibald], 'If you ever see me jump off the bench to call a time-out in a situation where you need to create to get us a big basket, ignore me,'" Bob Cousy said. "There are no miracle plays. The academicians with the clipboards in this game are the most overrated. That's not basketball."

Many of these clipboard coaches had been the highest profiled and paid over the last fifteen years. By reputation, they were well-schooled. By extension, they were highly qualified to teach the game. Generally, the technocrats were white men with suburban or country roots who would take over a team and immediately implement their well-advertised "system." This was the self-aggrandizing catchword used as a means of controlling their environment. Black coaches who achieved varying degrees of success, such as Jones, Lenny Wilkens, Don Chaney, Bernie Bickerstaff, and Wes Unseld, never used the word "system." They generally got less media and public acclaim.

The Coach of the Year award in the eighties was won by a white man every year. Only one black head coach, Ray Scott of the Pistons in 1974, won the trophy in the award's first twenty-nine seasons. In 1990–91, young white men coaching the league's elite teams—Dunleavy in Los Angeles, Rick Adelman in Portland, Chris Ford in Boston—were acclaimed the young Turks of the coaching fraternity. By comparison, the solid work Don Chaney was doing with the Rockets went largely unnoticed outside Houston until his unheralded team exploded and nearly stole the Midwest Division title.

Chaney, the former Celtic backcourt general, had kept his team well over .500 despite losing All-League center Hakeem Olajuwon for much of the winter. Under his guidance, journeymen guards Kenny Smith and Vernon Maxwell had become solid, often spectacular, contributors. This time, the media voters had no other choice for Coach of the Year. On May 24, at halftime of a Lakers–Trail Blazers Western Conference final game, Chaney was presented with the Red Auerbach trophy, a statue of Auerbach sitting on a bench. By peeking at his trophy case, Chaney could forever be reminded of the man who wouldn't give him his deserved remuneration as a player, and of the city he had to leave to get the chance to embark on his coaching career.

With Chaney as Coach of the Year, there predictably was no league-wide celebration over another brilliant coaching system. But in New York, people were already gearing up for Riley's methodology. New York loved coaches—analyzing them, idolizing them, destroying them. In New York, three of the Knicks' previous four head coaches—excluding interim coach Bob Hill—were known for their "systems." The one coach who didn't have one was young Stu Jackson, the only black of the group.

Hubie Brown held tight to a rigid, half-court, work-the-low-post system. Rick Pitino used a popular helter-skelter, press-and-run system. John MacLeod had a half-court system, preferable to Brown's because he wasn't as strident in enforcing it. With all the different coaches and systems, the Knicks never got out of the second round of the playoffs. For years, the debate raged in the locker room and in the media. Should the Knicks be running? Should they be playing more half-court?

Red Holzman was on the Knick payroll as a $100,000-a-year consultant throughout the eighties, then again beginning in 1991. If anyone had bothered to ask, Holzman would have been happy to explain that basketball is a game of ebb and flow, of opportunities created by defense, of rebounding, unselfish execution, and good judgment. To mold one's team in any exaggerated fashion, be it Brown's slowdown or Paul Westhead's Denver free-for-all, was self-serving gimmickry. The best teams could always play *any* style. The Celtics of the eighties performed up-tempo basketball when they needed it, even with the slow-footed Bird, Kevin McHale, and Dennis Johnson. The Lakers of the eighties were known for their high-speed showtime, but Magic Johnson and James Worthy were underrated half-court players who won games with their defense.

For technocrats like Hubie Brown and his slew of protégés, including Pitino, Richie Adubato, and Ron Rothstein, the "system" was built-in protection against personal failure. If the team won, the system was brilliant. If it lost, the players didn't fit the system. The coach was prepared, one way or another. Diligent preparation and single-minded dedication were part of Hubie Brown's hard sell, and his players were to follow in line. Sooner or later, however, they realized the man standing on such high moral ground was a flawed human being just like everyone else. While these coaches were busy selling themselves as hardworking family men, they couldn't resist the temptations of celebrity any more than the players. The moment the clipboard was in the briefcase, out came Mr. Hyde.

One NBA coach had a hooker in every city, and almost nightly fed his kinky appetite by sucking stockinged feet. Another NBA coach confessed he hated his wife but kept her around for image's sake. He was hoping for a college job and needed the family as a prop.

Taskmaster coaches were always big on punctuality and time management until it involved themselves. Once, when the Knicks were in Cleveland to play an afternoon conference game against the Cavaliers, Brown violated league policy and team decorum by staying behind for a personal engagement the night before. He had failed to notify Knick management about this, fearing reprisals. When his morning flight was rerouted to Pittsburgh due to bad weather, Brown recognized a newspaper reporter in the same predicament.

"We'll rent a car," he said. Setting records for violating speed limits, Brown pulled the car into the toll booth of the Ohio Turnpike, one hour before game time. "How long to Richfield?" he asked.

"About ninety minutes," the woman in the booth said.

"Fuck!" Brown yelled in the woman's face. "We're screwed." The reporter, sitting on a bigger story than the game, resisted the temptation to say, "What do you mean *we?*"

The same season, one of Brown's players, Darrell Walker, grew tired of the verbal whipping he was taking and suddenly refused to move from his spot on the practice floor at the Omni in Atlanta. While players went on shooting around them, Walker and Brown went face-to-face, Brown attacking Walker's effort and Walker informing Brown the players all knew he was no boy scout and that his "rap was bullshit." Brown didn't know Walker had come to practice burning mad. The player had heard that Brown was calling him "nigger" and other slurs behind his back. "I was younger, not as mature then, so part of it was my fault," said Walker, who eventually became a solid player for Wes Unseld, another solid but largely ignored coach in Washington. "But Hubie was crazy."

Black players often felt an undercurrent of racism with coaches such as Brown. When Brown coached in Atlanta, Tree Rollins, the starting center, said Brown's attempts to "relate" to them were painfully obvious and condescending. The black players, he said, believed many of the southern fans only came to the games to see Brown humiliate them. Most white coaches in this black sport are not racist, but few understand black culture and can be embarrassingly awkward trying to embrace it. And some are much, much worse than others. One former NBA coach, stumbling around the hotel lobby one night after drowning away the sorrow of another loss, decided to plead his case to a couple of reporters.

"Who knew we had a bunch of liggers?" the coach said.

"Bunch of what?" said one reporter.

"Liggers," said the coach. "Lazy, fucking niggers."

Sitting around an airport terminal one afternoon, discussing with a few writers the best neighborhoods in greater New York, Hubie Brown carefully enunciated some advice: "Fort Lee [New Jersey] is a great neighborhood. It is in a great location, has great schools, great parks, and no blacks." Brown stated this quite matter-of-factly, probably as a means of saying the neighborhood was safe. In his own mind, he had said nothing wrong or controversial. Coaching blacks was one thing; golfing with them at Red Auerbach's country club or sharing Hubie Brown's street was another. This kind of mentality seemed fine for networks such as CBS and TBS, which have employed Brown as lead analyst and surely have heard of his reputation through industry sources. In the final analysis, broadcasting was the perfect job for Hubie Brown, the coaching genius and industry know-it-all who retired from the sidelines with an NBA winning percentage of 45.4. On TV, he lectured to millions who couldn't talk back.

Clearly, despite some progress, despite being the most racially enlightened pro sports league in America, the NBA still had a long way to go. By the All-Star break in 1991, there were five black head coaches on twenty-seven teams, down from six out of twenty-three teams in 1988. There were fourteen black assistants out of seventy-nine in 1991, an insignificant increase, percentage-wise, from nine of fifty-three in 1988. "Black players will ask white teammates, 'If you get a coaching job, will you hire me as an assistant?'" said former Hawk guard Mike Glenn. Black trainers and PR directors were virtually nonexistent in the NBA. Mitch Kupchak, a likable white center whose promising career was cut short by knee and back ailments, became assistant GM with the Lakers at the remarkable age of thirty-four.

By his thirty-fifth birthday in 1991, David Checketts, a bishop in the Mormon church, had been a top administrator of the Utah Jazz, the Denver Nuggets, the NBA office, and—his greatest coup—the New York Knicks, where he was named executive vice president. His first hire there was thirty-six-year-old Ernie Grunfeld as director of player personnel. Grunfeld, a white player, came to the Knicks as a heady veteran player, a Hubie Brown favorite, in 1982. He retired into the broadcasting booth and was added to the coaching staff as an assistant in 1989. To that point, his career paralleled that of Butch Beard, a black, who finished a well-traveled but creditable career with the Knicks and subsequently became a broadcaster and assistant coach. That, however, was where Beard's budding management career came to an abrupt halt. He was out of basketball, then an assistant coach for the New Jersey Nets, finally the head coach at a black university, Howard.

"Butch Beard at Howard," old friend and admirer Bob McAdoo said of Beard's relegation to small-time college ball. "That's terrible, really depressing."

Blacks couldn't win because the sport wouldn't let them. Charles Grantham, who is black, believes disenfranchised blacks are paying now for past sins of omission. "Twenty years ago, the pressure groups didn't pressure sports into minority hiring. They just pressured corporations," Grantham said. "The NBA was more like a ma and pa business. The league would say, 'Hey, we have 70 percent black players. We gave at the office.' That was supposed to be enough. Remember, you have all these different franchises responding to their own market, like a Wendy's or a McDonald's. It's difficult to get a hold on them."

Clearly, it required more than basketball smarts for a black coaching applicant. Four of the five NBA black head coaches, Jones, Don Chaney, Wes Unseld, and Lenny Wilkens, had truly distinguished pro careers, like former black head coaches Bill Russell, Willis Reed, and Al Attles. Of the twenty-three white head coaches, the same could be said only for Chris Ford and Don Nelson. "If you're black, you need a couple of championship rings before you get an offer to coach or be an executive," said Mike Glenn, now an Atlanta Hawks broadcaster, who is certain that had he been a white player, he would have been considered coaching material. White coaches were preschooled in coaching; blacks were not. This unequal selection process led to another sterotype: black coaches as unprepared and unqualified celebrities, as laissez-faire "players' coaches."

The implication was that coaches like K. C. Jones lacked teaching skills but might compensate for that by getting along with the players. This was generally nonsense. "You've got to understand, K. C. Jones was a players' coach, but no one has as much patience with teaching and learning as he does," Robert Parish said. "He can coach, in my book, a veteran team like ours, or a young team like Seattle's."

In 1987–88, Jones's last season coaching the Celtics, Larry Bird was playing with bad heels, the backcourt was old and slow, and the bench was thin. The Celtics won fifty-seven games and lost in the conference finals to Detroit. Despite averaging sixty-one wins in his five years, this was somehow below expectations. In Jones's words, "Here came *jaws*." Under media criticism for not developing his rookies—especially Reggie Lewis—for the playoffs, Jones knew management was eager to replace him with assistant Jimmy Rodgers. He accepted the ceremonial front office seat of vice president of basketball operations. With Cohen, Volk, and Rodgers making the big decisions, the position was worthless. This plot development infuriated most of the players on the team, including Larry Bird, who resented Rodgers for some time.

"K. C. felt pressure to leave, but not from the players," Danny Ainge said. "Other people might not have wanted to give him credit; that's not how I saw it. He let Jimmy coach a little. He didn't have to, he didn't need him, but he knew Jimmy wanted to. You could always go to K. C. and say, 'Let's try this.' He gave respect. He had no ego hangups."

It was not within Jones's nature to protest, and it was with his trademark cool, clever detachment that he recalled the obvious manipulation. At the 1983 press conference when he originally had taken the head coaching job, he had said that he probably would coach a couple of years and retire. He really hadn't given the subject much thought. Now the Celtics were holding him to it.

"You said you'd retire in a couple of years," Volk said.

"Oh, I *did*?" Jones replied.

Jones preferred the belief—for public consumption, anyway—that the move was made because of Volk's close friendship with Rodgers. "It was not that Jan thought Jimmy was better," Jones said. He hoped it had little to do with the notion that the aging Celtics needed to develop young talent and Rodgers was the more qualified "teacher." To keep life uncomplicated, Jones out of habit refused any suggestion that Auerbach was involved, as if Volk would ever have had the authority to make a decision like that without Auerbach's approval. But whatever he was feeling deep inside, Jones typically made his point quite well without raising a stink. He left the Celtics a year later to be the assistant for another black coach, Bernie Bickerstaff, in Seattle. Bickerstaff had been Jones's assistant with the Bullets; the two were old friends.

Why would Jones leave the Celtic family, uproot at fifty-seven and move clear across the country? His ability to defer to others didn't mean he was without great pride. He wouldn't stay in a scouting position he knew was irrelevant. "It wasn't [the position] I expected," Jones said. "The media didn't call me up or ask my opinion. There wasn't much to do."

"It surprised me that K. C. left," Bob Cousy said. "I would've just taken the check and forgotten about it. But that's me. I guess the fire still burned for him and he didn't like being shoved upstairs."

After one season, Bickerstaff moved on to Denver, leaving the struggling young Sonics in Jones's capable, diplomatic hands. That early December night in New Jersey at the Sheraton Hotel, Jones excused himself from his two visitors to make a call. He dialed another room, and when the other line picked up, he said, "Quintin, what time is the bus tonight?... Okay, see you there." The two puzzled visitors looked at each other. What kind of head coach would need to call Quintin Dailey, one of the most troubled NBA players in recent years, to find out when the team bus was leaving for the arena? Then the visitors suddenly understood. Jones was tactfully making certain that Dailey knew the bus departure time so he would have no excuses later. Jones returned. "Now where were we?" he said.

Jones was in the middle of another successful season with a club that did not have the talent to own the respectable record it had in the powerful Western Conference. Young players such as Shawn Kemp and Gary Payton were developing nicely. Acquired during the season, veterans like Eddie Johnson and Ricky Pierce were thrilled to be away from Cotton Fitzsimmons in Phoenix and Del Harris in Milwaukee. The Sonics looked and played as a team under control, with a future. They surprisingly extended Portland, the team with the NBA's best regular-season record, to the five-game limit in the first round of the playoffs. K. C. Jones, as usual, took no credit, and few seemed interested in giving him any.

❈   ❈   ❈

The Celtics' two seasons under Jimmy Rodgers were unhappy and unproductive. He was not the teacher they hoped he'd be, and his communication skills as head coach weren't very good either. Worse, he couldn't balance the preferential treatment Larry Bird demanded with the needs of the other team members. Under Rodgers, the man the Celtics were so desperate to jettison K. C. Jones for, the Celtics were eliminated twice in the first round of the playoffs. He was fired after the 1989–90 season. "We wanted to do it the year before," Alan Cohen said. "I'm sorry we waited."

The Celtics were now viewed around the country as old and tired, the Bird era seemingly having run its course. It was impossible not to dwell on what might have been if Len Bias hadn't died of a cocaine overdose in June 1986. He would have been in his prime, the fresh set of superstar legs the team desperately sought. It was a shame, a bum deal for everyone involved. Auerbach appeared paralyzed by the disaster. He and Volk sat around for years, watching their backcourt and bench strength dissipate. They made no important transactions. All the ideas were gone. "Bias changes everything," Auerbach said. "If I've got him, I can make other moves from strength." He shook his head. "This kid was not a druggie. That was the first or second time he'd used drugs."

It didn't really matter anymore, but such naivete was almost a plaintive cry for what *Globe* columnist Bob Ryan called an "insight transfusion" the day the Celtics introduced Dave Gavitt as their senior executive vice president on May 30, 1990. The whole thing was set up by Gavitt and Cohen to sound like Auerbach's idea, one last stretching of the truth for the sake of the legend. "Red sat right over there and suggested it," Cohen said in his Manhattan office one day in late 1990. But years before, Cohen had tried to bring Gavitt to the New Jersey Nets. Gavitt had only become a hotter property since then. Cohen clearly had never discarded his number.

Gavitt fit and looked the position of a Celtic head of state. Born in Westerly, Rhode Island, he was the definitive New Englander.

His career in basketball began at Worcester Academy and took him to Providence College; Dartmouth in Hanover, New Hampshire; back to Providence; and on to his office with the Big East, which he stationed in Providence. He had a rugged, bulldog, working-class look to him. His ruddy complexion gave him the appearance of a man who'd survived many forbidding New England winters. He smoked cigars.

Gavitt for Auerbach was still a delicate operation for the Celtics, the unofficial exorcism of a legend. "We're not talking about a dinosaur," the ever-loyal Jan Volk said of Auerbach, but the evidence said otherwise. It was time to step aside, if not down. "Bullshit!" Auerbach blustered when asked if Gavitt's opinion on personnel matters would weigh more heavily than his. But in a private moment, he conceded, "Look, I'm realistic. I'm getting older."

Auerbach and the Bird-era Celtics never looked older than on May 6, 1990. The Celtics were hosting the Knicks in a decisive fifth game of their first-round playoff series. The Knicks had lost their last twenty-six games over seven years at Boston Garden, and their general manager, Al Bianchi, had been cursed in the building all the way back to his Syracuse National days in the 1950s. "See this?" Bianchi said, standing in the corridor hours before the game. He was holding a copy of the *Sunday Globe* in his left hand and slapping it with his right. The headline on the sports page was something about Boston Garden ghosts haunting opponents in crucial playoff games. "This is my fucking life they're talking about."

Anxious to write another chapter for Bianchi, the Celtics spurted to an early lead, and the fans seemed to relax. But when the Knicks rallied behind forward Johnny Newman, an uneasiness reclaimed the building. Newman repeatedly was beating Bird off the dribble, breaking down the Celtic interior defense. A heavyset, redheaded fan behind that basket, a regular for years, didn't quite see it that way. "Ca-mahn, Chief," he screamed at Robert Parish. "Get back on D." By the fourth quarter, the Knicks held a 2-point lead. Bird navigated the baseline, left to right, and went in for an uncontested dunk. The ball mysteriously popped out. As it hung in the stale, smoky air, there was an inescapable feeling that something was changing in Boston Garden.

The hero of the Knick victory was the quiet, respected veteran point guard, Maurice Cheeks. Cheeks won his only championship with Philadelphia in 1983, but had always said his most cherished NBA memory was beating the Celtics at Boston Garden in game seven of the Eastern Conference finals in 1982. Bianchi had traded for Cheeks's leadership in February, at the expense of Rod Strickland, ten years Cheeks's junior, a future star. It was a deal that helped unravel a young, exciting team, putting Bianchi's head on the chopping block. The ax would come ten months later.

Bianchi, in essence, had sold his soul to the devil for that afternoon in Boston Garden. A cynic might have said he'd mortgaged the team's future at the expense of his personal vendetta. It all seemed worth it, though. For once, he'd beaten the hated Red Auerbach, driven away all the ghosts. While Auerbach walked sadly down the narrow corridor, defeated in his final game as commander-in-chief of the Boston Celtics, Bianchi stood at the other end of the hall, puffing away contentedly on his victory cigar. He could have been at War Memorial, in Syracuse.

Chapter 9

Three Steals

JOHN Havlicek stole the ball. Gerald Henderson stole the ball. Larry Bird stole the ball. Only two found glory.

There were three uncommon steals in the illustrious Celtic history. They led to two Eastern Conference championships and an NBA title—and decidedly different aftershocks. From the moment Havlicek stole the inbounds pass from Hal Greer to Chet Walker in the seventh game of the 1965 East final, he became an unparalelled Boston legend. Five months after Henderson stole James Worthy's pass and rescued game two of the finals in 1984, he was tricked by Jan Volk, badmouthed by Red Auerbach, and sent packing to the Seattle SuperSonics. Two days after Bird stole the pass from Isiah Thomas in game five of the Eastern Conference finals, Thomas was jetting around the country performing damage control after making a post-game statement about Bird that would follow him for seasons to come. Another Detroit Piston, rookie Dennis Rodman, was suffering a similar image problem that he was still too young to comprehend. The resulting equation: Three Celtic steals equaled two white heroes, Havlicek and Bird, plus three black victims, Henderson, Rodman, and Thomas.

Chronologically, and in the hearts of most diehard Celtic fans, Havlicek's steal will always come first. Hondo was a thirteen-time All-Star, a member of eight championship teams, a remarkably durable star who averaged 18.3 points per game in 1977 at the advanced basketball age of thirty-seven. Havlicek, a man who never stood still on the basketball court or in life, would like to think a single steal against the archrival 76ers did not define his entire athletic career. Not in his own mind, anyway. "The only thing that came out of it was a great deal of notoriety, as far as I was concerned," Havlicek said.

The play itself, on April 15, 1965, was a genuine pearl, set up by one of those wonderful oddities of sport. Havlicek had keyed a third-quarter Celtic rally, scoring 15 of his 26 points in that period. Wilt Chamberlain hit a basket with five seconds left in the game to cut the Celtic lead to 1 point, 110–109. Bill Russell's routine inbounds pass then struck one of the guide wires leading to the basket, posing an officiating dilemma. The wire had been placed there two years earlier, after the already outmoded Boston Garden floor was extended by ten feet to conform with the rest of the NBA. These cross wires would be eliminated after this series, before the finals against the Lakers. But for the time being, Earl Strom, the referee in game seven and one of the premier NBA officials for the next twenty-five seasons, would have to make a grounds ruling. He gave possession to the 76ers. It was not an easy call to make at Boston Garden, but Strom made it. "Thank God what happened next happened, or I wouldn't have gotten out of that arena alive," Strom said.

What transpired was a combination of typical Celtic good fortune and pure Havlicek instinct. Havlicek first decided he would cover big man Johnny Kerr on the 76ers' inbounds play, but was talked out of it by Sam Jones. "Sam had more senior leadership than I did, so I listened," Havlicek said. "Sam said he would keep him off the boards, and told me to take a guard." Chet Walker was swinging back to the guard position in the 76ers' big lineup, so Havlicek stuck with him. Greer tried to inbound the ball, was pestered by K. C. Jones, and found all his teammates covered. He had five seconds to throw the pass, and Havlicek, counting to himself, noticed that Greer was having trouble. "Usually, the passer doesn't get past one-thousand-three when I'm counting," Havlicek said. "He was having trouble, and my antenna went up." The lob was short, though not badly misdirected. "It was the sort of pass that could have been easily received [by Walker] if I had my back turned," Havlicek said. Instead, Havlicek deflected the ball, controlled it, then knocked it over to Sam Jones as the game was sealed. Havlicek, Red Auerbach, and Bill Russell were unwillingly hoisted onto the shoulders of fans and carried off the parquet floor into the beery hallway.

Courtside, screaming into his microphone, the coarse vocal cords of Celtic radio announcer Johnny Most were telling the world about the enormity of this play. "Havlicek stole the ball!" If this was not the defining moment for Havlicek, then maybe it was for Most, the mythical chronicler of the Celtics. Most's voice, and Havlicek's play, were united forever in cosmic synergism, radio waves bounding toward uncharted galaxies beyond the realm of twenty-four-second clocks. Nobody, least of all Most, would mention that Havlicek had played a generally disappointing series against Philadelphia; that he had shot 32.9 percent from the field over seven games. "They were playing the recording of that steal every fifteen or twenty minutes the next day, and that's when I realized this would not go away," Havlicek said. "Then they put out an album and called it 'Havlicek stole the ball!' I still hear it more than you'd think." At every NBA highlight show, at every league gathering, the recording or the film is rewound and shoved into another projector or VCR. Sometimes, on All-Star weekends, Most on Havlicek is piped into the elevators of NBA hotels.

The retelling is loud, it is stirring, it is always the same: "Havlicek stole the ball!" In the *Boston Herald* the day after the steal, too,

Havlicek got his due. HAVLICEK SEALS CELTIC WIN AT FINISH, the headline read, and the lead by reporter Jack Sheehan spoke about "a fantastic last second defensive gamble by John Havlicek." Two days after the triumph, Havlicek was pictured in the *Herald* smoking a victory cigar with K. C. Jones. The sports page explosion of the eighties had not yet hit Boston, but the coverage gave Havlicek about as much one-event publicity as any Boston athlete had ever received, Ted Williams included.

Havlicek was a classic Celtic by Auerbach's definition. A lifer. Asked to play the role of the sixth man, he obeyed. In his first four seasons, when Tom Heinsohn and Sam Jones were still around to score points, Havlicek curbed his offensive instincts and scored fewer than 20 points per game. When he was asked to score in later years, when the team fell on hard times, Havlicek averaged in the high 20s and missed a total of just five games in his last seven seasons. Asked to guard bigger forwards or smaller guards, the six-five swingman did what he was told. Asked to scoot around the floor chasing shooting guards, he did this too. "I had the ability to run and not get tired," Havlicek said.

He was, in other words, quite worthy of the praise heaped on him. And yet so were other Celtics who were either traded unceremoniously or generally ignored. While the steal was no immediate financial bonanza for Havlicek, it did assure him of his place in Celtic lore and a lifetime of career opportunities in Boston. There were never any trade rumors with Havlicek, not after his second season, in 1963, when Auerbach actually flirted with the awful idea of sending Havlicek and Tom Sanders to the Knicks for Richie Guerin, an established scoring guard. Havlicek played on into his late thirties, retiring when he was still a real force on the court. He continued to work out with the team, a special status approved by both the coaching staff and Auerbach. At age forty, in 1980, Havlicek was approached by coach Bill Fitch and asked whether he would like to come out of retirement to play with the new kid, Larry Bird. Havlicek declined the honor, but he will never be forgotten in

Boston. Most's voice still finds its way onto every retrospective sports show in the area. Havlicek still lives there, owns a couple of Wendy's restaurants, and does promotional work for Nabisco. He has a pair of season tickets to Boston Garden and a standing invitation to sit next to Auerbach and the Celtic brass in loge one whenever he comes to a game.

Havlicek was there watching at the Garden when Henderson stole the ball from Worthy. He was a little surprised there wasn't more of a fuss. "I guess Johnny Most came up with all the adjectives for me, and ran out for the others," he said. "You know, Henderson not only made the steal, he made the shot."

Henderson remembers that, and more. He remembers that his play saved a championship, while Havlicek's and Bird's steals simply preserved Eastern Conference titles. "They're always showing Havlicek and Bird stealing the ball in video and radio highlights," Henderson said. "They can play it up or down in Celtic history. I don't give a crap about how they play it. The fans play it the way they want to.

"The steal Havlicek made, Boston was already up by a point. It just secured the game," Henderson said. "Larry's was a great steal, but it didn't win a championship that year. But it shouldn't matter how the media portray my play. The whole country should know how important it was."

Henderson's steal in 1984 turned around what was the most important Celtic series of the 1980s. If Boston had lost that year to Los Angeles, then Larry Bird's Celtics would have dropped all three series in the eighties to Magic Johnson's Lakers. Bird didn't beat Johnson as a collegian and he would not have beaten him as a pro. The Celtics' claim to uninterrupted glory, through every decade, would have been severely tested. "If not for that pass," said Byron Scott, the Laker guard, "they never would have beaten us head-to-head." Instead, with one victory for the Celtics in three championship meetings, the result was respectable.

The finals did not start off that hopefully in 1984 at Boston Garden, where the Lakers broke the home court edge immediately with a 115–109 victory in game one. On May 31, Los Angeles held a 2-point lead with twenty seconds to play in regulation of game two. A second straight victory for the Lakers at Boston Garden would almost certainly have been decisive, with three games still scheduled for the Forum. During a gloomy time-out huddle, K. C. Jones inserted M. L. Carr on defense at guard and told Henderson to roam around, maybe make something happen. "The feeling was like, 'We blew it. We're dead,'" Cedric Maxwell said. "And then all of a sudden, we're back, we're tied, we win in OT."

Unlike Havlicek, who can recall precisely what he was thinking about in the seconds leading to his steal, Henderson is a little fuzzy on details. He rotated off his man, but he can't remember if his man was Scott or Michael Cooper. He remembers Worthy taking Johnson's inbounds pass, then trying to lob the ball crosscourt to somebody. It was Scott, who would regret this whole episode for years. "I remember in our huddle there was this incredible feeling of excitement, that we were going home 2–0," Scott said. "We were all hyper—'Yeah, yeah, yeah.' We were so close. I was on the right side, myself and Earvin [Johnson] split, and I was going upcourt, in the other direction from the ball, which was a rookie mistake. If I'd been moving to the ball, Henderson wouldn't have had the time to get there, or maybe he'd have run into me and committed the foul. We ended up throwing away the championship."

Henderson stepped in front of Scott, soared for the layup at the other end ahead of Worthy. "I took a swat at him, but the angle wasn't good," Worthy said. "I felt terrible. It stayed with me until after the season, when Magic and I talked about it and put it behind us." The Celtics won that game in overtime, 124–121, and went on to take the series, 4–3. As game seven ended with Johnson dribbling away the Lakers' last chance, the media seemed to celebrate Bird's personal triumph. "Tragic Johnson," Magic was called. Forgotten was his remarkable trifecta—state high school, NCAA, and NBA championships over a four-year span.

The day after game two, reporter Dan Shaughnessy's lead game story in the *Boston Globe* did not mention Henderson until the third paragraph. Then it divided credit among several players. "The Celtics had more heroes than a Philadelphia deli," Shaughnessy wrote. Henderson already was being written out of the script.

At the time of this great triumph, the Celtics were using a three-guard rotation with Henderson, Dennis Johnson, and Danny Ainge. All three players could swing to either backcourt position, but Ainge and Henderson generally shared time at the playmaking spot. Henderson was a wiry six-two point guard with unselfish instincts who in 1979 had been rescued from the Continental Basketball Association by Bill Fitch. He was, before the upcoming betrayal, a loyal employee who bought into the Celtic Mystique. Henderson's four-year contract signed in 1980 expired a few weeks after his remarkable steal, and negotiations dragged on through the summer. The Celtics came up with a stingy offer in the $350,000-per-year range, and Auerbach vowed publicly, "not a penny more." Ainge, the brash former infielder out of Brigham Young University, was earning an inflated— for the time—$650,000 per season. Ainge had been a major disappointment during the 1983–84 regular season, his third in the NBA, averaging 5.4 points. He already was resented among opposing players as the whining crown prince of Boston and was actually targeted by a few teams for occasional blindside picks.

Henderson, earning half of Ainge's pay in his fifth season, had shot 52.4 percent and averaged 11.6 points. Still, Celtic brass was willing to bet on the development of Ainge, a solid white player who was already a big hit with Boston fans. Auerbach and Volk began looking for creative ways to trade Henderson, to open a starting spot for Ainge. "They try to recruit the best white guys who play the game," Henderson said later. "They're catering to the paying fans. It's a format that's worked for them for years. Why go against it, especially if it's accepted by surrounding society?"

Henderson's agent, Scott Lang from New Bedford, Massachusetts, shopped Henderson around the league, trying to force the Celtics to bid higher for his client's services. This strategy, common practice in the NBA, did not really work. Henderson was a restricted free agent. Other teams understood the Celtics would simply match their offer and retain his rights—even if it was just to trade him later for some equitable compensation. Lang began protracted negotiations with Volk, a man Lang now regrets ever trusting.

Early in the talks with Volk, Lang asked for a no-trade clause in the contract, which was still legal back in 1984. The Celtics refused. Training camp was three-quarters done, two exhibitions had been played, and Henderson was getting itchy. Ainge buried eight straight shots against Houston in a preseason game, and coach K. C. Jones sent a message to Henderson the next day by saying that Ainge "has looked awfully impressive." Lang felt the heat, along with Henderson. The Celtics had them boxed. "I asked Jan Volk at the time, 'You don't have any intention of trading Gerald, do you?'" Lang said. "He gave me a look like, 'You've got to be kidding.' He said he had no intention of doing that."

Before a Friday night exhibition game on October 12, Lang and Henderson huddled with Celtic officials in Auerbach's cozy office at Boston Garden. When the talks began around noon, Auerbach sat down at his desk to make his one and only speech to Henderson. He argued that Henderson could not afford to pass up the playoff and endorsement opportunities with the Celtics; that he would come out ahead, regardless of his salary. Henderson was wanted in Boston. "The tone was friendly and sincere," Lang remembered. Then, after about an hour, Auerbach excused himself. This was not 1960. He was above crunching specific numbers in contract negotiations. He would leave that to Volk.

After six hours of talks, Henderson signed a pact. It was for three years, at $350,000, $375,000 and $400,000, plus an option year. The deal was not nearly as sweet as Ainge's, Lang realized, but Henderson, twenty-eight, wanted another shot at a title, playoff money, and television exposure. A big mistake. "Throughout that era, and later too, championship teams had a tendency to count the playoff money in their salary offers," said Players Association president Charles Grantham. "We say contracts shouldn't be negotiated that way. We try to tell players they can be on any one of twenty-seven teams after a trade, with the same contract. There should be a bonus trade clause in the contract." There wasn't this time, but the loyal Henderson took the deal and reported to practice. After all, Volk had given his assurances. Lang had taken the bait.

Soon, the other sneaker dropped. The vaunted hero of the 1984 series, the man who stole the ball from Worthy, became the victim of a lightning-strike smear campaign. Auerbach complained about Henderson's playing shape to reporters. Clearly, the Celtics were preparing their public for what was to come: the dumping of Henderson less than a week after he signed the contract. Henderson had worked out on his own at Boston College, had played just six minutes of one exhibition game on Sunday against Utah at Las Vegas. But the deal was already coming down. "The *Globe* always backed management, and Red had his ways of manipulating the *Globe*," Henderson said. "That's how he did things. Red said I was out of shape, fed this information to the press. I've never been out of shape. You can't get into NBA shape playing against lesser talent, like I'd been doing during the holdout, but I was in decent shape."

Even Ainge, the greatest beneficiary of the upcoming Henderson deal, was turned off by the Celtics' propaganda campaign. "Gerald was definitely in shape," Ainge said after his own rebirth as a title contender again with the Portland Trail Blazers. "He was a hard worker, and that was just management's excuse. It was a PR move by the Celtics."

Before an exhibition game on that Tuesday, four days after his signing, Henderson practiced with the Celtics at the Summit. Hours later, at the Westin Galleria, coach K. C. Jones told Henderson he'd been traded to Seattle for a first-round draft pick. Henderson thought it was a joke. His teammates thought it was, too. His agent, Lang, thought it wasn't even remotely amusing when Volk called him to relate the news. The contract Lang had negotiated was only acceptable to Henderson because it was with the Celtics, not a particularly wise move by the agent, who might have negotiated a no-trade clause. Now Henderson was a Seattle SuperSonic, lost in the great Northwest with a down-turning team, far from the possibility of an NBA championship or big endorsement money. "They took away Gerald's free agent rights, then traded him," Lang said. "If there was such a thing as green blood, Gerald Henderson had it. And what Volk did to us was the equivalent of me bringing Gerald in with a severe injury and not telling them before they signed the contract. I haven't had too many experiences like that. People who run the clubs know and respect each other. There is a code of faith, and you do not violate that faith. I thought I knew Jan."

At the time, Volk all but gloated about his triumph over Lang. "That sounds to me like someone feeling very bad about the job they did for their client," he said, when told of Lang's bitterness. "I said I had no intention of trading Gerald Henderson *at that time.*" The Auerbach public relations machine kicked into high gear. "He [Henderson] made one mistake," Auerbach told reporters. "He told K. C. he was in shape, and he came in in horrible shape. Missing training camp really hurt him."

The Godfather had spoken. By Thursday, October 18, the *Globe* had abandoned all pretexts of neutrality and swung fully behind the franchise. Under the headline CHANGING OF THE GUARDS, the newspaper ran an amnestic feature by Shaughnessy about rookie replacement Rick Carlisle and a truly malevolent anti-Henderson column by Will McDonough. Shaughnessy's piece, accompanied by a lead photo of the untalented Carlisle, began, "The newest member of the Boston Celtics is prep-school handsome, a self-taught pianist, and has a degree in psychology from one of America's finest academic institutions. Meet Rick Carlisle, a 6-foot-5 guard from the University of Virginia ..." Henderson was all but forgotten. A very white, third-round savior—one who could not push the ball downcourt, but could play the piano—had been found.

McDonough's spiel, straight from the self-serving cerebral cortex of Auerbach as usual, was an attack on Henderson and Lang. "Pardon me for just a moment, will you?" it began. "I have to wipe my hands before I start. They are wet from the tears that poured out of the newspapers I've read the past 24 hours. And goodness, everytime I touched my TV dial last night to watch the sports on the 6 o'clock news, they were crying again. Scott Lang and Gerald Henderson. The Kleenex Twins. You'd need a whole box of tissues just to get through a one minute interview about how terrible it was that Henderson got shuffled off to Seattle ..." McDonough went on to write that Henderson deserved to be traded for being a willing party to Lang's free agency marketing attempts. In two days of reporting this deal and in ignoring its dreadful, dehumanizing facets, the only mention in the *Globe* of Henderson's steal against the Lakers came from Larry Bird—who was not paid to be a journalist and could easily have ignored the issue. "He saved our ass," Bird said. "I just wish he could be around after doing what he did last year." When the championship banner was raised at the Garden on opening night, Bird grabbed the microphone and said it again.

The Henderson double-cross had repercussions for the next several years that Volk, Auerbach, and the rest of the NBA did not see coming. Larry Fleisher, then head of the Players Association, used the transaction as a bloody flag for unrestricted free agency, a campaign he won, in large part, during collective bargaining four years later. Then, players with Henderson's playing experience and contractual standing would be free to shop around their talents without threats of reprisal. Also because of the Henderson deal, Celtics like Bird and Cedric Maxwell began to view the green uniform and Volk's contractual offers in a different, more skeptical way.

Henderson, suddenly three thousand miles away from the parquet, certainly viewed his basketball career in a more jaded light. He had believed in the Celtic Pride concept, but when it all came tumbling down, Henderson was a changed man. This wide-eyed enthusiast became, understandably, one of the game's great cynics and locker room lobbyists. Henderson wanted clubhouses at practice sites closed to the press. He wanted people out of his face. "I finally understood things, then," he said. "They're going to be tough. You be tough. You've got to handle it like a business, then get out. Back then, I thought you had an obligation to the team. But it doesn't matter if you have twelve guys playing for a common goal. When management gets involved, it all breaks down."

By the fall of 1990, after brief stints in New York, Philadelphia, and Detroit, Henderson was on the sidelines, an unemployed journeyman, deprived of the glories and endorsements that come with single-team career tenure. He and his wife began a different business in Philadelphia, in some ways a more rewarding one. They transported elderly and handicapped people. He would be picked up again by the Pistons in February 1991 when Isiah Thomas was injured. He would start next to Joe Dumars in the backcourt. But nobody was doing Henderson any favors, making any long-term commitments. And Red Auerbach wasn't reaching out to take care of his own.

Scott Lang believed the Celtics treated Henderson so badly not because of race, but strictly because of economics. Auerbach thought Henderson, a starter, would not easily accept less money than Ainge, a reserve. But as several studies have concluded, and as black players have long understood, race and NBA salary are clearly interrelated.

In 1988, two University of Illinois professors, Lawrence M. Kahn and Peter D. Sherer, conducted a study titled "Racial Differences in Professional Basketball Players' Compensation." Their conclusion— again, no surprise to any studious observer—was that "black NBA players earn significantly less than white players [of the same playing talent] by about 20 percent." The study found that home attendance was correlated to white representation on the team and therefore concluded that "as long as fans prefer to see white players, profit-oriented teams will make discriminatory salary offers." Another study done during the same season, by Eleanor Brown of

Pomona College, Diane Keenan of Claremont Graduate School, and Richard Spiro of First Boston Corporation, confirmed the earlier findings. It found earnings penalties in the range of 14 to 16 percent for black players in the NBA.

By the 1990–91 season, NBA players were averaging nearly $1 million, and virtually everybody was making a good living. Yet discrimination still existed. Looking at salaries league-wide, many players clearly were overpaid considering their statistical contributions, their experience, and their potential. The most flagrant examples: Mark Jackson of New York earned $1.75 million; John Williams of Cleveland, $3.785 million; Danny Ferry of Cleveland, $2.64 million; Blair Rasmussen of Denver, $2.185 million; Alton Lister of Golden State, $1.7 million; Jim Petersen of Golden State, $1.235 million; George McCloud of Indiana, $940,000; Willie Burton of Miami, $2 million; Alex Kessler of Miami, $1.6 million; Brad Lohaus of Milwaukee, $1.275 million; Randy Breuer of Minnesota, $1.15 million; Jon Koncak of Atlanta, $1.55 million; Dennis Scott of Orlando, $1.56 million; Ralph Sampson of Sacramento, $2.25 million; and Pervis Ellison of Washington, $2.3 million. Out of these fifteen fortunate players, seven were white (46.7 percent), in a league that had fewer than 28 percent white players overall.

Henderson realized all this when he was negotiating with the Celtics back in 1984. He was willing to accept far less than Ainge. But Auerbach did not believe him, did not think Henderson could possibly live with this situation. Perhaps this was because Auerbach himself realized how unjustified such a pay differential was.

From strictly a player personnel viewpoint, the Henderson deal was a tremendous gamble that looked great after eight months and lousy after nine months. Ainge developed quickly, leaving the Celtics with a strong, albeit thin, backcourt through the mideighties. The Sonics, a 42–40 team in 1983–84, fell apart on cue. They finished out of the playoffs and in the lottery. The Celtics suddenly owned the second overall pick in the draft, which they used to draft Len Bias after Philadelphia picked, and traded, Brad Daugherty. But this was the terrible drug draft of 1986, when Bias died from a cocaine overdose, and William Bedford, Chris Washburn, and Roy Tarpley suffered great problems because of the same drug. Bias's death, Golden State coach Don Nelson said, "cost the Celtics a decade of dominance."

Without Henderson, and without Bias, the Celtics struggled with bench problems from 1984 to 1990. They looked at reserve guards like Jerry Sichting, Jim Paxson, John Bagley, and Charles Smith. None was worthy of feeding Bird, McHale, or Parish. The Celtics even flirted with the idea of trading for Henderson again, but backed off. "The Celtics didn't meet their potential for the eighties," Lang said, "and maybe it was better for basketball that they didn't."

In the face of terrible, inexplicable tragedy, it is humankind's nature to construct simple, causative chains. Lonise Bias believed that the death of her son Len from cocaine intoxication was an anti-drug message from God. After his death, she embarked on an enervating, year-round crusade against drugs on behalf of Christ, speaking throughout the country at banquets and fund-raisers. Her second oldest son, Jay, was shot in the back in a suburban Washington, D.C., parking lot after an argument over a woman on December 4, 1990. Jay, twenty years old, died in the same Leland Memorial Hospital where Len had died. At Jay's funeral inside the packed A.M.E. Zion Church in Temple Hills, Maryland, Lonise Bias waved her arms and shouted to the heavens, "Hallelujah! Thank you Lord." The minister, the Reverend John Cherry, told Lonise and James Bias that both their sons had died so that mourners would come to his church, hear his sermon, and experience a rebirth in Christ's name.

For Gerald Henderson and Cedric Maxwell, too, Len Bias's death was predestined. It was, in their minds, an awful, just punishment from God against the Celtics' deadly sins of greed and envy.

"The deal wasn't right for anyone involved," Henderson said. "You just don't know how the Lord works."

Maxwell was more specific, more bitter. "I've always said, 'God doesn't like ugly things,'" Maxwell said. "I hate to say this, but maybe that's why it all turned out the way it did. They got their draft pick, but look what happened. I think God was saying, 'You didn't give the man any credit? Okay, I'm telling you from upstairs that I don't like what you did.' Gerald was a very good player for us. He wasn't old. There was no reason to trade him other than making room for Danny and not having to pay him. But again, if he were white, would they have dared trade him after he'd been such a big part of a championship team?"

By the late eighties, the Celtics and Pistons had surpassed the Lakers-Celtics as the hottest rivalry in the NBA—whether or not CBS and its stubborn audience was yet willing to admit it. Of the eight highest-rated playoff games ever on television, five were broadcasts of Celtics-Lakers finals. The 1987 finals between the Celtics and Lakers recorded a record average Nielsen rating of 15.9 points.

But by this time there was simply too much respect, too little machismo, when Bird met Magic. Both sides, particularly Boston, considered the season a success merely if they reached the finals. The Pistons, on the other hand, were a hungry, disrespectful bunch. They were not yet so cocksure that they were dubbing themselves "Bad Boys," but they were anxious to test their growing skills and ample energies against the aging, injured Celtics. Bill Laimbeer was honing his leer and his villainous wrestler persona. Rick Mahorn was a careless bruiser with another big mouth. Isiah Thomas was the breathtaking little man with a huge chip on his shoulder.

In 1987, during a seven-game Eastern Conference championship series, the two teams put on the ultimate grudge match between upstart and champion. In game three at the sterile, cavernous Silverdome in Pontiac, Michigan, Laimbeer grabbed Bird in a headlock on his way to the hoop. Bird bopped Laimbeer in the face with the ball. They were both ejected. When it was time to return to Boston Garden, Laimbeer said he knew what to expect. "I'll never be small or cuddly," he said during one private interview. "I might as well play my part when I come to Boston Garden. If I gave 60 points on defense, the fans at Boston Garden would still think I'm a fuck. If I were somebody else looking at me, I'd think I was a fuck, too."

Game five was arguably the single most intense playoff game in recent league history. Neither team could push out to an advantage as the level of physical roughness escalated. Directly in front of referee Jess Kersey, after a few relatively minor pushes, Robert Parish knocked down Laimbeer with a quick boxing combination. The Boston fans cheered a black man punching a white man, proving a uniform can sometimes overcome even the most ingrained prejudice. Incredibly, Kersey ignored the incident. No technical. No ejection. If ever there was a case of Boston Garden intimidation, this was it. Finally, the Pistons seemed to have conquered even this inequitable moment. They held a 107–106 lead with five seconds remaining, and Thomas was set to inbound the ball. Whether it was the incessant, cumulative pressure of that evening or the false ecstasy of imminent victory, Thomas relaxed too soon. Instead of calling a time-out, as his coach, Chuck Daly, was urging, he lofted a lazy inbounds pass toward Laimbeer. Al Attles, the Warrior vice president, remembered watching Thomas's terrible instant and grimacing, recalling so many of his own mistakes against the Celtics at the worst of times. "It makes sense to call time-out, but he's thinking, 'I'm so close to finally beating these guys, I can taste it.' He can't wait," Attles said. "He's thinking, 'Get it in. Get it in. Get this over.' He loses his perspective on the moment. He's affected by where he is. The whole thing, all the frustration, has crept into his psyche."

From nowhere, from somewhere near the foul line and the right-hand side of America's television sets, Bird raced off his man, Joe Dumars, to intercept the ball. "It seemed to hang up there forever," Bird said. "I got my left hand on the ball. I thought about shooting but the ball was going the other way."

Instead, he turned and flipped a pass to Dennis Johnson, who had the presence of mind to cut for the hoop. Johnson made the layup, the Celtics won. "It was a lucky play," insisted Bird. "That was all it was." The newspapers thought it was more than that. MAN OF STEAL! shouted the *Herald.* "The message is clear," wrote Bob Ryan in the *Globe.* "If you want to beat Larry Bird in a big game, you've got to play the full 48 minutes."

Bird scored 37 points in the decisive game seven at steamy Boston Garden, and the Celtics held on for another tight victory, 117–114. He grabbed 9 rebounds, handed out 9 assists, and played for the full forty-eight minutes. Afterward, the shell shocked young Pistons were swallowed whole in the tiny, stifling dressing room. They had come so close, and might have won if Adrian Dantley had not been knocked out of the game after a freak head-on collision with Vinnie Johnson in the third quarter. Dennis Rodman, a talented rookie driven by spontaneous combustion, reacted indignantly to yet more questions about Larry Bird. "He's a smart player. I give him all the credit in the world. He takes advantage of his strengths. He can read picks, and he can go around picks for dish-offs, but other than that, he's a decent player. He ain't God, he ain't the best player in the league." Somebody asked Rodman why Bird had received three MVP trophies, and this was where the trouble really began. "He's white," Rodman said. "That's the only reason he gets it. I don't care … Go right ahead and tell him."

The pack of reporters, doing its job, took this quote to another locker, to Thomas. Thomas, like Rodman, has never been a good loser. Both players proved that all over again in 1991, during and after a four-game sweep by the Bulls. Rodman committed a flagrant push against Scottie Pippen, badmouthed the Chicago forward, and was eventually fined $5,000 by the NBA for his unsportsmanlike behavior. Thomas discredited Michael Jordan's victory over the Pistons and led a "Go L.A." cheer against the Bulls at the Pontiac Silverdome. The Pistons correctly were criticized for this behavior, but it could be argued that their sour persecution complex might never have manifested itself without the events of 1987.

After that game seven against the Celtics, Thomas was dead tired, heartbroken, still reeling psychologically from his mental lapse in game five. He backed up his teammate, Rodman. "I think Larry Bird is a very, very good basketball talent, but I have to agree with Rodman," Thomas said. "If he were black, he'd be just another good guy."

As absurd as the notion was, Thomas's statement was perhaps the most important comment by a black player in any sport in the eighties. With one conditional phrase about Bird—which Thomas insisted later was sarcasm—the Piston star had laid bare the underlying bitterness of black athletes in this country. Finally, somebody was standing up and saying that he was sick of this white role model constantly being held up before him.

Another Piston, the dour but dependable Dantley, wasn't available to the press that afternoon in the locker room. He was getting medical treatment after the collision. If Dantley had been there, he might have explained firsthand why so many black players had a Bird complex; why, through no fault of Bird's, they were dead tired of his sacrosanct image.

Strangely enough, Dantley was once suspended for rebelling against a Larry Bird comparison. Back in March 1986, late in a tight game at Phoenix, the Suns intentionally fouled rookie Utah Jazz star Karl Malone. The Suns called a time-out to make Malone think about his upcoming free throws during the two-minute break. Jazz coach Frank Layden was annoyed with Malone's attitude for one reason or another and screamed at him, "Do you think they'd call time-out to ice Larry Bird?" This tirade came at a very inopportune time, it seemed to Jazz forward Dantley. He intervened on Malone's behalf, telling Layden to stop his lecture on Bird. For this insurrection, Dantley was humiliated. Layden later suspended him from the team, and announced a fine of thirty dimes. Layden told reporters if they had any question about the terms of the penalty, they should refer to the Bible. Dantley was cast as Judas; his fine was thirty pieces of silver.

The lesson was clear, to the black athlete: Don't mess with white coaches, or with Larry Bird. America wasn't about to let Thomas get away with his indiscretion, either. In newspapers across the country, Thomas was reviled as a reverse racist, or at best as a fool. Only two reporters bothered to call up Thomas the next day for a cooler second-day reaction. Thomas had little opportunity to put his spin on the matter, although he opened up to Ira Berkow of the *New York Times*, telling him he had been more sensitive to the black-white issues because Boston has more white players than any other pro team.

"When Bird makes a great play, [people say] it's due to his thinking and his work habits," Thomas said. "It's not the case for blacks. All we do is run and jump. We never practice or give a thought to how we play. It's like I came dribbling out of my mother's womb. It's like we're animals, lions and tigers, who run around wild in a jungle.

"This white guy on the other team who is supposed to be very slow, with little coordination, who can't jump, all of a sudden appears out of nowhere, jumps in, grabs the ball, leaps up in the air as he's falling out of bounds, looks over the court in the space of 2 or 3 seconds, picks out a player cutting for the basket and hits him with a picture-perfect pass to win the game. You tell me this white guy—Bird—did that with no God-given talent?"

Game one of the finals between Boston and Los Angeles was played two days later. After a press conference at the Silverdome, Thomas jetted out to Los Angeles for what would become a more humbling apology session on Thursday, before game two. As hundreds of reporters and cameramen jammed into a ballroom in the Los Angeles Marriott, Thomas squirmed on the dais next to Bird, explaining that he meant nothing at all by his remark.

Lights. Camera. Retraction. Thomas played a tape recording of his quote on Bird, prepared by the peacemaking, image-conscious NBA office, and told everyone to listen carefully. There was a laugh, a cynical giggle, on the tape. Reporters who had been there in the Piston locker room insisted that Thomas had been dead serious. Thomas continued to plead, saying his mother had cried over this incident and could take no more. Black fans all over the country grimaced at this sad spectacle. "One day Isiah's saying he's going to kick the Celtics' ass, and then the next day he's saying, 'Oh, I'm sorry, I didn't mean it,'" said Spike Lee. "The NBA must have really read him the riot act."

Thomas insisted they had not, that he wanted to say these things and the NBA just facilitated matters. While he spoke into the mike that day, Bird looked uncomfortably out of place. Bird was a decent man with a working man's insatiable appetite for sports. With his low-income upbringing, with his deep-rooted family problems, Bird was oblivious of racial barriers. Anything outside the basketball court that did not involve a simple commercial endorsement was both confusing and irrelevant. Even Kevin McHale, an uncomplex man with a few ancillary hobbies, befuddled Bird. How could he comprehend the tortured Thomas, from a different culture and even a different time? Later, Bird commented, "I felt so bad for Isiah. I like the kid. His whole life was hanging on that game. He's got to answer these questions for the rest of his life." Here in the ballroom, at this ludicrous press conference, Bird did what he had to do, showed a real sense of decency just by attending. He said he forgave Thomas, even joked about it. "I knew right off the bat those remarks didn't come from his heart, they came from his mouth," Bird said. "Isiah's not stupid. He knows I'm a *baaad* player."

Thomas continued his press conference, tried to turn it around again to the stereotyping issue. He said again that black players were perceived as one-dimensional athletes while whites were commonly described by white commentators as intelligent or hardworking. "Larry Bird worked very hard to get here, but so did I," Thomas said. This only got him in further trouble with the agitated media, and was not at all what the NBA had in mind when it choreographed Thomas's appearance in Los Angeles. The resulting controversy did Thomas a great deal of harm from a public relations standpoint. Endorsements were very slow to come. This youthful, teddy bear player was suddenly viewed with great suspicion by TV-watching America. He had gone from phenom to phony. Thomas was jeered at virtually every arena, asked the same questions about Bird time and again. "To say all that didn't affect me personally, that's not true," Thomas said years later. "People still talked to me, and they still asked for my autograph. But you have to understand. To be called a racist in our society is one of the worst things, especially if you're black."

Rodman, too, had apologized, in a letter—as he did four years later to Pippen—but he was not forgiven so easily. He was not yet one of the marketed elite. He also had played some *baaad* defense against Bird, which seemed to bug the Celtic superstar more than a little. Before he left that Thomas press conference early for practice, for something within the realm of sanity, Bird mentioned that he'd like to bust Rodman "upside the head." Bird didn't speak with Rodman until the 1991 All-Star Game, and then he merely said, "Good job," in passing.

Like Thomas, Rodman paid a heavy price for this brief verbal skirmish. Maybe a heavier one. Thomas was an established superstar and was granted several post-incident forums for his views. The NBA didn't bother setting up a press conference for Rodman the rookie, didn't prepare any tapes. "I did something that was crazy," Rodman would say about his Bird quotes four years later. "At the time, I was young and dumb." For years afterward, this great defensive player carried around a hot-dog image that was reinforced by early-career fits of fist-pumping and leaping about the court. His Q score wasn't what it might have been.

"The endorsements that are here now weren't there then," Rodman's agent, Bill Pollak, noted during a game at Madison Square Garden in February 1991. "It hurt Dennis that a person as fairminded as Bird would believe it was racial, when what he said was said in a moment of emotion and did not reflect his feelings."

Unlike Laimbeer, who gloried in his bad-guy image, Rodman never enjoyed his newfound notoriety. Yet, to achieve some level of commercial success, he was forced to accept the role of a national knucklehead. That was the way Madison Avenue could sell Dennis

Rodman, who was really a sensitive kid from little Southeastern Oklahoma State with an interracial upbringing. He had cried in front of a full house at the Palace when he received his first Defensive Player of the Year award. But an ad campaign for Reebok Pumps featuring Rodman, the Defensive Player of the Year in 1990, had him swatting the air with a pair of sneakers and beginning his endorsement with these words: "I may hot dog ..."

Whatever progress he might have made since 1987 was lost in these commercials and the several roughhouse tantrums during the Bulls' four-game sweep in 1991. When Rodman and Thomas gracelessly stalked off the floor seven seconds before Chicago won the crown, they walked right back into the Boston Garden locker room. On NBC, Pat Riley dismissed Rodman as a player who had learned nothing in four years. America shook its collective head and said, "What did we tell you about these guys?"

Only a blind man would argue that Bird's remarkable team talents were overrated. But Thomas's other points that day at the Marriott were clearly on the money and opened a dialogue that would receive more attention when Dodger executive Al Campanis announced that black athletes were not really meant for swimming—or thinking.

Bird was great, sure. He worked hard, but ... "People would have you think Larry Bird has no physical ability," said David Lee, a black Boston architect who followed the Celtics closely. "He's big, he has wonderful hand-eye coordination, and he can shoot the lights out. That's physical ability."

The NBA was littered with examples of black athletes who were branded as underachievers, slackers, or no-brainers. Likewise, uncountable whites were labeled scrappers, ideal role players, or high-IQers. The Celtics, like much of the NBA, always seemed to save a few spots, and a few words of unconditional praise, for this kind of white player—from Conner Henry to Rick Carlisle. They always seemed to have more patience for the physical rehabilitation of front-line white players like Bill Walton and Larry Bird than that of Cedric Maxwell and Jo Jo White.

They were not the only guilty ones. In New York, a couple of years after the Celtics lost patience with Maxwell, the shortsighted Knicks cut Bernard King loose. King had ripped a ligament in his right knee in 1985 and missed the 1985–86 season, plus most of 1986–87, working hard to recover from what would have been a career-ending injury for most players. In 1987, the Knicks insisted that he was not worth the $1.2 million per year he was demanding; that he had insulted the franchise by working at his rehab in secret.

King, a black man blessed with great depth of character, had already demonstrated he was capable of remaking himself in the face of tremendous adversity. A recovering alcoholic who had experienced several brushes with the law, King worked passionately and successfully to rebuild his reputation—years before he rebuilt his knee. After speaking candidly of his drinking problems for several months, King declared the subject closed. However unreasonable, he told reporters he would no longer speak to them if they dared mention his past. Once he was back in his hometown, starring with the Knicks, King was the model of deportment. He would not so much as loosen his tie in public, even in the midst of a noisy card game in the first-class section of an airplane.

Tragically for the team, King and his remarkable game face would be cast aside by the incoming regime of Al Bianchi and Rick Pitino. Yet it was almost predictable that this would happen. Once King had been told by two reporters that the general manager, Scotty Stirling, had instructed them to spy on his rehabilitation and private practices at Upsala College. "Fuck Scotty," King said simply, and he meant this message to be no secret. A black player with this sort of self-confidence was a real threat to a couple of newcomers like Bianchi and Pitino, who were trying to make a personal imprint on New York. King would find a new home with the Washington Bullets.

In search of a scorer to replace King, the Knicks were frustrated in their persistent efforts to land one of the legitimate, young, white superstars of the league; Brooklyn's Chris Mullin. The Knicks finally turned to Kiki Vandeweghe, a white player with all the hardness and emotion of a wet noodle. With his former Knick father, Ernie, running political interference, Vandeweghe had whined his way out of Dallas after the college draft. He had whined his way out of Portland, where the Trail Blazers immediately became a better team without him. He could never pass as well as King, couldn't grab hold of a game in the fourth quarter. Suffering from mysterious back pains, he would disappear to California for private therapy treatments from an unlisted personal physician. Yet the Knicks never lost patience with Vandeweghe as they had done with King. Prior to the 1990–91 season, they let one of their few exciting players, Johnny Newman, walk away as a free agent, granting Vandeweghe undeserved security at his position and further weakening a deteriorating team. Words like "arrogant" and "selfish," used so often by the New York media and Knick fans to describe King, were never applied to the soft-spoken Vandeweghe. The fans never jeered him, even as King rounded into shape and scored 49 points against Vandeweghe and the Knicks on January 31, 1991, at Madison Square Garden. King returned to the starting All-Star lineup in 1991, while Vandeweghe averaged under 2 assists per game again.

Back at the press conference in Los Angeles, minutes after Thomas had completed his mea culpa confession, Jawann Oldham, then a Knick center, dropped by to make small talk poolside at the Marriott with a couple of reporters he knew from New York. Oldham, a graceful seven-one shotblocker with embarrassingly weak offensive skills, was another living example of how black athletes were characterized or caricatured in demeaning terms. Oldham was a highly intelligent man with a great sense of humor and adventure. He flew helicopters in the offseason—the ultimate flipside tidbit for an NBA trading card. He had an opinion on almost everything and spoke colorfully about all matters, in worldly terms. For Oldham, road trips were "forays into Vietnam." Oldham's personality was somewhat reminiscent of a former NBA center named Rich Kelley. Kelley, being white, was celebrated by the media as one of the bright, funky, fascinating characters of his time. He became a cable broadcaster in Sacramento for the Kings. For many of these same attributes, Oldham had been rewarded with this nickname from reporters: ALF, or Alien Life Form. Poolside in Los Angeles, Oldham had an opinion on Thomas's press conference, too. He figured the media would simply lynch the offending point guard from Detroit. "You can't say anything about Larry Bird," Oldham said. "That's like saying something about the Grand Wizard himself."

Thomas would later say that his gaffe and apologetic press conference had opened a dialogue on this subject of black versus white perception. It had, but Thomas paid a steep public relations price—like several players before him who had confronted the Celtics or posed a competitive threat. Auerbach took special pleasure in belittling Wilt Chamberlain with the "loser" label, which stuck with him unfairly for most of his career. Tree Rollins wrestled with his own image for years after brawling with Celtic guard Danny Ainge on April 24, 1983. The fight, midway through the third quarter of deciding game three in a preliminary round series between the Celtics and Hawks, ended with the seven-foot center biting Ainge's hand. Rollins was fined $5,000 by the NBA and suspended without pay for five games. Ainge was fined just $1,000, with no suspension.

Reruns of the fight and a freeze frame of the actual bite were shown in an eighty-eight-second halftime package on CBS's televised playoff games that season. It was another nightmare for black players, who remembered all too well the publicity when Kermit Washington nearly killed Rudy Tomjanovich a few years earlier. "CBS made it look like the big black guy jumped on the little white guy," said Rollins, who has no argument with Ainge anymore, just CBS. "We [the Hawks] sent them tape showing what happened, and they didn't use it. Nobody saw him with a clenched fist, taking a swing." Ainge himself admitted punching Rollins in the chest, although he said "it wasn't hard enough to hurt my wife." In the

Boston newspapers the next day, Rollins was compared unfavorably to a dog. He had wronged the wrong basketball team.

Three years later, sensitive, underachieving Ralph Sampson of the Rockets experienced similar treatment. He never recovered. On June 5, 1986, in the fifth game of the finals at Houston, Sampson was ejected in the third minute of the second period for landing a punch to the face of Boston guard Jerry Sichting. Sampson was seven-four, Sichting six-one. Sampson was black, Sichting white. The resulting sixteen-player brawl played big-time on TV and in newspaper accounts.

The fight was a disastrous temper tantrum by Sampson. He and Sichting had bodied each other for position in the paint. Sichting turned and told the big center, "I'll get you for that elbow." Sampson reacted. Then somebody pushed Dennis Johnson. "My momentum took me forward into Ralph," Johnson said. "He threw a punch. I may have thrown one first." By now, Sampson was chasing Sichting, swinging. "I'm really sorry this happened," Sampson said. "Someone jumped in and I did what I had to do to protect myself."

Now, however, game six was to be in Boston and Sampson was heading for major trouble. The Celtics played on his fear. "He'd better wear his hard hat come Sunday," Bird told reporters. The Boston papers couldn't resist the story of the bully beanpole. In one cartoon caricature, Sampson was depicted in a wide-brim hat wielding a blackjack.

When Sampson got to Boston Garden that Sunday, he was jeered during warmup drills. A fan screamed, "We're gonna kill ya, Ralph." The Celtics saw vulnerability in his eyes, swarming at him on defense and forcing Sampson into mistake after mistake. "They knew he had to be thinking," M.L. Carr said. "So they hounded him." Sampson missed his first seven shots, finishing with only eight points. When the Celtics were well ahead in the final period, Sampson took his place on the Houston bench and the Boston crowd chanted, "We want Ralph."

Sampson, a proud man, never admitted the Celtic crowd had reached into his psyche and tinkered with his heart that afternoon. But he was never the same player after that game, after that series. All the grace and potential seeped out of his game. The Celtics and Boston Garden could do that to a man.

Chapter 10

A Tale of Two Bostons

R OXBURY Crossing is just nine "T" stops south on the
Orange Line from North Station and Boston Garden. But
this is another universe, a hungry black and Hispanic world
that most Celtic players do not venture out to see.

Like most American cities, arguably more so, Boston is segregat-
ed, neatly delineated by income and race. In June 1974, when a federal court forced school busing on the white population as a tool for
integration, fights broke out in the streets and 10 percent of the student population stayed home. Private schools flourished. Wounds
festered. Financial redlining and housing discrimination drew the
racial lines sharp and cold into the city landscape. Blacks lived in
Roxbury. Whites lived in West Roxbury. "In Boston," Dave Cowens
said, "you not only have racial barriers, you have ethnic barriers.
Everyone is separated."

Traditionally, the Celtic organization has not attempted to tran-
scend those boundaries. In the fall of 1974, when the club could
have tried to mend some fences in the schools, it was too busy winning another championship with Cowens and John Havlicek. During the eighties, when the franchise was reborn with Bird, it stood

passively by while a few other pro sports teams developed a growing awareness about community relations. In return, there are few Celtic rooters in black Boston. In the midst of the franchise's glorious eighties, an informal *Boston Globe* poll discovered that black youths were rooting for the Lakers against the Celtics in the finals. Such blasphemy existed both inside and outside the city limits. Patrick Ewing grew up nearby in Cambridge, a Philadelphia 76er fan. Little has changed. Among today's black kids, only a select few have seen Bird in person. Their heroes are other players from network television: Michael Jordan, Charles Barkley, or one of the young, black San Antonio Spurs. Maybe in a season or two, Reggie Lewis or Dee Brown might catch on in Roxbury. But not yet.

A few miles from where Bird goes one-on-one with Dominique Wilkins, youth gangs battle in Roxbury and Dorchester for turf, for women, for pride. The gangs name themselves after professional teams in different sports: the Orchard Park Blazers, the Humboldt Raiders. Attire is carefully coordinated. It is dangerous to wear the wrong sports team's jacket here or the wrong cap in the wrong place. Walk along these broad avenues, past the projects and the sprawling, concrete schools, and you see gangly kids in the official gear of most college and professional teams. They are rarely in the uniform or accessories of the Boston Celtics.

In front of English High School in Lower Roxbury, minority students hang out during lunch hour while white motorcycle cops eye them suspiciously from across the street. There are jackets from the Seattle Mariners, from the Detroit Pistons, from the Georgetown Hoyas. "The Celtics are too old, too slow, and too old-fashioned," said Jose Santiago, a student at English. "Any gang member can wear a Celtic cap, because it's considered neutral. But nobody does. If a gang called itself the Celtics, they'd get laughed at. That's corny. What kind of name is that?"

One small clandestine Boston gang defies this taboo. The Castlegate Celtics, a splinter group from the Castlegate G Boys, has found that the name serves its purposes. Since the Castlegate Celtics do most of their business in New York, the name gives them instant geographic recognition with outsiders. And nobody is about to mock the Castlegate Celtics in Boston or anywhere else, because they deal in guns.

"They go to New York, they get guns, they sell guns from their cars," said Henry Fernandez, Jr., a former member of the Humboldt Raiders and later a counselor to other youths in gangs. "That's their specialty. The other gang members get them from the Celtics. These days, everybody carries something. Life is that way in Boston."

Fernandez was raised on Humboldt Avenue, three blocks away from what Boston cops call the war zone, by the Castlegate projects near the Dorchester-Roxbury border. Once in 1988, the Raiders had a gun battle with the Celtics at a local schoolyard. A woman was shot trying to protect her baby. "I dropped out that night," said Fernandez, a senior at Madison High in the spring of 1991. "I got involved in the church and in football." When the Kings and the Heath Street gangs clashed over drug territory during the fall of 1990 at Madison High, Fernandez stayed far away from the action.

So have the Boston Celtics, with the exception of a few pioneer players like Tom Sanders, Dave Cowens, Paul Silas, M. L. Carr, Scott Wedman, Reggie Lewis, and Robert Parish, who struck out on their own. It is not an easy thing to do, and there is a large area to cover. Where does one start? In Chicago, Michael Jordan never quite made it across the street from Chicago Stadium, where children in the Henry Horner Homes, an impoverished housing complex, dream aloud of meeting him, according to Alex Kotlowitz's touching book, *There Are No Children Here*.

Several NBA teams help their players reach out, help them find a starting point. For the past six summers, the New York Knicks have sponsored a summer caravan through largely minority neighborhoods in their city. They get players to touch these communities, teach skills, and expand the franchise's base. Nearly every player on the Knick roster has become involved in the project, first conceived by general manager Al Bianchi and coordinated by public relations director John Cirillo. It is not that unusual for a young black Knick fan to poke his head through the baseline crowd before a game at Madison Square Garden, to yell, "Remember me, Patrick?" It hasn't worked that way in Boston. "The Celtics didn't get too involved," said Silas, an assistant coach with the Knicks. "Nothing like the caravan. That was unfortunate. It would be nice for some of those kids to meet Larry Bird."

In 1989 at Wellesley College, instructor Phil Weisner taught a summer exploration course on running a pro sports franchise. Students in the class quizzed Tod Rosensweig, vice president of marketing and communications for the Celtics, about what the club was doing for the community. Rosensweig, a former public relations director for the team, surprised everyone with his brusque replies. He said the club had no specific projects planned, that building or developing playground space was not one of the Celtics' prime objectives. The Celtics established a recreation fund in Red Auerbach's name, contributed to the Jimmy Fund, but rarely got their hands dirty. The Celtics' modest financial contributions were meager compared to savings of $50 million that came with the tax dodge of a limited partnership in 1986. At least until Dave Gavitt took over in 1990—and even then, to a great extent—much of the Celtic organization remained haughtily aloof from their black backyard.

"We can't expect basketball players to take the role of politicians, lawyers, or preachers," said the Reverend Al Owens, director of the NAACP in Boston. "But here, they could have more influence if they came into the community. If I was a kid with drug problems, then Larry Bird is just a hero I see on Channel 25, or CBS on Sunday. He's never visited my high school, or my neighborhood."

"They being the Celtics, you'd think they'd hold some clinics in these areas," Owens said. "But they never contacted us."

Owens is a thin reed of a man with an infectious smile and a sharp twang, presiding energetically over the second-story NAACP office on Massachusetts Avenue. People come to him to organize charity events, hunt for jobs, get their resumes in order, down a slice of pizza and a lukewarm Coke on a summer day. Much of Boston, fighting through a deep recession in the early nineties, has found its way to his door. Not the Boston Celtics, however. Never. They have kept their distance from Owens.

"I've been around for fifteen years, since I was a kid until now, and there has been no special reach-out program in my neighborhoods by the Celtics," Owens said. "Two or three times, maybe a player came by. Reggie Lewis decided not to disavow his friendships. Dennis Johnson, you can see him in a restaurant. You might see Dennis Johnson and Brian Shaw having a pickup game at Brookline. But there's nothing organized by the Celtics."

Lewis, who went to college at Northeastern in Boston, has remained something of a fixture in the minority community. He lives in a residential Boston neighborhood year-round. At the suggestion of agent Jerome Stanley, Lewis and Brian Shaw handed out turkeys in Roxbury at Thanksgiving. Lewis and his fiancée, Donna Harris, formed the Reggie Lewis Foundation for disadvantaged youth. By spring 1991, Lewis, on his own initiative, had become the official spokesman for the Boys and Girls Clubs of greater Boston. He brought with him to these clubs, at times, other members of the Celtics. "I want the people in every neighborhood to feel like the Celtics are their team," Lewis said. "I want to help rebuild some of the playgrounds, like the ones I played in when I was a kid."

In his black BMW, Lewis could be spotted driving Wednesday nights to The Gallery, a black club on Massachusetts Avenue near the NAACP headquarters, where he danced until the late hours to reggae and rap music. Lewis kept going to the same barbershop on Tremont Street and brought some of his new Celtic teammates, Ed Pinckney and Kevin Gamble. Boston barbershops are where players like Silas met black community leaders, where they became involved, on their own initiative and not the team's, with Boys Clubs and school clinics. On Tremont Street, the man manipulating the barber shears was always Robert Foggie, a weathered curmudgeon who once cut the tight, black curls of Bill Russell and Sam Jones.

"Yeah, I cut their hair, and it's no big fucking deal," Foggie said at his little shop behind a red cement facade. "White players go to white shops, black to black. It's a different grain of hair.

"The Celtics had a lot of white players, then they had to do something because they weren't winning," Foggie said. "So now I have more customers again."

Foggie and his head barber, Lennie, charged Lewis the same price as they charged any customer. The tip was usually bigger. Because Lewis was now a Celtic, there was some jealousy in the neighborhood. "He pulls up at the barbershop in his 733i BMW, then he keeps on moving," said Reginald Garner, a local resident. "He's like the rest of the bunch: white-man niggers. K. C. [Jones] married a white woman and moved to Wellesley. The only time we really see the Celtics, any Celtic, is when they win a championship and hold a parade." Obviously, it was going to be a long climb for Lewis, for Shaw, for Dee Brown.

This alienation of the black community was reinforced daily by the unavailability of tickets at cozy Boston Garden. There are different ways for a professional sports team to move out of a city. It can steal away a thousand miles in the middle of the night and break hearts quickly, the way Robert Irsay did with the Baltimore Colts. It can move to the suburbs, land of skyboxes and oversized parking lots, like the Pistons of Auburn Hills. The Cavaliers moved so far away from Cleveland, to the farmlands of Richfield, Ohio, that opposing center Mike Gminski regularly would get bus-sick during the one-hour drive from his team's hotel. But a sports organization can stay inside city limits and still remove itself from the urban heartbeat. It can raise ticket prices, sell box seats to corporations, redesign its own arena to provide more expensive seats, and make those seats virtually impossible to obtain. That was, essentially, the Celtic modus operandi. If this last method was somewhat less reprehensible than the other two, it was hardly enlightened.

Within the context of major professional sports officials in America, David Stern is a progressive-thinking commissioner. He does not try to smash the players' union or demand conformity from all players and franchises. Yet on the subject of the NBA losing sight of its community roots, Stern remains a shortsighted apologist. He seems to view the issue only in terms of television viewer perception. The Detroit chapter of the NAACP was infuriated by the Pistons' move out of downtown, first to Pontiac, then to even more distant Auburn Hills. Stern does not see it as a problem. "I think the thing was somewhat overstated," he said. "The New York Giants play in New Jersey. The Lions play in Pontiac. With the Pistons, they still talk about Motor City Madness, not the Auburn Hills Holiday. I think the Pistons still have an emotional attachment to greater Detroit, since the great majority of NBA fans see their games on television, rather than live.

"Fifty percent of the country doesn't have an NBA team within a good distance," Stern said. "It's an interesting balancing act. Look at the success of the NFL. Their success stems from season tickets sold out forever and TV that's more widely viewed than we could ever aspire. That means tens of millions of people have never been to an NFL game."

By this cold, economic logic, the inner city might need an NBA franchise, but the franchise doesn't need an inner city. Ticket prices at Boston Garden in 1990–91 ranged from $11 for obstructed view seats to $34 for seats right behind press row—by comparison, in Philadelphia, the 76ers lowered their cheapest seats in 1990 from $6 to $4. By the 1991–92 season, the average ticket price to a Celtic game was $24.80, another annual increase of more than three dollars. That was the sixth highest average price in the NBA. The league-wide average ticket price for all its twenty-seven franchises was an overblown $22.52. The costs in Boston virtually exclude the low-income residents, who would need to spend a minimum of almost $25 for a father-daughter night out behind metal I-beams. Those cheapest ticket prices have crept up incessantly at Boston Garden through the years. In 1985, obstructed seats went for $8. In

1986, $9. In 1988, $10. Because the Celtics never blocked out a section for possible community reach-out use, the pattern is likely to continue at least until the team moves into its new arena.

"I just don't know what we're going to do, or any sport's going to do, about the pricing structure," Stern said. "I see the same inevitable flow of success that is going to occur, and that is that small numbers of people will be able to afford tickets. Whatever the prices have been, that's always been the case. There's always a relatively small number of people. Portland has 12,666 seats, and most of them are sold on a season ticket basis. Portland has more than a million people. Maybe seventy thousand people, at most, will step into that arena. Most of them will take their game from the TV, the newspapers, the radio."

But somehow there was a distinction here that Stern ignored: It is one thing when physical limitations keep spectators out in random fashion. It is another matter when ticket prices disqualify a whole income level from attending. All Celtic home games were sold out again last season, 40 percent of the tickets going to corporations. There was a time, even after Bird arrived in 1979, when the Celtics would give away tickets to make the building appear full and let the right people know this was a happening place. When Jan Volk became ticket director in 1971, there were only eight hundred season ticket holders. Now there are 12,500. Only the $11 obstructed vision seats are available in advance at the box office. The Celtic ticket sales telephone recording impersonally informs any caller that even these obstructed seats are unavailable for dates against the glamour teams like Chicago, Detroit, Philadelphia, Portland, and Los Angeles. So it is a matter of whom you know, or how much you are willing to pay backroom dealers or Causeway Street scalpers. Obviously, this precludes much of black Boston. And even when black spectators make it inside, they do not often feel comfortable.

Rickety, perpetual lame-duck Boston Garden is home to both the Bruins and the Celtics. Much has been made in the local papers about the difference between the two crowds: how the Bruin fans are rowdy lunch-pail types, stumbling about with their paper cups filled with beer, and how the Celtic fans are trendy, laid-back yuppies who enjoy their Steve's Ice Cream bars. But this is a press-table view of things, down below where Ted Kennedy hobnobs with the Celtic brass, and where corporate suits clap politely at a Brian Shaw fast break. Higher up in the arena, there are still plenty of drunks, plenty of rednecks. They are not particularly knowledgeable, even after all these years of great basketball. During one regular-season game at Boston Garden in 1990 against the Knicks, the fans loudly jeered a foul call against Bird in the final seconds. It was a kneejerk reaction. Bird had fouled deliberately. The Celtics were nursing a narrow lead, and the team had one to give. Blindly loyal to Bird, many of these spectators are simply not as sophisticated as they like to pretend. What these fans are very good at, when roused from their slumber, is sheer intimidation. They still rattle the opposition and the badly outnumbered black spectators.

Although the city of Boston is 22 percent black, the demographics of Boston Garden are very different. This racial ratio is something that the fans, the players, and NBA Players Association president Charles Grantham could never help but notice. "All you have to do is go to Boston Garden to understand the Celtics' hiring practices, I guess," Grantham said. "Whenever I go, it's like me and the players on the court and maybe seven or eight other blacks in the whole place. I look around, I say, 'Holy shit.'"

This void was obvious, also, to blacks bouncing the ball on the parquet floor. "The black players would always joke around," Cedric Maxwell said. "We'd say, 'If there's a black person in the crowd, you can find him fast because he's the one yelling, 'Peanuts! Peanuts! Get your peanuts!'"

Game five of the Celtics–Pistons Eastern Conference finals in 1987 was a wild game, ended by Bird's dramatic steal and Dennis Johnson's layup. Emotions were raw, on the court and in the stands. "People were hollering things about the mothers of the African-American players," said David Lee, the black architect, who has lived in Boston for twenty years. "I mean every vituperative insult you could imagine. I grew up in Chicago, and it just wasn't as mean and personal there. In Boston, people are venting some other kinds of problems."

Kristina Perez of Brighton was at a game last season against Utah. There weren't many blacks in the stands, and a lot of drunks. "I look around me at these games, I think, 'These people could be trouble if I speak out here,'" Perez said. "You feel you have to be careful. It's the same crowd I've seen on St. Patrick's Day, and I was scared to death of them, too."

Reginald Garner remembered being taken to a game by his brother-in-law. Garner hates the Celtics, so he cheered after Bird fouled out. The guy behind him said, "Nigger, sit down."

Garner never went to Boston Garden again.

At Somerville High School in the largely white, working-class suburb just north of Cambridge and Boston, there is a real sense of connection with the Celtic organization. Building master John Silk, captain of the Boston College basketball team in 1953, once tried out for the Celtics. Like Boston mayor Ray Flynn, Silk nearly made the team. Wide-eyed students at the school now find this hard to believe about their stout school official, but Silk roomed with Tom Heinsohn during the exhibition season and played in several preseason games. Silk attacked the basket, he was ambidextrous, but he was also very skinny in his prime. He endured the double sessions, the road trips, and the tough talk from Red Auerbach. He remembers an Auerbach speech following a couple of meaningless exhibition losses. The coach had become livid after discovering that several of the players went golfing despite a defeat. "We'll get rid of Cousy or Sharman before we get rid of the redhead," Auerbach said. Silk was one of Auerbach's warnings to the other, front-line players. If they misbehaved enough, Auerbach just might keep this thin intruder. In the end, it was an empty threat. Silk was one of Auerbach's final cuts in 1956, the season that Bill Russell arrived.

"I went to Walter Brown before that year and told him I thought I could make the team," Silk said. "He asked me, 'What do you think of Bill Russell?'" I told him, 'The day you get Russell is the day you win your first championship.'"

When Silk was cut, he lost the opportunity to earn about $5,000 from the Celtics that season. He didn't get paid at all for his preseason games. Yet Silk still marvels at Auerbach, still roots hard for the Celtics. He never misses a game on television, and he'll relate his experiences to anybody who will sit back in his school office and listen.

Brian O'Riordan, an amicable social studies teacher at Somerville High, said he has deep ancestral ties with the Celtics. He offered some little-known lore, a historic scoop. O'Riordan's father, John, was president of the original Boston Celtics in the twenties. John O'Riordan was one of the founders of the New England Soccer Association and part-owner of the Celtics soccer team. The league included teams of Irish, English, Scottish, and Welsh descent. Many league officials didn't want to let the Portuguese in, but John O'Riordan insisted. "This is America," he told his fellow owners. "You can't do that here." The Portuguese were welcomed, and dominated the league after that. At John O'Riordan's wake, most of the Portuguese population in Boston showed up.

John O'Riordan weighed about 135 pounds in his soaking wet hurling boots. His ankles were both split through the bones from the hurling sticks that would pound around his legs and feet. But when the Celtic basketball team was formed immediately after World War II, when Walter Brown decided to usurp the basketball nickname established in World War I and the twenties by the New York Celtics and then the Original Celtics from New York, he had to negotiate with the limping little Irishman for local rights to the moniker.

Here, at Somerville, the kids have seen Bird and McHale. The students have gone to Celtic games regularly. "Getting tickets depends on who you know," said Kevin White, a senior. "I know a neighbor with season tickets. Nobody buys a Celtic ticket."

"My cousin's father's company has sky boxes," said Marc Taddia. "I get in sometimes."

"My father's friends have season's tickets," said Chris Antonelli. "My grandfather knows the ticket sales guy."

In recent years, a growing Haitian community had begun to settle in parts of Somerville. The schools had been integrated peacefully, although there was some fallout on the athletic fields. A soccer coach from rival Arlington called several black players on the Somerville team "jungle bunnies" and "niggers." A protest was lodged with the school.

During lunch hour at Somerville High, black students sit with black students, white students with white students. Among the things that separate them, apparently, is their taste in NBA basketball teams.

"Most of the black kids like the Bulls, they like the black players," Kevin White said. "The white kids like the white players."

This concept, bent but not broken by crossover superstars like Michael Jordan and Magic Johnson, is not a new one. During his volatile reign in the early eighties, former Cleveland Cavalier owner Ted Stepien once made a startling proclamation. "This is not to sound prejudiced," he said, "but half the squad should be white. I think people are afraid to speak out on that subject. White people have to have white heroes. I'll be truthful, I respect them [blacks], but I need white people. It's in me."

Stepien was always a loose cannon, a man whom NBA officials understandably did not want around trumpeting his theories on marketing and race. He was enough of a problem running his own team, trading away first-round draft choices and firing coaches. Once, head coach Chuck Daly, who would go on to much bigger and more pleasant things with the Detroit Pistons, called a team practice for the Cavaliers and noticed that his assistant coaches were missing. Stepien was holding a meeting with the other coaches, discussing the possibility of firing Daly. Daly fined his assistants for missing practice, then quickly became another Stepien casualty. On the subject of white basketball players, Stepien later amended his statement by saying he meant it was easier to market a white team to white fans. The NBA finally had enough of Stepien, just as baseball had enough of George Steinbrenner, and basically chased him away by placing a hold on many of his player transactions. Maverick owner that he was, there remained the feeling that Stepien's very public ideas on marketing a largely black league to white spectators were not so very far removed from the private beliefs held by other NBA club owners. Stepien claimed he knew his audience, the target of his ticket sales, and that it was white.

The Celtics, with a predominantly white following throughout New England, didn't need to advertise themselves too hard or too directly. Their games were already sold out. But television stations and newspaper companies, inside and outside the Celtic corporate family, boldly promoted their own coverage of the team in white neighborhoods. Black communities were bereft of any such advertising or billboards. Driving through Cambridge toward Somerville during the 1990–91 season, you could see a huge *Boston Globe* billboard aimed at commuters near the Massachusetts Turnpike: LEARN ABOUT THE BIRD AND THE B'S [Bruins]. An oversized headline shouted: BIRD SAVES CELTICS. The *Globe* never was too proud to link itself with the right home teams in the right neighborhoods.

Chapter 11

The Outsiders

MAKING a home in Boston, or in the ring of wealthy suburbs that surrounds this hub city, is no easy matter for a black professional athlete. He might have the income to enjoy the luxuries of the white communities, but he does not own the skin color of preference. When neighbors in Framingham burned a cross on K. C. Jones's front lawn, he took it in stride, the way he approached all of life's vile treats. Russell had a longer memory than Jones about such things. When it was time for his uniform to be retired at Boston Garden, the Celtics' great center understandably decided he did not want to share the moment with Celtic fans. The banner was raised in the afternoon, with the Garden empty of all tormentors and autograph seekers.

The years passed, the ugly incidents did not. Curtis Rowe and Sidney Wicks were called every name under the New England sun, right there at the Garden, because the Celtics were losing. When the club started winning again after Bird came, the heckling moved back outside the building. Gerald Henderson's family was harassed on a beach.

Then on September 21, 1990, came what would be called "the Dee Brown incident."

When Brown came to Boston, he was a rookie inexperienced with prejudice. He grew up in an integrated neighborhood in Jacksonville, Florida, and was the only black in his graduating class at the exclusive Bollis Prep School. His mother, Charlene, was a computer analyst who taught her son to love programming. His father, Dee Brown, Sr., was a successful commercial printer.

Brown hadn't signed yet with the Celtics in the fall of 1990, and he wasn't yet married to his fiancée, Jill Edmondson, a white woman who had been a student and cheerleader at Northeastern when Reggie Lewis played there. But Edmondson suggested the couple search for a house in the affluent suburban town of Wellesley. While they looked, the pair stayed at a hotel. Their mail was sent to the Wellesley post office across the street from a bank that had been robbed of $1,800 on September 18 by a man described as black, six-two, with a light complexion.

Brown was six-one and black, but dark-skinned. When Brown left the post office with some mail, a secretary at the bank told the manager she thought she had spotted someone resembling the bank robber. The manager called the police. When Brown was confronted, the police dealt with him as if he had been confirmed as the culprit. As Brown and Edmondson sat in their car, shuffling through the mail, nine local police officers confronted them with five guns, loaded and cocked. "It was like a scene from a movie," said Jill Edmondson Brown.

Brown was ordered outside the car, told to lie down on his stomach. "I heard them say, 'Bank robber,'" Jill Brown recalled, "and I started screaming, 'He's not a bank robber! He's a basketball player! He's a player for the Celtics!'"

At the urging of many of Wellesley's rightfully embarrassed citizens, the Browns eventually decided to settle in the community. They also settled something else—a complaint against the police—for $5,000, which covered legal expenses. There were only 250 black residents of Wellesley in a town of 27,000. But in the wake of the Dee Brown incident, several of these minority citizens formed the Wellesley African-American Citizens Group to improve community relations with police and officials in the deeply divided town.

"What happened is that when many of the town's black residents who didn't know each other got together, they realized that many of them had similar stories to tell," said Buzz Luttrell, a former TV talk show host and a member of the group.

Michele Gibbons-Carr had some stories. The corporate consultant told how her husband, Richard, had been routinely followed in his Mercedes and occasionally stopped by Wellesley police for twelve years. "Who was he going to tell and who was going to listen?" Carr said. "He's not a basketball player. He's a dentist."

Another nightmare began along with the New England spring. In the early morning hours of March 22, 1991, Celtic reserve guard Charles Smith left the Zanzibar disco on Boylston Street and got behind the wheel of his rented Dodge Caravan with passenger Ben Gillery, the former pro and Georgetown player. Driving west on Commonwealth Avenue, Smith's vehicle allegedly struck and killed two Boston University students—An Trinh, twenty-one, a Vietnamese refugee from Placentia, California, and Michelle Dartley, twenty, of Ridgewood, New Jersey.

Smith was arrested about twelve minutes later on Boylston Street and Massachusetts Avenue on a tip from a cabbie who had followed the blue van. There was damage to the front grill and windshield, and strands of the women's hair were found in the damaged windshield. Smith pleaded not guilty to eight charges, including vehicular homicide, leaving the scene of an accident, and driving under the influence. This last charge fell into a particularly gray legal area. Smith's blood alcohol level had been measured at .06 after the accident. In the state of Massachusetts, it is not a crime to drive with a blood alcohol level up to .05. At .10, the driver is legally intoxicated. But between the measurements of .05 and .10, the driver's legal status must be determined by a court of law. Smith was released on a $100,000 personal bond, and faced between two and a half and fifteen years on each of the major counts.

For years, there had been problems with speeding cars in the thirty-mile-per-hour zone, and Boston University president John Silber had protested that university police didn't have the authority to enforce traffic laws. Now the skid marks on Commonwealth Avenue showed it was too late for this debate. Here was a disaster for everyone—for the students' families, for blacks in Boston, for the Celtics. The attorney for the Dartley family, Michael Mone, planned civil suits against Smith and National Rental Car, and possibly the Zanzibar disco. "It's not beyond the realm of possibility," Mone said, that the Celtics would also be sued, because he believed they might have rented the car for Smith.

Smith was a marginal NBA performer, backcourt insurance in case of injury or foul trouble. He was not, as many TV news broadcasts would describe him, "a Celtic star." He had been near the end of his second ten-day contract with the Celtics, and they had been expected to pick him up for the rest of the season. Now, of course, they wouldn't. The franchise was in a no-win situation. Back the player, and it would be accused of insensitivity toward the students. Back the students, and it would be accused of turning its back on yet another black player in his worst time of need.

It was a time for great clarity and tact, until Smith's case came to its judicial conclusion. But Red Auerbach couldn't keep his mouth shut. Asked about Smith's dilemma, the Celtic president did what came naturally. He wrote the kid off, talked about him in the past tense, and pleaded innocent himself. All within twenty-four hours of the accident. "I'm surprised like everyone else," he told the Globe, sounding the same chords he once struck over Len Bias's death. "His reputation was 100 percent clean. He was a good kid. John [Thompson] said the kid was never in any kind of trouble while he was there [at Georgetown]. He said he was a helluva kid."

Dave Gavitt and the Celtic organization were busy with some

quick damage control. They helped post Smith's bond (Smith supposedly could raise no more than $4,000 cash himself) and arranged for a defense attorney, Dennis Kelly. They issued "sincere and heartfelt sympathies to the families" involved.

But the Celtics never bothered to start a scholarship fund in the victims' names. They never did anything for the families. "All they did was release the statement," Mone said.

In the end, Auerbach couldn't hope to negotiate this delicate situation because he had little idea how to interact with the outside community, with any real-life issue, or with his own players outside the basketball arena. Smith was left dangling, his contract expired, his future in the NBA probably destroyed before a judge or jury could decide his guilt or innocence. He was banned in Boston, and everywhere else.

Even after his own awful episode, Dee Brown said he would stay in the Boston area at least while he was a Celtic. Afterward, history said, he would travel far away to get on with his life.

"I think the thing that stands out in my mind, and I think this is something that should be asked, is of the majority of the outstanding black players, how many of them stayed in the area?" asked Al Attles, the former Warrior star. "Russ? Sam? K. C.? Satch?"

No, no, no, and no. While John Havlicek, Dave Cowens, Bob Cousy, Tom Heinsohn, and even Henry Finkel have put down residential and career roots in the area, not many blacks have stayed in Boston past their playing days. Then again, not many have been asked by the Celtics to stay in any official capacity. The one most visible exception has been Michael Leon Carr, listed as a scout in the Celtic directory through 1991 but used vaguely as a black-of-all-trades. When the Celtics needed a former black player to talk with Brian Shaw, to coax and convince him that Celtic green was more glorifying than Il Messaggero red, they turned to M. L. Carr. When they needed a black speaker at a chamber of commerce function, Carr was the man again.

Here was the city's most ebullient entrepreneur. After his retirement in 1985, Carr hooked on with Bank of Boston as a community relations representative. He started the Wellesley-based Carr Company, selling stain removers and paper and plastic products. He gave motivational speeches before corporate executives and fund-raising events. About the only thing Carr did not do was scout or have any input into Celtic player personnel decisions. "No question, I'm up front on that," Carr said. "I get a tremendous benefit from my connection with the Celtics, and they get a benefit from me, too. I speak to the United Way in Worcester, I speak about the Celtics, the camaraderie. I am an ambassador for the Boston Celtics."

The Celtics rescued Carr, a classic role player, from the moribund clutches of the Detroit Pistons in 1979. In return, Carr gave them quality bench time and a buoyant cheerleader's spirit. Unjustly, Carr is remembered more as a frantic towel-waver on the Celtic bench than as the man who knew how to get under the skin of any opposing player and stay there. Carr, a stocky six-six swingman from little Guilford College, shot only 45 percent from the field and averaged just 6.3 points per game as a Celtic. Yet he knew precisely how to jostle and pester pure scorers like Julius Erving or Bernard King. King, still irked, refused to address the anything-goes tactics of M. L. Carr. "There are better things in life to discuss," he said coldly. Carr was a poor man's K. C. Jones, lacking some of the athleticism but with some extra tricks up his sleeveless shirt. He also recognized a good thing when he saw one. He would carve a career from that towel. He would walk through life swinging it over his head at all comers.

"You know what I bring to this company?" Carr said about his post-Celtic venture in capitalism. "I bring the towel. I pick people up because I'm not going to accept losing."

Before he created his own eleven-employee company, and before he hooked on with Bank of Boston, Carr would still travel with the Celtics. He would make impromptu speeches in hotel lobbies, auditioning for the corporate auditoriums he'd later work. At the Los

Angeles Airport Marriott in 1987, Carr got really cranked up one night before a Celtic-Laker playoff game and started screaming in his suit and tie about how fans in every city in America, how the Irish, how the Jews, how the Methodists, all loved the Celtics, the lunch-bucket team. Onlookers stared and laughed, which only encouraged Carr. "New Yorkers love the Celtics. All of Los Angeles loves the Celtics," Carr said. "They just don't know it yet. The Celtics represent everything that is worth winning in life." His speeches before the CEOs and junior executives became a bit more refined, but most of them still included the basics: teamwork, hustle, victory against all odds, including race.

Even Carr admitted, however, that not enough of these speeches were ever directed toward minority kids while he was a player. "In my mind, there's no doubt teams like the Celtics need to do more in the community," he said. "I know not everyone's an extrovert like I am. But to a certain degree there is a debt to be repaid. There's a greater obligation than to put the ball in the basket."

Unfortunately, by now Carr is viewed as an ex-player by the kids in Boston, not as a sneaker-sponsoring star. His impact, his Q score, is not what it once was. Sitting in front of English High in Lower Roxbury, a student tried to remember the two former Celtics who had visited the local Boys Club during the past year. One Celtic, he said, was tall and skinny. Probably Tom Sanders. The other was the guy with the towel. The kid couldn't remember Carr's name.

A pro basketball team is defined, in part, by how it presents itself over the airwaves to its public. In these days of crossover ownership and broadcast control, franchises are able to determine their own image by hiring the television and radio announcers of their choice, then molding them to fit an image. The Lakers are slick and smooth with Chick Hearn and Stu Lantz. The Knicks are street-wise with Marv Albert on TV, stylish and frenetic with Walt Frazier on radio. Some teams exert tighter control than others, but virtually all NBA franchises have some say in who gets hired, who gets reprimanded for being overly critical. In Boston, the Celtics have selected an assortment of purely white faces and voices to bring basketball to their viewers and listeners in white New England.

For the 1990–91 season, there were six Celtic broadcasters—three for radio (Glenn Ordway, Doug Brown, and Johnny Most), two for commercial station Channel 25 (Tom Heinsohn and Bob Cousy), two for cable SportsChannel (Mike Gorman and Heinsohn). None of them was black. Johnny Most, the gravelly-voiced legend who made homerism the right thing to do in Boston, all but retired before the start of the season. Here was a chance to bring in a fresh, very different voice. Maybe a former black Celtic like Dennis Johnson or Sam Jones. Instead Doug Brown, a white weeknight sports talk show host from Marblehead, Massachusetts, was hired. It was a slap in the face to a lot of people, and did not go unnoticed around the league.

"I know the Celtics could come up with one black," said Charles Grantham. "When you look at the host of great players, and good people, who have played for that team, it's almost a statistical impossibility that they can't find a black broadcaster. The broadcasters, the management, the coaching staff … after a while, you've got to figure there's some other factor involved."

The Celtics are not the only offenders in this area, only the most obvious. As recently as 1988, the twenty-three NBA teams did not yet employ a single black play-by-play man on a full-time basis—on radio, commercial TV, or cable. Out of a total seventy-five broadcasters, only nine were black. CBS had two all-white broadcast teams covering the playoffs. When NBC took over coverage in 1990, it quickly came up with an assortment of white broadcasters, former NBA coaches, a general manager, and a sports columnist for the plum assignments. Until playoff time, when Steve Jones was added to some B team telecasts, blacks were used only as peripheral interviewers, so-called sideline reporters. In his TV sports column in the now defunct sports daily, *The National,* Norman Chad correctly assessed the roles of Jones and Ahmad Rashad, the two blacks working the 1991 NBA finals, as "unspeakable intrusions." To help break through this embarrassing barrier, the NBA office sometimes circulated resumes of potential black broadcasters around the league. Its lobbying efforts met with negligible results. It was not as if qualified candidates weren't available. Clark Kellogg and Len Elmore, in particular, were incisive analysts with far more broadcast experience than bland, stumbling Bob Ferry and Pat Riley. Finally, after Riley left to coach the Knicks for the 1991–92 season, NBC hired Quinn Buckner, a black former Celtic, to replace him. The articulate Buckner had played for the Celtics during three glory seasons. After his retirement, he had been available to broadcast but never received an offer.

Butch Beard, a black NBA player and later coach at Howard University, tried broadcasting for a few years. He hired Lillian Wilder, a speech coach, to tone down his Kentucky accent. Wilder advised him to shave his mustache too, but Beard wouldn't do it in order to further his broadcasting career. "The network just doesn't give the black guy an opportunity," Beard said. "We're as good as guys like Tom Heinsohn, but it's a never-ending struggle."

The Celtics can be blamed directly for their white public face on television and radio, but they had little or no control over the assignment of writers to their beat by the two major newspapers in town, the *Boston Globe* and the *Boston Herald*. Yet while dailies in other major metropolitan areas were turning more to black reporters on NBA beats in the eighties and nineties, the *Globe* and *Herald* stubbornly assigned a string of white reporters like Bob Ryan, Jackie MacMullan, Peter May, Mike Carey, and Steve Bulpett to cover the Celtics. The sports reporting was largely competent, insightful in a basketball sense. But the *Globe*, the broadsheet of record in Boston, was painfully aligned with Auerbach and management. It did a lousy job of covering the tough black-white issues on the team and rarely dealt with community questions. Finally, in the summer of 1991, the *Globe* addressed the issue of racism on the Red Sox in a series of articles that should have been written long before. But once again the paper gave the Celtics a virtual pass. In fairness, such coverage is not always easy for a busy beat writer, who must file stories every day from twenty-seven different NBA outposts and maintain some sort of decent working relationship with club officials during a season. The writers travel with the coaches and depend on people like Auerbach and Volk for breaking trade rumors. Still, one would have hoped for more critical pieces at critical times. Certainly in New York local reporters had established a healthier adversarial relationship with the Knicks.

Even in the alternative weekly, the *Boston Phoenix*, the Celtics were treated far too gently from a sociopolitical perspective—also by predominantly white reporters and columnists. As one *Phoenix* editor explained, the Celtics were extended a certain reservoir of goodwill not offered any other home sports team. This was a championship team many times over, the crown jewel in the family of Boston's sports franchises. And the Red Sox had been so much worse, for so long, in a hundred different ways.

The Red Sox were the last team in major league baseball to integrate their team. They had mistreated their few black players so grossly that pitcher Oil Can Boyd finally erupted in a tirade during an interview with Lisa Olson of the *Hérald* (again, notably, not the *Globe*). "What the bleep do you think the Red Sox would do if Roger Clemens was black?" Boyd said. "Think he'd be Mr. Wonderful right now? Roger's their great white hope. He can rob a bank if he wants and so can Wade Boggs. Hide your women and children, Wade's coming through. Man, look at Lee Smith [another black pitcher then on the team]. He gets diarrhea and can't pitch and they ship him out. If Roger gets diarrhea, they'd be wiping his white ass for him."

The Celtics were better, certainly. Relatively speaking, the Celtics looked like John F. Kennedy to the Red Sox's George Wallace.

"I'm inclined to defend the Celts," said the *Phoenix* editor. "It's easy to accuse them of pandering, of hiding behind the 'sophisticated' basketball code word, which would be a word for appreciating white basketball. But I wouldn't credit them with everything. They are no more guilty than Notre Dame football, Yankee baseball, Canadien hockey. The demographics of whiteness caught on in Nebraska, Iowa, and everywhere else. Everybody in a bar in Northern Michigan and Detroit, the redneck element across the country, will root now for the Celtics, because of the Havlicek, Cowens, and Bird years."

The editor's argument was that bigoted Celtic fans were a symptom of society and that the disease had little to do with Boston or the Celtics. Not everybody agreed. After Len Elmore finished with the NBA and then Harvard Law School, he practiced at the district attorney's office in Brooklyn, New York, before returning to basketball as a college broadcaster. While he was living in Boston, Elmore viewed the Celtic organization suspiciously. "The way that Red Auerbach organized and marketed that team was perfect for Boston," Elmore said. "If it had been another city, he would have organized it a very different way."

If he is not being snubbed by award-givers at the Cannes Film Festival, director Spike Lee is sitting courtside at Madison Square Garden on celebrity row for all the biggest Knick games. He is a sight to behold: a spindly five-five fanatic, urging on the home team giants with high fives and cynical headshakes.

Over the years, Lee's seat has improved with his growing celebrity status. Before *Do the Right Thing*, he was often seen scrambling, one step ahead of the ushers, for a place behind the basket. After that movie's great success, Lee was welcomed as a bonafide star by the white Paramount hierarchy that owns the club. He was featured on network NBA promos, offered locker room privileges of the rich and famous. If dispassionate, aloof Woody Allen had been the Knicks' greatest cultural booster in the heyday of the sixties and seventies, then the more outspoken Lee easily supplanted him in the funkier, blacker nineties. Madison Square Garden has overpriced seats, growing more outrageously expensive each season. But at least its tickets remain physically accessible. Unlike its cousin at North Station in Boston, New York's Garden is a well-integrated arena—unless the Rangers are in town.

Lee is a big-time sports fan, a man who loves his baseball and his basketball and his boxing. Football is more problematic. He went to the Super Bowl in 1991 in the midst of the Gulf War frenzy and found it distasteful.

"It was a lot like a Nazi rally, with everybody waving flags and singing," he said. "The NBA is a lot more progressive."

Political perspectives like these have offended more than a few conservative and moderate whites, who charge Lee with anti-Semitism, reverse racism, and demagoguery. To most blacks, however, Lee represents both a rare success story and a racial conscience in the highest places. Lee can trace his roots to slavery, to his great-great-great-great-grandparents in Alabama. His great-grandfather, Willie Edwards, founded the Snow Hill Institute in Alabama, a top black school. His father, Bill Lee, was a standup bass player who played with Duke Ellington and Billie Holliday. Spike Lee's influence extends from a movie studio in Brooklyn into NBA arenas everywhere, where Lee maintains contacts with several top NBA players like Patrick Ewing and Michael Jordan—in part because of his Nike sneaker commercials, which more often than not feature Jordan. He has strong opinions about the Celtics, a team that receives no respect whatsoever in his movies.

"When I hear the name Celtics," Lee said before a Knick-Piston game at Madison Square Garden in February 1991, "I see the American flag, I see Elvis Presley, I see Mom and apple pie, I see the bus with black schoolchildren being overturned during the whole busing thing in Boston.

"All the players talk about the Celtics, but they can't come out and express what they feel. They are the most hated team in the NBA. I'm not talking about the players on the Celtics, but I'm talking about the team, and the image. The players know what they represent, and they go harder when they play the Celtics. When the

Lakers are playing the Celtics in a championship series, the brothers are praying that Magic or Jabbar or somebody is going to pull it out. I'm not going to say all of white America, but a large part of it is saying, 'Come on Celtics, you can't let these niggers beat you.' There are no blacks for the Celtics. There are a couple of black people that wear Celtic stuff. I give 'em a look, it says, 'You gotta know what's up, man. You wearin' this green over here?'" In Lee's *Do the Right Thing,* a white character named Clifton is openly mocked in a black Brooklyn neighborhood because he is wearing a Larry Bird uniform shirt. Lee says he has no trouble with Bird personally, a player he generally respects. He hopes the feeling is mutual. Asked by *Sports Illustrated* to pose with Bird for a photo, Lee was wary that Bird might harbor a grudge or two. Bird did not, and Lee appreciated that. But Lee is unapologetic on one front: He says black fans and players have been inundated with too much Bird, too much of the time.

"I mean, Larry Bird is a great ballplayer, and I'd never say he wasn't a great player," Lee said. "My problem was the way the media pushed him up. I don't think he was a part of it. The media, like, they got to hold Larry Bird up to the world like he is a great white hope on CBS, ABC, NBC, whoever has the NBA contract at the time." Lee has studied basketball history. He knows that the Celtics integrated the NBA on both the player and coaching fronts. But he remains suspicious of their motives.

"The first thing that the Celtics are going to say is, 'We had Bill Russell as a coach, and we had the first black player, blah, blah, blah, blah, blah,'" Lee said. "Why? Because it was to their advantage. And when it became their advantage to put eight white players on the team, then they did that. If you're a halfway decent white ballplayer, the Celtics will find your ass.

"They have that tradition," Lee said. "If they can get a white ballplayer, Bill Walton, anybody, they will. The Celtics, all these businesses for the most part, are owned by white corporate America. When it comes down to it, they're going to do what the hell they want, because it's their business."

✵ ✵ ✵

Of all the great white Celtic players to wear the green, only Dave Cowens really immersed himself in the black community of Boston. Others did their share in other ways. Bob Cousy was Big Brother to two black children and provided a sympathetic ear to his black teammates. Larry Bird played in Magic Johnson's charity All-Star games out on the West Coast, helping to raise money with the annual high-scoring spectacle. He organized Larry's Game in Indianapolis to aid poor Indiana kids who needed scholarships. But only Cowens dove into Roxbury and Dorchester without the slightest prodding from the laissez-faire Boston franchise. Not surprisingly, he was welcomed graciously at the schools and the Boys Clubs in black Boston. His enterprise and openness were appreciated by those who understood he could so easily have been like the others.

Cowens, as single-minded as he was redheaded, had always gone his own way. A southern Republican with a strong work ethic, he quickly learned to respect the toughness and unselfishness of his black teammates on the Celtics. As a rookie, before the season even started, he became involved in the Maurice Stokes charity game in the New York Catskills and played so hard, with his hallmark roughness, that he won the MVP trophy. When he became Celtic player-coach in 1978, he expected every player to play as he did. They weren't even close, so he quit.

They didn't always run hard. They didn't always get back on defense. And they wouldn't go out into the neighborhoods, where there was another sort of job to be done. Cowens, the individualist, the six-eight NBA center, never thought it was the duty of the team or the coach to act as social director. He felt the players should have gone out on their own, or be forced to do so by the Collective Bargaining Agreement between the league and the Players Association. "My feeling is that all of the players in the NBA should have a clause in their contracts—a give-back clause—that forces them to do X amount of work in the community," Cowens said. "That's the kind of stuff Satch Sanders is doing now for the NBA. Some guys want to give money, and that's fine, too. Do something.

"If the players are willing to do that then I think it's up to the guys who give them the contracts—the owners—to do something too. Keep some of the ticket prices reasonable, make sure a number of tickets each game are available for kids in the inner cities. That's where basketball comes from, doesn't it? Shouldn't people who don't have a lot of money get a chance to see Larry Bird and Robert Parish up close?"

Cowens has come full circle, going back into the community with his work at the New England Sports Museum. Like Carr, he no longer plays basketball, and a few of the kids have never heard of him. But he was once the starting center on the NBA champions. He is white and trying, which counts for something in communities that rarely get to reach out and touch the Celtic Mystique.

Adidas is the basketball shoe of choice in Boston, not Larry Bird's Converse or Reggie Lewis's Reeboks or even Michael Jordan's Nikes. Nobody is certain how or where this tradition began, but black Boston became an Adidas town sometime in the eighties and stayed that way. The kids wear light Adidas warmup jackets even when the blustery weather begs for more. They wear Adidas caps. The sneakers, however, make the wardrobe. Three stripes is the only way to go south of Ruggles Street.

In recent years, since Michael Jordan did Spike Lee's commercials in a national television advertising campaign, a tempest has whirled around this whole subject of sneakers. Not much came of it here in Boston, really, but the subject was batted around for a few months in the national media. Around the country, there had been a few inner-city homicides involving $100-plus shoes. A columnist at the *New York Post,* Phil Mushnick, screamed about the connection between footdress and murder. He blamed Jordan and Lee for endorsing such expensive and potentially hazardous products. *Sports Illustrated* did a cover story on the subject. Suddenly, successful black role models were being told they should endorse nothing more valuable than a soda can, or they would become accomplices to heinous crime. White journalists were telling black parents that their children could not afford or handle the responsibility of an expensive shoe.

Lee started fighting back, writing editorials on the subject when ever he could. "This is thinly veiled racism," Lee wrote in *The National*. "Only when black athletes or entertainers get big visibility do they have to be the moral conscience of America. It is crazy to think all black kids can't afford the sneakers and resort to selling crack to buy them." The sneaker companies, suddenly immersed in a controversy they had not foreseen, poured money into community relations programs to polish the image. Like most American corporations, they were not doing this to be good guys but to be perceived as good guys. Some real good came out of it anyway. Richard Lapchick's Institute for the Study of Sport at Northeastern received a large grant from Reebok for its neighborhood Project Teamwork program when the loud debate began.

"There was the immediate accusation there that Reebok was giving us blood money," said Lapchick. "*Sports Illustrated* did all this research and documented nine murders and about 110 robberies that were sneaker-related. But I have this hangup about going back to this perspective thing. They documented those nine murders from 1983, and since then there were 120,000 murders in America and there were over 640,000 robberies with assault involved. Any social scientist would say those nine murders and 110 robberies were statistically insignificant.

"Ripping Michael Jordan—who, from my understanding, went back to school to get his degree—sets a double standard for athletes who are making money in society," Lapchick said.

Lapchick is no corporate shill. When he was growing up in New York City, Lapchick heard his dad sobbing one morning in another room, over his coffee. The boy walked in on his famous coaching father from St. John's, Joe Lapchick, former star of the Original Celtics, and asked him what was wrong. The father explained that for the first time, he realized that his players were having terrible problems with their classes, and that he had done nothing to help them. He had not even been aware of the situation. He had been wrong.

From this moralistic background emerged Richard Lapchick, vegetarian and activist. In 1978, while a political science professor at Virginia Wesleyan, Lapchick, a white, tried to prevent a Davis Cup meeting between the United States and South Africa, in protest of that country's apartheid policies. On Valentine's Day that year, two men broke into his office, beat him up, and carved the word "nigger" on his stomach with a knife. Lapchick proceeded with his cause, sporting a scar but no bitterness. It is Lapchick's benevolent theory, maybe because of his experience with his father many years ago, that colleges and professional franchises like the Celtics generally want to do the right thing for minorities. It is just that they don't even realize there is a right thing to do. Some day, he hopes not too late, they too will be sobbing into their coffee.

"White society doesn't know black society," Lapchick said. Lapchick, who is echoed by Tom Sanders on the point, believes that Boston is not significantly worse in this regard than any other American city. But he has had a lot of trouble convincing most blacks on this particular issue. When he first founded the institute, he tried to hire Anita DeFrantz, the first black woman on the International Olympic Committee, an attorney, and the first black rower to make the Olympic team. She was a pioneer, a woman who organized the protest against President Carter's decision to pull out of the Moscow Olympics. DeFrantz was unemployed at the time of Lapchick's offer, and still she would not come to Boston. "Even though this was something she believed in and this was something she wanted to do, she was black and this was Boston," Lapchick said. "That was my introduction to this city."

DeFrantz never came to Boston, where she might have bridged some of the rigid boundaries that divided people by religion, income, and race. In the tale of two Bostons, another black athlete had fallen through the cracks.

Chapter 12

Building the Empire

FOR his birthday in 1986, Robert Willens was given 110 shares of the Boston Celtics at $18.50 a pop. By comparison to the other ninety-five thousand Celtic unitholders, Willens had to be considered a major investor, a big spender. When Celtic Pride went up for sale on the big board that December, trading as "BOS" on the New York Stock Exchange, it had many takers. Most of the Celtic stockholders, more than fifty thousand of them, either purchased or were presented with exactly one stock share as a tack-it-on-the-wall birthday, Christmas, or bar mitzvah gift. Unlike these more passive recipients, Willens began to study the stock and the Celtics' corporate moves with great curiosity. Yes, he was a Larry Bird fan. But Willens was also a senior vice president of Lehman Brothers, a certified public accountant, and soon to become, probably, the world's only outside financial expert on the Boston Celtic master plan. The offering was too small to interest any other analysts, but Willens saw more to it than a $48.1 million sale. Willens, who worked high above Wall Street in the American Express Tower of the World Financial Center, had an accountant's respect for what Alan Cohen and the Celtics were doing. What they were doing, basically, was dodging taxes like no other pro sports franchise had ever done, and never would be able to do again.

The Celtics were the only sports team in America trading on any stock exchange, the only one with a master limited partnership and a communications sister company. They would remain unique in this fashion indefinitely, because the tax loops were sewn tight as soon as the Celtics slipped through them. "The Celtics are not like Jack Kent Cooke, simple fans cheering like hell on Sundays," said Willens, who issued regular memos at American Express on the precedent-setting tax and accounting issues posed by the Celtics. "These guys are running the team like a real business."

The man whose mind Willens most enjoyed shadowing from afar was Alan Cohen. If the NBA boom was sparked by Larry Bird and Magic Johnson, if it was intelligently nurtured by Players Association head Larry Fleisher and commissioner David Stern, then it was best financially exploited for private interests by Cohen. Cohen was no simple creation of Auerbach's, no favorite friend of the family's with insurmountable debts of loyalty to pay. Cohen was a brilliant opportunist, well-connected with commissioner David Stern, and a man who wielded strong influence over no fewer than three NBA teams: the New York Knicks, the New Jersey Nets, and the Boston Celtics. So omnipotent was Cohen, so seemingly indifferent to the possibility of conflict of interest charges, that he helped negotiate for the purchase of the Celtics in 1983, while he was still chairman and NBA governor for the Nets. The purchase was for the ridiculously low price of $17 million, including liabilities, and was made on behalf of former associates from Madison Square Garden. Four years later, then the vice chairman of the board and treasurer for the Celtics, Cohen was one of several Celtic officials approached by Madison Square Garden president Richard Evans when Evans was looking for advice on a new coach and general manager. Somehow, Evans came out of these consultations coveting Boston assistant coach Jimmy Rodgers, who could only be acquired if the Knicks gave the Celtics steep compensation. A year later, Cohen, the Celtic vice chairman, was advising Net CEO Alan Aufzien on important team matters when the New Jersey franchise was unraveling because of drug charges and an in-house mutiny. Aufzien denied that Cohen gave him personnel advice, but former Net coach Dave Wohl said it was his impression that Cohen had a powerful say in all affairs. "Aufzien keeps going back to Alan Cohen," Wohl said. "When I was there, I told him, 'He's in our division. Do you really believe he's going to help you?'" The Net ownership was so influenced by Cohen and the Celtic organization, it installed a parquet floor at Meadowlands Arena in a feeble attempt to duplicate the tradition and success in Boston.

Cohen, fifty-two years old when he first bought into the Celtics, was a product of the hard-edged North Jersey towns of Clifton and Passaic. Bald, physically unimposing, he was nonetheless a formidable, driven man. A graduate of Columbia Law School, like Volk, he specialized in tax and corporate law and became an associate with the Democratic-leaning cutthroat Manhattan law firm of Paul, Weiss, Rifkind, Wharton & Garrison. He advanced to partner and was remembered as something of a tyrant by those who worked beneath him. His office was off-limits, his own little fiefdom. One former co-worker remembered introducing his wife to Cohen with a touch of irony totally lost on Cohen: "Meet Alan Cohen," the employee said, "without whom Paul, Weiss would not have the reputation it now enjoys."

As a basketball operations director, Cohen had been known to oppose the most benign giveaway promotions on budgetary grounds. An unconfirmed story circulated with knowing smiles among Madison Square Garden cronies goes like this: One season, Cohen fought other Net directors about the idea of handing out free basketballs to kids at a game. According to this account, Net principal owner Joe Taub finally slapped a few hundred dollars on the table and shouted, "If it matters so much to you, I'll pay for the basketballs."

But because he had a way of making big money for those who

associated with him, Cohen always engendered a real loyalty among his peers. Philanthropists like Taub might grimace a bit at Cohen's bottom-line thinking, but Taub and other past partners retained a real respect for Cohen's Darwinistic business acumen. When he left the Nets, he did so with the blessing of Taub, who eventually sold the team because of Cohen's departure and the carping of minority owners. Cohen told Taub of his departure over dinner, on the night of Taub's thirtieth wedding anniversary.

"Would you buy me out, if that makes sense?" Cohen said.

Taub replied, "Is that good for Alan Cohen?"

Cohen told him it was. The deal was done, sadly, even though Taub correctly understood that it might mean the end of the New Jersey owners' fragile alliance. When Cohen escaped from New Jersey, the Nets were a young, forty-nine-victory team on their way to great things. They never got there, and front-office problems were one of the reasons.

Cohen was a man clearly obsessed with acquiring money. At the same time, however, he found himself attracted to running operations that were in the entertainment or luxury fields: Warner Brothers, moviemakers; the Palladium, a giant rock and roll establishment in lower Manhattan; Steve's Homemade Ice Cream, crunchy and fruity; last, but not least, NBA teams, with all their inherent glamour and potential pitfalls. His interest in pro basketball was more than casual. Cohen would come to most home games at Boston Garden, commuting from New York to do so. While on the Board of Governors for the Nets, he once fought with Red Auerbach about eliminating the backcourt foul. When Cohen helped set up the purchase of the Celtics in 1983 on behalf of Don Gaston and Paul Dupee, Cohen worried that his past tiffs with Auerbach would sour the deal, which required Auerbach's approval. Instead, Auerbach welcomed Cohen, recognized him as a sly businessman who would, in turn, recognize a sly personnel manipulator.

Cohen made powerful friends at Madison Square Garden and its parent corporation, Gulf + Western, during his three years there.

Gaston and Dupee had been two of them. After Harry Mangurian announced he was going to sell the team, and after a proposed sale to a local Boston businessman collapsed, Mangurian phoned Cohen. It took Cohen just two hours to read the contract language offered by Mangurian and to advise his two trusting associates to grab this bargain. "It was $15 million, plus assuming the deferred," Cohen said. "I thought it was an extraordinarily low amount. I thought it was such a good deal. Coming back from looking at the books, Don Gaston said, 'Are you going to take a piece of it?'" I said, 'I'd love to.'"

The deal was set in August. By September, Larry Bird was locked up in a new seven-year contract. It was important, perhaps crucial, to keep Bird around as long as possible, or at least until the team acquired a similar draw.

David Falk, the well-connected and influential ProServ agent who represented Patrick Ewing, argued during Ewing's 1991 arbitration case against the Knicks that a $4.9 million bonus in a 1988 one-year extension of Bird's contract placed Bird above Ewing as one of the four highest-paid players in the league. Falk believed the NBA actually bent its complicated salary-cap rules to keep Bird from quitting.

He contended that the Celtics and the NBA secretly conspired to circumvent the cap in 1988 because both parties knew Bird would retire unless he could reap a financial bonanza the capped-out Celtics were in no position to offer

While denying that loopholes in the cap were deliberately created, the NBA's general counsel and salary-cap whiz, Garry Bettman, admitted to assisting the Celtics—in itself a questionable act. Said Falk: "I can't prove this, of course, but my belief is that the league thought Bird was going to retire after the 1989–90 season and didn't want him out until it had negotiated its next mega-TV contract." Which, Falk pointed out, would be with NBC for the 1990–91 season.

In addition, there was the issue of the 1992 Summer Olympics in Barcelona, which presented the burgeoning league with a fantastic global marketing opportunity. The NBA wanted Bird to be a part of its global expansion and marketing. It wanted him out there selling, like Michael Jordan and Magic Johnson.

"I don't like any of it," Bird said. "I'm a private person. I hear it all the time from people in the league how I should do more. I just can't see myself doing that, be Mr. Nice Guy, go around and shake everybody's hand, and you can make $1 million.

"I think the league sometimes is disappointed in me because I'm the most visible white player and I don't do more."

League officials practically begged the wavering Bird to play. He was extended one of ten invitations during the summer of 1991, despite having undergone back surgery in May. When it was apparent the surgery had been a success, Bird's contract was again extended, for two more years, in October 1991 for $10 million.

By 1985, the new triumvirate of owners began to wonder how it could make big money without reselling the team—an entity that already had brought a new level of prestige and success to Cohen and his partners. "The franchise had prospered beyond our wildest dreams," Cohen said. "Don and I were never going to sell, so we're sitting with this team." Cohen raised ticket prices dramatically, virtually shutting out low-income fans, but that wasn't enough. He went to California, talked to Drexel about raising some money. One plan was to take out a large loan in the name of the Celtics. Cohen returned from his trip and presented the idea for approval to Stern, another former tax attorney. "Fine," Stern told Cohen about the loan proposal. "But I've got something to talk to you about." The commissioner of basketball was about to make the Celtic owners very rich men, and years later they would repay the favor by supporting a $5.1 million per year salary for Stern.

"Anytime you want something done in the NBA," said NBA Players Association president Charles Grantham, "you have to go through the Celtics." Stern, more than anybody, always understood this. He told Cohen that a representative from Smith Barney had come to the commissioner's office with an idea for using a professional sports team in a master limited partnership. In order to make it work, the team would have to be popular enough nationally to sell millions of stock shares on novelty alone. It certainly would not be viewed as a great investment by brokers. Stern told the Smith Barney rep that there were probably only two teams that could pull it off in the NBA, Boston and Los Angeles, and that the Celtics were the prime candidate. Stern had thrown the business their way. With their championship banners and their ten white faces on the 1986–87 roster, they were America's team, with followings from Maine to Montana. "Would you be interested?" Stern asked Cohen. He already knew the answer.

Under the master limited partnership (MLP), Gaston, Dupee, and Cohen would still retain control of the team. They would just sell off forty percent of their team to the public in 2.6 million shares, make a quick cash killing, and continue on their merry administrative way. After the sale went down, Gaston would still own 32.5 percent of the Celtics, Dupee would own 14.7 percent, Cohen would own 11.8 percent. But they had to push the transaction through in a hurry. The General Utilities Doctrine, which came about as a result of a 1935 Supreme Court case, was about to be repealed beginning in 1987. Under the doctrine, a company could still liquidate on a tax-free basis. The shareholder tax rate of 20 percent would go up to 52.5 percent on January 1, 1987. Under the MLP, a company would pay just 28 percent in taxes, not 34 percent on income, plus 28 percent on dividends. A lot of companies, nearly a hundred of them, liquidated at the end of 1986, hoping to come in under the wire. The Celtics hired the law firm of Ropes and Gray to get out the message, to drum up some interest among potential investors. They put out a 122-page prospectus detailing their finances. Suddenly everybody would know that Red Auerbach, cornerstone and symbol of the franchise, was earning a relatively modest $250,000 in 1986, the amount he would receive for his lifetime; that Jan Volk was earning $190,000, which would increase to $246,000 by 1990.

At about the same time, the Denver Nuggets tried to go public with Paine Webber as their underwriter. Nugget management traveled around the country for a week or so to twenty cities and discovered there was little or no interest. "Everybody thought the Nuggets were overpriced," Willens said. "The Celtics are the Celtics. The

Nuggets are the Nuggets." Very late in 1986, the Lakers started making noise about going MLP. But they did not have an Alan Cohen in their corner, and apparently had not been given the same early advisory by Stern. The Lakers, who probably could have pulled it off based on their popularity, did not get the MLP done by January 1, 1987. The Celtics were the only ones. The door slammed shut on everybody else.

Even the Celtics underestimated the novelty value of these stocks. There was no real investment thesis here. The Celtics were not going to increase their sold-out attendance in the near future, and it seemed unlikely they would get much better TV contracts. The stock purchasers simply wanted to consider themselves part owners of the Celtics. "It was fun just to get the reports," Willens said. "You can't look at this thing rationally." There had been nothing like this before. The shares sold out immediately. They went so fast, they could have been sold at more than $18.50, and the Celtic ownership could have earned more than the $44.746 million in proceeds from the sale. "Smith Barney left some money on the table," Willens said. "The Celtics were probably pissed off, but they couldn't do another offering."

Once the stocks were sold, Cohen discovered a few new problems he did not expect. Because there were all these one-unit stockholders, the cost of sending out the thousands of quarterly dividend checks for 35 cents was costing the organization over $1 million a year. "It became an administrative nightmare," Cohen said. "People come to me and say they've given the stock as presents to children, and I tell these people, 'I really wish you hadn't.'" The Celtics amended everything to once-a-year mailings. The stock plunged with the rest of the market during the crash of 1987, going down to as low as ten points, and suddenly the Celtics had a public relations problem. Then just as quickly the stock recovered and averaged a healthy, if unspectacular, 11 percent return over the next four years. The unitholders, loyal fans, wouldn't think of selling their certificates, regardless of profits. On what was a typical trading day, Willens checked the monitor outside his office and noted that only 1,500 units of Celtic stock had been traded. By comparison, there had been 425,000 units traded that day in a similarly sized stock offering.

The fortunes of the stock were largely irrelevant to the Celtic triumvirate. The three owners had their money, and their families were assured of it even after death. The Celtics had an advantage over all the other NBA teams. They had eliminated 34 percent of the entity tax on their income and had a greater free cash flow to invest in players and the franchise. The NBA supported their plan, had even suggested it. There was one danger. Under the Revenue Act of 1987, the Celtics could lose their MLP status if they added a substantial new line of business. They would lose $5 million in 1989 taxes, and up to $50 million over a ten-year period, if they branched out. And yet the ever-aggressive Cohen was now in the market for TV and radio stations.

When the Celtics had moved in 1985 to Channel 56, WLVI, it was an independent UHF station owned by Gannett that was, by Cohen's measure, "muddling along." When the Celtics signed a five-year contract with that station, its estimated value immediately increased from $50 to $75 million. Cohen was not a man who enjoyed making money for others without a piece of the profits. He and Gaston began discussing the idea of buying their own station and putting the Celtics on it. In late 1987 into early 1988, Channel 25, WFXT, became available. Rupert Murdoch had to sell the local Fox network station because of an FCC ruling that prevented him from owning both a newspaper (the *Herald*) and a TV affiliate in the same city. It was Senator Ted Kennedy, a regular guest of the Celtic brass at Boston Garden and a long-time political nemesis of Murdoch, who fought hardest against giving the Australian magnate any sort of waiver around the rule. The Celtics purchased the station for $10 million, plus liabilities, after a very quick negotiating session in New York one Tuesday afternoon. Cohen's business tentacles again had facilitated matters. The man running and selling the station was Barry Diller, a former Gulf + Western associate. Volk and Auerbach knew little about this business deal until it was completed. Auerbach didn't care. Volk kept his ego bruises to himself.

The Celtics later would sell their own station the rights to broadcast Celtic games at the rate of $30,000 per preseason game, $150,000 per regular season game, $200,000 per playoff game. To pull this off and avoid losing the tax-exempt status of the MLP, Cohen founded a sister partnership, the Boston Celtics Communications Limited Partnership, and held a rights offering to the Boston Celtic stockholders on September 14, 1990. For $1.20 in subscription rights, unitholders could now buy into this new limited partnership and make claim to owning a piece of television and radio stations. It was the BCCLP that purchased Channel 25 and later bought WEEI radio—which would pay the Celtics an annual fee of $1.4 million through 1992, then $2.4 and $2.5 million the following two seasons for radio broadcasting rights. The Celtics had created their own communications network, controlling when and how they would be presented to the New England public over the airwaves. "It wasn't so much about building a basketball empire as much as it is building a business, or businesses, that get their jump start from the Celtics," Cohen said.

The new businesses also assured the Celtics of guaranteed access that might otherwise have been lost. WFXT remained a Fox affiliate, and once Fox became successful enough with shows like "The Simpsons" and "Married with Children," network officials started pressuring the Celtics to preempt their basketball games for higher-rated programming. The Celtics owned the station, however, and didn't have to listen. They could say what they wanted on the air about any player transaction, about any disappointing loss, about any scandal in the front office. The message would get through, on radio and TV. In addition, since the TV station was still with the Fox network, certain programming originated in Boston and was broadcast nationwide. On February 3, 1991, for example, Fox network aired a bizarre hybrid version of "Comic Strip Live" from the Celtic practice site at the Hellenic College gym in Brookline. As comedian Joe Piscopo cracked jokes and Queen Latifah performed rap songs, the camera panned a puzzled, vaguely appreciative group of past and present Celtic players in the crowd.

Even more troubling than this monopoly of information dissemination was the ethical question of the Celtic tax dodge through the creation of a sister communications company. The Celtics, relatively inactive in the area of community outreach, were basically avoiding $50 million in tax payments to local and federal governments. "They got the job done," Willens said. "This will slip through the cracks. They'll get an extension of sorts to the year 2000, with the help of some Massachusetts congressman on the Ways and Means Committee.

"When the Celtics write their assets off, they might have a problem," Willens said. "They will amortize TV contracts, broadcast rights, player contracts, uniforms, and the franchise itself. They could have a tax deficiency—provided they don't dazzle the auditor with free tickets."

By the fall of 1991, Cohen and the other Celtic owners found themselves overextended in the broadcast business during one of Boston's most severe depressions. Cohen, never shy in seeking out the rich and famous, went on an aggressive safari for fresh investors in the franchise's radio and television holdings. If at all possible, the Celtics wanted to hold on to these assets, which gave them a stranglehold on the New England audience.

Having assured themselves of fast cash through the public stock sale, and of tax dodges with the sister communications company, Cohen and the Celtics still had one more fiscal bonanza to reap: a new, more lucrative arena. Ever since the Celtics drew 14,570 fans to a game against the Houston Rockets on December 19, 1980, they had been selling out the well-worn arena on Causeway Street. The Celtic owners had nothing against the cracking, erratic parquet floor or the overhanging balconies or the gritty background organ music. These were welcome home court edges. But the Garden's capacity of 14,890 was the second smallest in the league, greater only than Portland's Memorial Coliseum. There were no true luxury boxes, the backbone of windfall gate profits around the league. And most frustrating of all to the Celtics, they were merely tenants in a building owned and leased by the New Boston Garden Corporation—a subsidiary of Delaware North Corporation, which also owned the Boston Bruins. The Bruins were leasing space from their own parent corporation, much like the Celtics' new radio and TV station was paying the team for broadcast rights. The Celtics, meanwhile, were paying a fixed per game fee to the NBGC—amounting to a cost of about $1 million per season—and were not sharing in revenues from concessions or parking lots.

For a franchise as powerful and haughty as the Boston Celtics, this sort of poor-sister relationship would not do. Scheduling was a roll of the dice. At playoff time, there were unexpected conflicts like Bruin Stanley Cup games and a 1991 figure skating extravaganza that pushed a game against the Pistons to a weekday afternoon.

For much of the seventies and eighties, owners like Harry Mangurian and Cohen dropped hints they might be forced to take the team elsewhere, to suburbia or beyond. To drive this point home, and to expand their power base, the Celtics had agreed as far back as in 1974 to play a limited number of regular season home games at the 15,134-seat Hartford Civic Center in central Connecticut. This was an arrangement that was very clearly bad for the team, which performed better at Boston Garden than at the Civic Center. From 1974 to 1990, the Celtics were 1,479–126 at the Garden, for an astounding .921 winning percentage. They were 36–15 (.706) at Hartford. There was money to be made and a threat to be carried out, however, and Boston brass was not about to let a few extra defeats and the possible loss of the home court advantage in the playoffs stand in its way.

Cohen and Gaston threatened to build their own arena for the Celtics as owner Jack Kent Cooke had done more than twenty years earlier for his Lakers. Finally, after a great many tantrums and a few false starts, a new Garden was officially advertised for bidders in 1985. In January 1989, it became a designated project. It was the position of the mayor's office from the start that the construction should be a private operation. "We wanted to avoid a city-franchise trap," said John Connolly, Mayor Ray Flynn's development adviser. "This is not Oakland."

Nobody wanted to be Oakland, California. There, desperate city officials had attempted in 1990 to woo back the Raiders from Los Angeles only to embarrass themselves and their hometown. A revolt by taxpayers and activists in that city killed the outrageously expensive deal with Raider owner Al Davis and finally drew a monetary line in the sand against the most powerful civic blackmailers of all—professional sports team owners. Slowly, inevitably, some cities were getting the message that these nomadic franchises did not in any way belong to their fans; that they displayed no loyalty, and that they were ultimately expendable. They were less important than a good school system or a safe railway bridge across the Charles River.

To Boston, of course, the Celtics were significantly more important than an average pro team. The team's incredible success, achieved in the lifetime of most of the city's residents, made the team a precious resource. And although the city did not want to get involved with the Celtics' expansion plans, it could not entirely avoid an indirect role. Boston Garden was built over North Station. The arena and the railway system of the Metro Boston Transit Authority were dependent on each other to provide a flow of business. Eventually, an $86.3 million contract was awarded for a new station and an underground parking lot. A new eighteen-thousand-seat basketball arena was planned, which would bring the project cost to $142 million. It would be finished in September 1993. This arena and surrounding office buildings were on MBTA land, and encroached city air rights. Boston became involved in the talks between the

Celtics and Delaware North because it was in Boston's self-inter-est—to the tune of $13 million in tax revenues from the project. Those negotiations between Cohen and Garden Corporation chair-man Larry Moulter broke down on Labor Day weekend, 1989, jeop-ardizing the city's take, when the Celtics balked at paying any form of rent on the new building.

Finally, Delaware North agreed to the Celtics' demands. Incredi-bly, the Celtics had themselves a sweet ten-year deal in which they would receive, absolutely free of charge from the New Boston Garden Corporation, use of the arena and six thousand square feet of office space. In addition, the Garden would have to maintain the new arena, providing administrative personnel such as ushers, ticket takers, police, and security personnel. It would even pay for announcers, scorers, and statisticians. The Garden would be respon-sible for all box office ticket sales and remit the proceeds to the Celtics. The Celtics could still sell programs at the games. In return for all this, the Garden's take seemed paltry. It would receive rev-enues from the new executive suites, which the company hoped would be rented to very rich fans and corporate boosters at prices ranging from $120,000 to $200,000 a year. It would also receive gate receipts from two thousand "premium" seats. It would retain rev-enue from food and beverage concessions and be licensed by the Celtics to sell merchandise bearing the team logo—subject to pay-ment of a commission to the Celtics. The deal amounted to almost unconditional surrender by the New Boston Garden Corporation, which needed the Celtics or faced the loss of the whole project. "Alan is just ruthless," Moulter said with a businessman's sense of respect.

Moulter had been fleeced and he knew it. He also realized that he had no options. A new Boston Garden without the Celtics was an impossibility, a bad joke. By the summer of 1991, the Garden had successfully rented forty-five of its eighty-nine seats and twelve hun-dred of its two thousand premium seats. That prime real estate would have been empty without the Celts.

The new Garden was still not out of its Causeway Street mire. The economic recession in Boston caused a multi-million-dollar financing gap that Delaware North worked hard to close. But if the financing, or the local job outlook, could be straightened out in the early nineties, Cohen's empire would be complete: a projected new eighteen-thousand-seat arena, costing nothing per month through 2004; a network contract, through the NBA, that paid out nearly $5 million to the Celtics in 1990–91; a cable TV contract with Turner Network Television, worth about $2 million in 1990–91; a limited local pay-TV agreement with SportsChannel; local TV and radio rights, sold to the Celtics' sister broadcasting companies; and even a renovated charter Boeing 727 jet, more convenient and less costly than transporting the Celtics on commercial airlines.

In 1989–90, the Celtics received $8.341 million for just its local television, cable, and radio contracts. The team's declared net income for that season was very close to that: $8,021,707. The potential for more profit-taking existed. Every time the league expanded by one team, the Celtics could expect to earn another $1.5 million in the shared franchising fee. For every home playoff game the Celtics played, they could expect to clear an additional $500,000 after expenses. The Celtics hiked their ticket prices 7 percent in 1990. They would have three thousand more seats to sell when the new arena finally opened. None of those seats would be obstructed. All of them would be expensive. Alan Cohen would see to that.

The news of this luxurious future, for both the Celtics and the Bruins, received virtually no play in the sports pages of the *Boston Globe,* which came as no surprise. Sports editors in most cities long ago bought into the public's mindset that local pro teams were not profiteering corporations, but rather friendly, hometown entities. In New York, during the 1986 World Series, the Mets won game six over the Red Sox in dramatic fashion, forcing a game seven. The front page headline in the *New York Daily News* read, WE AIN'T DEAD YET, and had nothing to do with that tabloid's tenuous financial situation. The newspaper was trying to cash in on the public's good-will toward the team; on the blind loyalty that local fans usually display toward the home side. Two years later, a negative column about the Mets' policies toward black players appeared in the *Daily News* in the middle of a playoff series against the Dodgers. The managing editor had not known about it, and flipped out when he read it. The article was not part of the paper's puffy playoff package. Again, the editor's attitude was nothing unusual. Just good business and bad journalism.

This reportorial dishonesty might feed civic pride, but it also set a trap: What would happen if the team so loyally backed by local journalists decided it was more profitable to abandon the city? Residents and the media would feel betrayed. They should not. In the Japanese professional baseball league and in the Italian basketball league, there is greater honesty about these matters. Clubs are named not after the city where they happen to play, but after the sponsoring corporation. Thus they are not the Tokyo Giants and the Rome Reds, but the Yomiuri Giants and Il Messaggero, two newspaper companies. It probably should not have been the Boston Celtics, either, but the Brookwood Investments Celtics. For it was likely that Celtic owner Donald Gaston, Texas-raised and New York–oriented, was more loyal to his international conglomerate than he was to the Back Bay, Roxbury, or South Boston.

Few Celtic owners or officials understood the gold mine they were sitting on in the seventies and eighties. If they did, they just didn't have the stomach for gambling or the mind for business maneuvering. Among those who missed out on the gravy train were Harry Mangurian, steel-eyed horse trader; John Y. Brown, the public man with private vices; and Red Auerbach, who proved far less than ingenious or insightful in financial matters concerning himself.

Harry Mangurian should have known better. He had followed the fortunes of basketball since he was a kid, since he was growing up in Rochester, New York. He went to the 1954 All-Star Game in

New York and remembered how Bob Cousy stole the game in over-time for the East with three steals. The Celtics were something special to Mangurian. Yet he gave them up in a fit of administrative pique. To this day, Mangurian rues selling the Celtics to Gaston, Dupee, and Cohen for $17 million in 1983—just as the NBA was exploding and the Celtics were at their playing peak. Three years later, the 40 percent stock sale would value the Celtics' total price at more than $120 million. By 1987, primitive NBA expansion teams Miami, Charlotte, Minnesota, and Orlando were being sold for $32.5 million and strong bidders from other cities were being turned away, wanting to throw many more millions at established owners.

"Nobody has a crystal ball," Mangurian said. "When I sold the Celtics, I got the largest price for any pro basketball team ever sold. Who knew that four years later they'd be worth at least four times as much? I guess the way I have to look at it is that buying into the Celtics was one of the best deals I made and selling was one of the worst."

Mangurian sold for a number of reasons, all of which he now admits sound pretty stupid. He was frustrated about the arrangement the Celtics had with the equally arrogant Boston Garden Corporation. The franchise was paying more money for its arena than most other teams—although one could reasonably argue it was still a bargain—and there didn't seem to be any construction options. "They'd been talking about a new facility for thirty years," Mangurian said. He worried about the way salaries were going, about free agency, about the deferred money. The way NBA owners often got around immediate cash crunches was simply to defer much of the players' salaries to a later time, perhaps five or six years down the road, then sell the team before those payments came due. These were not tremendously rich men, as a rule. Several owners were rumored to be on the brink of financial ruin, and were quite fond of selling off or dumping top players. Flamboyant Franklin Mieuli of Golden State admitted he could not compete financially with a corporate-owned team like the Knicks, so he gave away star Bernard King for inadequate compensation.

Tax depreciations were usually good for five years, at which point the team was sold and the next owner would start the deferment-depreciation cycle all over again. In the early eighties, before the salary cap and the big network contracts, the NBA office was fond of publicizing that seventeen of its twenty-three teams were losing money, that it needed big concessions from the Players Association to survive. Mangurian wondered then whether owners weren't heading for some sort of deficit Armaggedon, like the savings and loan industry later. League salaries were zooming, nearly tripling from 1983 to 1991 to an average of $1 million per player. Everybody was worried. "We were the first sport to have these megasalaries and all kinds of negotiations and renegotiations," NBA commissioner David Stern said. "Certain ownerships were undercapitalized and did things to make payroll that weren't necessarily in the best long-term interest."

Mangurian, like too many other owners, could not justify paying this kind of money to those he perceived as average NBA players. There was no acknowledgment that these athletes were the very best three hundred basketball players out of many millions in the world, or that they were the show that was bringing in fans and revenues. "I had no problem paying Larry Bird a lot of money," Mangurian said. "But it was when you paid one guy, then the next guy's contract was running out and you had to pay him even more than Bird. And then you have Bird coming back in and where does it end?"

In Mangurian's case, it ended with a shortsighted sale to a more visionary Cohen—who had taken all of two hours to scour the Celtic books and realize what a mistake Mangurian was making. When Mangurian sold the Celtics, they were grossing about $8 million per season. By the time the team went public in 1986, just three years later, that figure had more than tripled through new broadcasting contracts, increased ticket prices, and licensing bonanzas that were unthinkable earlier. By 1989–90, annual revenues were up to nearly $30 million. The $54 million sewn up in future player and coaching contacts through 1996 suddenly appeared very manageable. "Obviously, the people I sold to were very astute," Mangurian said regretfully.

These customers were the New Age businessmen, acquisition-minded usurpers in the Reagan boom years. Men like Cohen and Gaston now recognized NBA franchises as good business holdings, not just toys. During the sixties, seventies, and early eighties, pro basketball teams were never considered serious investments. They were merely expensive sporting propositions, prestigious power bases, and quick resale items. John Y. Brown, one of a string of a half-dozen Celtic owners in the decade preceding Mangurian's purchase, was the most capricious owner of all. He still kicks himself just as hard as his successor, Mangurian, for dumping the Celtics. "I don't look too smart selling the Celtics, that much I'll give you," he said.

Brown was a slick, hands-on tycoon with strong, admitted connections to gamblers and to a convicted drug dealer. Brown had made his fortune by developing Kentucky Fried Chicken, by purchasing the hamburger recipe of Oliver Gleichenhaus and turning small portions of meat into big bread. He also developed some dangerous habits along the way. He often participated in legal, high-stakes card games in Las Vegas, and never denied the rumor he once lost $1 million at a single sitting. In 1981 and 1982, just a couple years after selling the Celtics, Brown withdrew $1.3 million in cash from the All America Bank of Miami to pay off gambling debts.

Brown played cards with too many people, made friends with all the wrong ones. He became a close associate of James Lambert, who was later indicted on fifty-nine drug counts. Brown was a co-owner with Lambert of a Cincinnati nightclub managed by Philip Block, who was later convicted of cocaine trafficking. When Brown ran for the Senate in 1984, his opponent, Walter D. Huddleston, said of Brown, he is "accustomed to carrying his money in $100 bills out of a Florida bank after hours."

Brown eventually became one of the targets of a federal investigation. Florida police officials described him as "an associate of organized crime and heavily involved in gambling." He was never charged. The NBA, which would bar Hot Rod Williams from the league in 1985 for point-shaving charges at Tulane that did not stick, either discovered nothing about Brown's habits in the late seventies or chose not to prosecute them. Brown, after all, was a moneyed owner in an era when investors were not that easy to come by for the NBA.

Despite his erratic resume, Brown remained a rich and popular Kentuckian. He might never have sold the Celtics, might have outlasted Auerbach, if he hadn't decided to run for governor of that state during his honeymoon with former Miss America Phyllis George in 1979. He waged a whirlwind two-month campaign and won. After his decision to run, before his election, a reporter asked him if he would be selling the Celtics. Brown, apparently untroubled by conflict of interest questions, suddenly developed a conscience at the wrong time. He hinted that he would indeed sell the club, and his quotes were plastered all over the Boston papers.

"Given the situation with Red and given the fact that almost no teams were making any money, I just decided, 'What the hell, I'll sell my half of the team to Harry Mangurian and concentrate on the governor's race,'" Brown said.

"I still wonder, though, to this day: If that reporter hadn't asked me about whether I was going to sell, would I have sold my half? It hurts too much when I think about that."

Auerbach breathed a sigh of relief at this sale, but he had managed to co-exist, even with this man, for as long as he needed to. The Celtics survived, too. Even thrived, despite the league-wide pessimism that was in vogue.

The Celtics were viewed for a surprising number of years as no different, no more potentially revenue-producing, than any other NBA franchise. They were all considered sad cousins of baseball and NFL clubs. As recently as 1988, Wilt Chamberlain predicted that no black man would ever own an NBA team, because it was not a profitable venture for such a high-capital, high-risk investment. "There are too many whites who get a vicarious thrill from being in control of players," Chamberlain said. "They are willing to pay too much money for a team in order to say, 'Michael Jordan plays for me.' If a black guy wants to rub shoulders with Jordan, he just goes to the disco. The white guy buys him."

Within two years, as the NBA became the hottest pro sports league in America, Chamberlain did not look like much of a soothsayer. A syndicate of black businessmen led by Bertram Lee of Boston negotiated to purchase the Denver Nuggets. Although they could not close on the deal without the big bucks of white businessman Robert Wussler, they became influential minority owners and were active in managing the club. Top players like Magic Johnson and Michael Jordan also began talking about purchasing a team, and had the money from NBA contracts and commercial endorsements to be taken very seriously. "I get the payrolls from the NBA and study the salary trends. I study the television numbers, the ratings, the dollars, the ticket prices," Johnson said. "I want the kids to look at me and think, 'He didn't throw his money away. He wasn't just a player to be used by white owners.' I want them to see me as an example that black Americans can make a lot of money without touching a ball." Johnson wanted to be an NBA owner—for the PR and for the money.

Before Red Auerbach was born, his father ran a little restaurant across from Radio City Music Hall in Manhattan. The owners of the building offered to sell the entire place to Hyman Auerbach for the bargain-basement price of $11,000, but the cautious Russian immigrant turned it down and eventually became a dry cleaner in Brooklyn. The senior Auerbach didn't want to risk a sure thing, albeit a modestly profitable enterprise, for the great unknown. Years later, after the New York City real estate boom, Hyman's son Arnold would muse, "Imagine how much that building would be worth today." He relentlessly teased his dad about that shortsighted moment.

If we are doomed always to repeat the mistakes of our parents, then Auerbach is a dramatic case in point. As one Boston Celtic owner blurred into another—as Marvin Kratter sold to Ballantine Breweries, sold to E. E. Erdman, sold to Investors Funding Corporation, sold to Bob Schmertz, sold to Irv Levin, sold to John Y. Brown, sold to Mangurian—Auerbach stood curiously on the sidelines from an investment point of view. This smart Brooklyn hustler, this managerial intimidator who had nickeled and dimed Celtic players in contractual negotiations for years, was not brave or wise enough to nose in on a piece of the Celtic action. "For years, I know Red had plenty of opportunities to own part of the team and never would," Irv Levin said. "They [the Gaston ownership] gave Red a contract for $250,000 lifetime, but that team was worth more than $100 million and three owners made a fortune from that public sale. The feeling at the time was that the team is nothing without Red. The stock deal would never have gone through if Red said the word. I was shocked that Red didn't get a piece. I mean, 10 percent and he's got $10 million. If I was closer to him, I would've called him and said, 'You schmuck, why didn't you get in there?' It was all his sweat, and those guys just cashed in."

Once, Auerbach actually owned a piece of the Celtics. Years would go by when Walter Brown still owed Auerbach half his salary, and Auerbach would just let it go. Auerbach knew he would get his money. He figured the aging Brown would leave him part of the team. When Brown died in 1964, however, he had not yet signed the papers that were drawn up giving Auerbach a minority partnership. Brown's widow, a generous woman, honored the agreement anyway. For a few brief months, Auerbach was part-owner of his Celtics. Yet he sold his share almost immediately as part of the transfer to Marvin Kratter and National Equities in 1965. Auerbach was clearly more comfortable with a well-defined employee-employer relationship, rolling his eyes and complaining quietly off the record, behind his boss's back. He took the $250,000 per year from Cohen because it was guaranteed for his lifetime and that of his wife, Dorothy. He took the sure thing, the tailor shop in Brooklyn over the building across the street from Radio City.

"After I had a piece of the Celtics and sold it, I wasn't interested in ownership anymore," Auerbach said. "I didn't like the way the salaries were escalating and the power of the Players Association. I didn't want to take my life savings and put it into that. I was too busy running the thing." Auerbach, like Mangurian and John Y. Brown, was unable to accept the notion that a pro league could succeed once its athletes earned more than its coaches or its presidents. He was, in more ways than he would like to admit, philosophically close to the very owners with whom he had waged his clandestine wars.

Traditionally, Auerbach has put down owners in public only after they have sold the team. That is a large part of his survival instinct, and that attitude has kept him associated with the same franchise longer than any other coach, official, or owner in the business. He continues to complain about men like Mangurian and John Y. Brown, about the faceless owners before them and after Walter Brown. Not surprisingly, again, he has nothing but wonderful things to say about the current Gaston-Dupee-Cohen triumvirate.

"I always resented when a guy would say, 'Well, so and so bought this team for $200 million,'" Auerbach said. "I don't care if he's worth $2 billion. The question is how much he's willing to spend.

"Mangurian, I liked him. Only the team was like his horses. Everything was for sale. These guys [Gaston et al.], from the very get-go, were not penny pinchers, they are concerned with people. They're the kind of owners you dream of having. They're fans. They're knowledgeable. They're not afraid of spending money. They established something for Johnny Most. They didn't have to do that. Dr. Thomas Silva [the Celtics' team physician], who's retired, they established something. They didn't have to do that."

The current regime, it could be noted, did nothing for Dennis

Johnson, Jimmy Rodgers, or K. C. Jones. But Auerbach will not get into this just yet. He will have to be approached about this subject after the next sale or after his official retirement. His habit of cozying up to whoever happens to be in power traditionally produced a blanket endorsement. In the past, his support even extended into the financial realm. While he was bargaining and intimidating his players out of a few thousand dollars during contract negotiations, Auerbach was more than willing to help subsidize ownership out of his own pocket. He clearly had a respect for power and authority that went beyond the call of duty. During the dark financial days after Brown's death, when the team was being guided ineptly by an absentee Ballantine administrator in New York, Auerbach would lay out his own money to keep the team afloat, or airborne toward its next road game. He paid a $3,000 team phone bill once, and laid out an $8,000 advance on a road trip.

Despite all the mismanagement, the Celtics kept growing in value with or without Auerbach's investments. From the estimated $10,000 that Walter Brown spent on his Celtics in 1946 to the pro-rated $120 million that Gaston, Dupee, and Cohen valued the team at their stock sale in 1986, the Celtics had increased in value more than 1 million percent in forty years. The owners came and went, they whined about player salaries and small arenas. But not a single one took a bath with this team. They just wished they had become a little richer.

Chapter 13

Changing of the Guards

O N FRIDAY, October 5, 1990, the city of Boston awaited the start of the American League Championship Series. The Oakland Athletics were in town to play the beloved Red Sox, the cursed Red Sox, the team guaranteed to break Boston's heart. Boston was excited and hopeful, yet the usual feelings of dread were just as pervasive. The city of trolley-car transit and cobblestone streets sensed unhappy history about to repeat itself.

Similar fears, unrelated to Dave Stewart's arm or Jose Canseco's bat, stirred inside several young men that very day in the sunny, leafy suburb of Brookline. Here, on the private campus of Hellenic College, the Celtics were holding their first official day of training camp. Reggie Lewis, Brian Shaw, Kevin Gamble, and Dee Brown were young Boston Celtics, and each already had tasted the harsh treatment reserved for black players on the world's most famous basketball team. Mixed with the anticipation of a new season, a fresh start, they had reason to wonder if the worst was still to come.

Media day at NBA training camp across the country is traditionally a good-natured session of introduction and reacquaintance, with all eyes on the lunch buffet. Not this year. This October, the Celtics were standing at the NBA crossroads. Their hopes of regaining prominence rested with an unpredictable, largely untested band of athletes the organization wasn't quite certain were "true" Celtics. Suspicions ran high. Not since the late seventies, the days of Wicks and Rowe, were as many black Celtics at once under inspection and siege.

Inside the boxlike gym at Hellenic, Robert Parish was the first veteran Celtic to venture outside the locker room in his freshly pressed 00 uniform, white with green trim. Less than ten steps beyond the door, he was pounced on by members of the media, asked to comment on the summer trade rumors that had him rejoining K. C. Jones in Seattle. At thirty-seven, Parish was about to begin his eleventh season in Boston. He had followed the remarkable lead of Kareem Abdul-Jabbar, performing near peak at an age when many peers were flabbing out at the Legends game during All-Star weekend. Three-time champion, nine-time All-Star, and loyal, indispensable, uncontroversial Celtic, the Chief played hard and he played hurt.

The Celtics lost their grip on the Eastern Conference to the Pistons in the late eighties—Bird on bad heels, McHale on a broken foot, and Parish on badly sprained ankles. All three limped heroically up and down the court, grimacing prime-time. All for the glory of the green. Lost on Auerbach was the strain he'd put on these rare players by filling his bench with the likes of Greg Kite, Mark Acres, and Michael Smith. And while he would always remember the dangerous sacrifices of Bird and McHale, Auerbach would often forget to mention Parish. Predictably it was Parish, not the younger, more marketable McHale, who wound up on the trade rumor mill following the sobering first-round 1990 playoff loss to the Knicks.

One might have expected Parish to have long since earned safe Celtic passage to Retired Number immortality, along with Bird and McHale. A Louisiana native, he even went against the black Celtic grain: He dared to move his off-season home to Boston.

Somehow, the trade speculation amused Parish more than it

upset him. He wasn't the most loquacious Celtic, but he was one of the more observant. He had witnessed the unceremonious departure of all key black players from the championship teams. He had seen firsthand what had happened to Dennis Johnson.

Larry Bird once called Johnson the best player he'd ever played with. When Bird stole Isiah Thomas's inbounds pass in the 1987 conference finals, Johnson intuitively bolted for the basket for the winning layup. He thereby not only tied himself spiritually to Bird but demonstrated his canniness, his depth, his place in the winner's circle. In fourteen NBA seasons, Dennis Johnson's teams won three championships, reached the finals six times, and failed to make the playoffs only once.

As much as it made sound basketball sense to replace the thirty-six-year-old Johnson, the passing of his seven-year, two-title Boston career was coldly marked at Hellenic by six paragraphs on official Celtic stationery. It was stacked on a table with training camp stats under the heading: CELTICS, JOHNSON CLARIFY FUTURE. Johnson was quoted, "The Celtics have decided not to renew my contract, and to go with the guard corps they have. That frees me up to field other offers."

Left unsaid was that by waiting until October, the Celtics had only "clarified" Johnson's future by nudging him into retirement. "It was too late to market him, and that was quite a disservice to a young man who had done so much for them," said Fred Slaughter, his agent. Johnson, Slaughter revealed, was upset, but silenced by the vague suggestion of a future assistant coaching job.

At least, as Parish said, "everyone knows D. J. was a great player." Black Celtics usually wound up convenient scapegoats of management. Johnson, Parish, and Cedric Maxwell had become accustomed to finding themselves featured in accompanying photos next to game stories in the *Globe* whenever the Celtics lost. When the Celtics won, they would predict, most often correctly, the lead photo would be of a white player. They laughed about such treatment because it did no good to cry. They would've been called whiners. Parish thus realized a long time ago that he had no special immunity in Boston. "I'm still here," he said of the trade talk, his bemused smile suggesting the realistic black Celtic's attitude—here today, gone tomorrow.

The oldest active Celtic understood the city's social forces, which only recently had been introduced at gunpoint to the youngest and smallest. Brown, the six-one point guard, was selected in the first round by the Celtics in the June 1991 draft, despite Auerbach's huffing and puffing about Florida's Dwayne Schintzius, a white seven-foot center. Just what they needed, Auerbach apparently figured: an heir to Joe Kleine. The *Globe*'s Bob Ryan, no sociologist but an astute basketball mind, had witnessed an electric performance by Brown at a predraft audition camp in Orlando. Brown dominated several more heralded guards and won the slam dunk competition. Ryan raved in print about Brown. And Gavitt, getting positive if not passionate reports from his scouts, knew that the Celtics were in dire need of some quickness. No one except Auerbach, still accorded resident-genius status by the media, wanted Schintzius.

Back home in Jacksonville, Brown heard from friends what Bob McAdoo said most young players hear. "That's a racist city; you're not going to be happy there," Brown was told. He remained hopeful. Now, having been mistaken for a black bank robber on September 21 while sitting in his car reading his mail, having been forced to kneel facedown, humiliated, in the Wellesley street, Brown found himself on media day discussing possible litigation—not his impressive vertical leap, which would earn him a very visible Reebok Pumps contract and the slam dunk championship.

"It really hasn't been resolved yet," Brown said. "It's up to the lawyers." He said he and Jill Edmondson still planned to move to Wellesley. "I didn't want to after the incident, but my family and friends have pretty much encouraged me to live in Wellesley after all," he said. "They've said, 'You can't let anyone run you out of the community that way, or you'll be running all your life.' There have been a lot of letters written. People have sincerely said they're sorry." He was more fortunate than most. He knew it. He was an up-close, personal teammate of Larry Bird's. Asked if such remorse would have been evident if he were a stockbroker or postal worker, Brown said softly, "Probably not."

While heartfelt apologies poured in for Brown, Boston was expecting no less an act of contrition from the Jerome Stanley twins, Lewis and Shaw. There was no mistaken identity here. These were backcourt partners in crime against New England's basketball community, guilty of acts injurious to the Celtic green, pride, and mystique. Now that they were back, they would have to earn their right to be there.

Everyone knew Shaw was there only because a court ordered him to drag his jumper from Italy to New England. The Celtics had ignored his demand for a trade and tried to discredit his agent, Stanley. Out of options, Shaw accepted the situation and returned to Boston. With Rome no longer in the rearview mirror, he took the offensive reins from Dennis Johnson. "This is a business and certain things are going to happen," Shaw, a lean and muscular six-six, explained on media day. This was also Boston, where a black player could expect excoriation for allowing those "certain things" to happen. Shaw was thus anticipating the start of the season, if only to get it over with. "Today is a piece of cake compared to what's coming," he said of his dreaded reunion with Celtic loyalists. But the boos turned to cheers as soon as the Shaw-led offense began to perk.

Lewis already had experienced a sampling of the city's wrath. On Tuesday, August 22, he announced at a press conference in Boston that he would not commit to the Celtics following the expiration of his current contract. He was merely following Stanley's lead. The agent had said two weeks before that negotiations were severed. As the contract still had another year remaining, this was an obvious tactic, commonly used in the era of unrestricted free agency. While it made for tiresome reading, there was nothing radical about it. This process was typically used to enforce one's leverage. It was the equivalent tactic, the other extreme, of Auerbach nailing a figure to a contract and asking his players, "Where else you gonna go?" It was the media's job to report these preemptive strikes in broader context.

The Lewis story naturally made headlines in the Wednesday Boston papers. What went unreported, however, was the Tuesday meeting, a couple of hours after Lewis's conference, at which Stanley, Jan Volk, and Dave Gavitt put the finishing touches on a five-year, $16.5 million extension. Wednesday, at press conference number two announcing the contract, Lewis claimed he didn't know Stanley was about to meet with the Celtics when he spoke his piece. Whatever the truthful order of events, Stanley's self-ascribed "thermonuclear war" plan was an unmitigated success. Lewis was a rich man.

"You're turning the hostility up," Gavitt had told Stanley before requesting the meeting at which their differences melted. It was, in the final analysis, smart business by both sides. Gavitt, who'd been extracting far larger sums from television networks as Big East commissioner, understood that. "I don't begrudge any player going after the best deal he can get," Gavitt said later. "It's a competitive market."

This contemporary, realistic posture was anathema to those who for decades had bowed and begrudged pennies in the presence of Auerbach. Writing on Thursday, August 23, in the *Globe*, Will McDonough attacked Lewis and Stanley as if they'd just beaten the rap for triple homicide. Condescendingly referring to them as "Reggie and Jerome," McDonough expressed thinly veiled horror that a couple of black men could wield such power over the Celtic establishment. "Street-smart city slickers who hustled the Celtics with a con game," he called them. Agents like Bob Woolf traditionally took all the Auerbachian heat for escalating the dollar wars for Bird and John Havlicek. This time, there was no distinction made between agent and client.

"Lewis, who built a reputation around here as a nice young man, does not carry the same persona anymore," McDonough announced. McDonough concluded this shameful piece by relating the tearful saga of a disillusioned friend, Boston developer Joe Corcoran, who claimed his teenage son, on account of Reggie Lewis, didn't want to watch the Celtics anymore. "Here was this smiling, likable young man, acting with such arrogance," McDonough quoted Corcoran. Naturally, there was no mention that Lewis would soon be earning roughly half of Bird's salary for the 1991–92 season.

Back at Hellenic College on media day, Lewis tried to make some sense of the attack. He couldn't. "I think, especially with the black players, a lot of people just see you as a player and not as an individual," he said. Lewis already had defended his contract maneuverings to the masses. Now he retreated to the top row of the wooden bleachers with a plate of chicken and salad. "We have needs, families, just like everyone else," he said. "It's no different for us than it is for Larry and Kevin. But sometimes you're made to feel like it should be. You're looked at one-dimensionally.

"I've been around Boston long enough to have seen a number of the Celtics redo their contracts. I can't remember anyone being accused of being the bad guy in the media they made me out to be: 'I used to be such a nice guy. I ruined my reputation in this town.' Some of the writers around here have to learn the difference between business and loyalty. You have loyalty after taking care of business."

Kevin Gamble eavesdropped while picking at his plate a foot to the right of Lewis. This was nouveau cuisine for thought. Just a couple of days before, Gamble had reluctantly signed a one-year, take-it-or-leave-it contract for $375,000. This didn't seem terribly severe for a player who averaged 5.1 points in fourteen minutes of playing time per game in 1989–90. But the central issue, as far as Gamble was concerned, wasn't what he'd done; it was getting a fair opportunity to do more.

A stocky six-five big guard or small forward, Gamble was drafted by Portland on the third round out of Iowa in 1987 and cut after nine games. He drifted to the Continental Basketball Association, then to a pro league in the Philippines and back to the CBA, which he led in scoring, before the Celtics signed him halfway through the 1988–89 season. After Gamble spent most of his time on the bench, watching others inadequately fill the position vacated by the injured Bird, Jimmy Rodgers inserted Gamble into the big guard position for the final six games of the regular season. Lewis, two inches taller, shifted to small forward. Gamble, a slashing driver with an above-average jump shot, was a revelation, averaging 22.8 points on 60 percent shooting, plus 5 rebounds and 5 assists. No one was quite ready to trade Bird, but Gamble figured he'd earned his place for the following season. He had, but that place was in the middle of a training-camp logjam for minutes, along with fading veteran Jim Paxson and disappointing number one draft pick Michael Smith.

Gamble was an overachieving black player who was struggling for time with two underachieving whites, and that was not lost on his agent, Ron Grinker, who wondered how it would have been for Gamble if he were white like Jeff Judkins, a rookie out of Utah he represented in 1978. "The year he was a rookie, Judkins had some very good games and looked like he would have a very good career there," Grinker said. "They hailed him as the 'next Havlicek.' The buildup was unbelievable, probably hurt the guy." The following year, Bird's rookie season, Judkins played less, making it easier for his wife to decide she didn't like the Northeast. He asked to be sent home to Utah. "The Celtics practically begged me to talk him out of it," Grinker said. "If Gamble had been white, they would have proclaimed him the next Havlicek, too."

There was no media day crowd for Gamble to charm. He posed for his team photo, had a couple of isolated chats with reporters, and watched from the bleachers. He noticed Jim Paxson was still around, despite word the Celtics were going to buy out his hefty contract. "Just let me play," Gamble said. "That's all I ask."

Lewis nodded in agreement. "I know how good Kevin is because

I go up against him every day in practice," he said. "He just needs the minutes. I don't know why he hasn't gotten them."

Grinker hoped Chris Ford, the new coach, would eventually realize what was obvious to most people outside of Boston—that the Celtics were best off with Bird at power forward, where he would avoid quicker opponents on defense, with McHale coming off the bench, and with Gamble and Lewis interchangeable at big guard and small forward. It would make the Celtics more versatile and potent in their projected up-tempo style. Gamble, Grinker was sure, would make the best of his chance. His contract would expire in June 1991, and he would be an unrestricted free agent, ready to shop himself to the highest bidder.

"Of course," Grinker said, "that's when they'll start talking about Celtic loyalty and all that."

It turned out that Dave Gavitt's first significant accomplishment as Celtic senior executive vice president, aside from selecting Dee Brown in the draft instead of Dwayne Schintzius, was to break from Celtic front-office policy and make peace with Jerome Stanley. The August contract extension for Reggie Lewis paved the way for Brian Shaw's peaceful return the following month. "Gavitt came in and disarmed me," Stanley said. "I like the man."

At the same time, Gavitt began the far more difficult task of attempting to "bring the Celtics into the twentieth century" before the start of the twenty-first. For public consumption, this meant modernizing facilities and replacing aged equipment. Gavitt was stunned at how primitive the Celtic operation was. He ordered a paint job for Hellenic, sofas, video equipment, new weights, better lighting, and additional training space. The Celtics, he discovered, had been without a serious weight training program and a nutritionist. Who knew what effect all this had had on their aging veterans?

Privately, Gavitt tried to rework the ancient personnel circuitry laid years ago by Auerbach. He began installing a program to deal efficiently with the NBA of the nineties. This was no simple chore.

Many of Auerbach's loyal, programmed soldiers still manned the front lines. There were exceptions, like the bright and principled public relations director, Jeff Twiss. But the operational laws, the blueprints, were still written on Auerbach's scrolls.

"Gavitt is probably saying, 'This is no way to run a team,'" said New Jersey Nets coach Bill Fitch, who nearly a decade earlier gave up his Celtic crusade in semi-disgust. "My guess is that Gavitt is probably up to his eyes in bullshit."

Gavitt discovered the Celtics had no full-time community liaison, which was a new priority of David Stern's. He called Alan Cohen and said he wanted to hire former NBA official Ken Hudson as the Celtic vice president of community affairs. Already filling that position for the Celtic-owned station, WEEI, the fifty-one-year-old Hudson became the first black in the higher administration. But Hudson was only the second black on the entire Celtic front office staff of forty-three, excluding M. L. Carr, phantom scout. "It shocks people," Hudson said, describing the reactions of those who ask what he does. "They're thinking, 'This guy's a VP with the Celtics? The Celtics can't find any black players and they have a black VP?'"

At one of their first meetings, Gavitt casually mentioned to Hudson, "You don't see black kids around town wearing Celtic jackets." Gavitt spotted plenty of Laker, Bull, Sixer and Georgetown jackets. Operating the Big East out of Providence, Gavitt had no way of knowing that to the average black teenager in Boston, a Celtic jacket ranked last in the NBA jacket ratings. Hudson was the creator of the legendary high school tournament, the Boston Shootout, donating profits to the Roxbury chapter of the Boston Boys and Girls Clubs, and had worked in Boston's black community for more than twenty years. He had not accepted the job to fill a quota. He was honest with his new boss. "The perception is that the Celtics are a white person's team," he said.

One had to look no further than the club's 1990–91 media guide to understand why. Of the six people featured on the cover, five were white—cartoon sketches of Gavitt, Auerbach, and Chris Ford backed by the front line of Bird, McHale, and Parish. Sprinkled throughout the book were photos of past and present Celtics. There were several of Bird but none of Parish, other than his biographical insert. There were action snapshots of Bob Cousy, Tom Heinsohn, Dave Cowens, and John Havlicek, and of the dynasty's black Celtics—Bill Russell, Satch Sanders, and Sam and K. C. Jones. The one black from the three-championship 1980s pictured in action was M. L. Carr. There were no photos of Jo Jo White, Cedric Maxwell, and Paul Silas. There was, however, a full-page shot of Danny Ainge and a one-third-page shot of Bill Walton with his first raised high on the Celtic bench. The one shot of a bench huddle starred Joe Kleine waving a towel, M. L. style. Under the page heading THE TRADITION was a four-photo spread, including Chris Ford ducking behind a double screen set by Bird and Rick Robey. Opposite this was the only advertisement in the book featuring a Celtic. Kleine, the uncuttable reserve center, was paid to let New England know he enjoyed Poland Spring water "at home and at courtside."

It was one thing to sell Larry Bird and Kevin McHale, Ken Hudson knew. These were the franchise superstars, regardless of color. But too many other marketing subtleties, conscious or not, were sending a powerfully negative message to the black community. He couldn't help but notice them. During the summer, for instance, one of the surprises of rookie camp was Eric McArthur, a six-six free agent forward out of Cal–Santa Barbara. According to Ron Grinker, McArthur, a black player, impressed Ford and his staff so much that they not only invited him to the veterans' camp but guaranteed him $75,000. Others, Ken Hudson among them, liked McArthur's athleticism but were unimpressed by his shooting and ball-handling skills. They didn't believe he would survive very long at the veterans' camp, and they were right. Eric McArthur was the first player cut.

"The coaches talk the kid up to the press, then comes the veteran camp and he's cut and you keep the two Yugoslavs [Stojan Vrankovic and Aleksandar Dordevic]," Hudson said. "I said to Chris, 'Look, I saw McArthur. I know what he could or couldn't do. But what is the message you're sending to the black community?'"

The same question could be asked of Ford's choice of assistant coaches. K. C. Jones may have been the head coach for half of the eighties, but the Celtics didn't put a black coach anywhere on the bench after he was replaced by Jimmy Rodgers. Ford's ascension to head coach and the departure of Lanny Van Eman left two assistant vacancies. Ford hastily filled both with whites. He hired former Los Angeles Clipper head coach Don Casey as his chief assistant. He promoted twenty-eight-year-old Jon Jennings, a former student-manager for Auerbach buddy Bob Knight at Indiana University, a video coordinator for the Celtics since 1986.

Assuming the role of organizational conscience, Hudson again asked Ford, "What are people supposed to think, that the Celtics cannot find one black man to be an assistant coach?" One was right in front of them. With the decision not to return Dennis Johnson to the backcourt came an obvious solution to two thorny issues. The Celtics could solve the black assistant problem while rewarding Johnson for his seven-year run as the brains and guts of the back-court. "His great defensive play and leadership were major reasons why we were so successful in the 1980s," Auerbach said in the media day statement. Given that, who better to work as an assistant with the young guards than Dennis Johnson?

"It would've been great to have him around as a coach, or a play-er-coach," Reggie Lewis said one early December night at Boston Garden before a game against the Denver Nuggets. "Everybody could relate to D. J., young and old. He was that bridge. He was the one veteran who would even listen to our music. The other guys say, 'Get that crap out of here.' D. J. would say, 'Let's see what it's like.' Personally, I think everyone here misses him." Ultimately, Johnson wasn't hired for 1990–91, Fred Slaughter believed, because Ford felt he might exert *too* great an influence on players such as Lewis and Brian Shaw.

There had been other qualified black candidates—Tiny Archibald, Ford's former backcourt running mate on the 1981 Celtic champions, for one. Archibald, after three years of assistant coaching at the University of Georgia and at Texas–El Paso, had returned to his native New York City and completed a master's degree in education at Fordham University. He was working nights toward his Ph.D. while spending his afternoons coordinating athletic programs and providing counseling at schools and homeless shelters.

When he was inducted into basketball's Hall of Fame on May 13, 1991, Archibald arranged for three busloads of schoolchildren and homeless men to make the trip with him to Springfield, Massachusetts, for the ceremony. Some of these homeless men he'd grown up with. He also invited a group from Boston's Roxbury Boys Club, where he'd donated time during his Celtic days.

For all this special man was accomplishing, however, Archibald still had basketball in his blood. He wanted to coach. "I would like to be an assistant coach in the NBA," he said. "But I don't have the connections and the network. It's a small fraternity." Very small for blacks.

How could the NBA afford not to retain men such as Archibald and Dennis Johnson, among the canniest at their craft? Ford, more than anyone else in the Celtic organization, should have appreciated their position. Like Johnson, Ford had come to the Celtics in midcareer. But when Ford retired before the 1982–83 season, people in the Boston area couldn't wait to employ him. When Johnny Most was sidelined by illness, Ford immediately joined the WRKO Celtic broadcast team. By the end of the season, he had assistant coaching offers from Gary Williams at Boston College and K. C. Jones with the Celtics. Dennis Johnson's experience was quite different. During the summer of 1990, when he was very available for any suggested career change, Johnson was passed over for coaching *and* broadcasting openings.

Institutionalized racism was insidiously entrenched, Ken Hudson believed, but black players also needed to be less accepting of these conditions. They needed to follow the lead of groundbreakers like

Julius Erving and Magic Johnson, who forced the sport to view them as more than mere showmen. Hudson had seen too much passivity, he thought. Too much acceptance of the white norms. Having left Boston to work for Coca Cola in Atlanta from 1987 to 1989, Hudson immediately familiarized himself with local basketball circles and was disturbed by what people were whispering about one of the Hawk star players. Without formal introduction, he called the player and asked that they meet for lunch.

"The word is out that you're playing with drugs," Hudson said after a while.

"I know what people are saying," the player said. "Believe me, it's not true."

The player explained that his sometimes erratic behavior had to do with depression resulting from the overwhelming loneliness of being far from home. The fast NBA scene frightened him, he didn't know whom he could trust, and he had been afraid to ask for help. Hudson challenged the player to do something about it. "Don't let people destroy your reputation with lies," Hudson said. He helped arrange for counseling, and by the following season, the player's career appeared to Hudson to be refocused.

Hudson had been close to many of the Celtics, black and white, since the mid-sixties. The alienation of black players in Boston—from Bill Russell to Cedric Maxwell—had always troubled him. Some of them, he thought, had made little or no effort to interact with the surrounding community because of preconceptions. With direction, this new group of players could significantly help themselves by accepting greater responsibility. Early in the season, Hudson noticed that Lewis, Shaw, Gamble, and Brown already had formed a natural clique. He made a point of broaching the subject with them. "That's what people start seeing," he said. "The problem starts all over again. I want these guys perceived as Celtics, not 'black Celtics.'"

Socially integrating the players would not be easy. Beyond the cultural differences, veteran players such as Bird and Parish were disinterested in the NBA "scene" and tended to distance themselves from the pack. Hudson instead looked to Kevin McHale to bridge the gap. Good-natured, open, and relaxed, from the Democratic state of Minnesota and Bob Dylan's hometown of Hibbing, McHale had always related well to black players. He loved free spirits like Maxwell and had developed close friendships with blacks on other teams—Charles Barkley, to name one.

For all of his career, McHale dressed on the opposite side of the Celtic locker room from Bird. Despite enormous respect for each other's ability, they were not friends. Bird, all-powerful in Boston, had often issued decrees against McHale from his throne: McHale didn't hustle enough, didn't dedicate himself enough, shouldn't be playing on a bad foot if he can only give 50 percent. "They hate each other, go to the bank on that," one Celtic insider insisted. Here were two white stars going at each other, yet their positioning seemed symbolic not only of their social stature within the team, but of a locker room division between races.

Despite a reputation as one who related well with blacks, Bird had for years been surrounded in the locker room by other white Celtics like Rick Robey, Jeff Judkins, Scott Wedman, Jerry Sichting, and Danny Ainge. McHale was ensconced in the opposite corner, wedged among Maxwell, Parish, and Dennis Johnson. The 1990–91 locker room lineup had yet another all-Caucasian strip: Bird, his good friend Joe Kleine, Michael Smith, and Dave Popson were at one end of the room; along the wall across the room were Shaw, Gamble, Lewis, Ed Pinckney, and Parish, with McHale in his corner, Dee Brown to his right, and the rookie Stojan Vrankovic, another alienated soul, to the right of Brown in D. J.'s old space.

"Keep your foot in the door with those three or four guys," Hudson told McHale. "You be the one." Hudson asked McHale to be seen on the town, out to dinner, with Kevin Gamble or Dee Brown. He asked him to spend time on the road with Lewis and Shaw. To the young black players, Hudson said, "You can play ten or twelve years, then live here the rest of your life." He suggested increased visibility in the black community and across Boston's rigid racial lines. The black players might even dare enter the bastion of the white working class, he suggested. They might want to go to some hockey games, get to know a few gap-toothed Bruins.

Years ago, in the mid-sixties, Hudson had accepted a public relations job in Boston with Gulf Oil and confronted these same classic divisions. He found himself shuttling between lily-white boardrooms and inner-city playgrounds. He related in both places. He liked to tell of the time *Globe* writer Dan Shaughnessy came to cover the Shootout and "misplaced" his wallet. Hudson turned to a couple of kids and said "Man here lost his wallet." There were denials all around, but a half hour later, the wallet reappeared. "How'd you do that?" Shaughnessy asked Hudson.

It never occurred then to Hudson that a white volunteer, a Celtic legend named Dave Cowens, would have a more difficult time relating to black kids than a black Celtic. One year at the Shootout, the star of the team, high school senior Patrick Ewing, arrived an hour late for the first practice. Cowens was furious.

"You ever heard of Robert Parish?" Cowens asked the young Ewing.

"Yeah, sure," Ewing said.

"Well, what about Dave Cowens, you ever heard of him?"

"No," Ewing said.

Cowens said, "See, they forgot about me around here already. You show up late one more time, they'll play the Boston Shootout without Patrick Ewing and they'll forget about you, too." Ewing, Hudson recalled, was never late again. For Hudson, the moral of the story was that effort and courage could overcome unfamilarity and mistrust.

Short and stocky, Hudson made a point all his adult life of looking people squarely in the eye. As a child growing up in Pittsburgh, he recalled his father telling him, "Don't ever forget your blackness, but never forget the world is not made up so much of colors as it's made up of people." Those were, he eventually understood, the words of an ideologue. He still found the advice constructive.

In the early seventies, he became the NBA's first full-time black referee. Hudson found himself one night in a restaurant with Jake O'Donnell, a tough Irishman, the best ref in the game, who grew up an orphan. "I hope you don't take this the wrong way, but I've never engaged in a real conversation with a black person," O'Donnell told him. Hudson was more curious than offended. Thirty-odd years and not one meaningful conversation with a black? How could that be? "We talked until three or four in the morning," Hudson said, "and developed a real, close friendship. That's change."

With the Celtics, Hudson knew, it had always been tough to hurdle racial barriers while maintaining one's blackness. It was a self-destructive process on a team marketed for whites. Cedric Maxwell had been no radical, just someone who, as he put it, wouldn't avoid the "obvious." In the eyes of Celtic patriots, Maxwell was a cancer. Jo Jo White was a complainer. Bill Russell was an enigma. Only black players who smiled for the white folks could be embraced within the Celtic family and in Will McDonough's column. M. L. Carr, a corporate climber who promoted the Celtic Mystique at business lunches, seemed to be Boston's ideal black athlete. Even Carr occasionally was reminded that a social ladder existed, that many believed his place was no higher than a couple of steps from the bottom. "You should be on television, or back with the Celtics doing public relations," he would hear when he started the Carr Corporation.

This could all now change, Hudson was convinced, because the Celtics were no longer struggling for acceptance in Boston. The city had developed an addiction in the past decade, since Bird. The spell cast over Boston was too strong. The list for season tickets was too long. "Black basketball" would not offend the fans, as long as the Celtics were prepared to sell it. Jerome Stanley truly believed the new Celtic administration was ready to do just that. "Gavitt is the new wave," Stanley decided. "He'll let the team play a black game."

Hudson thought so, too. He said the days of pandering to the vocal majority were coming to an end. Gavitt would personally see to it. Hudson held the same sort of admiration and loyalty toward Gavitt that others, for years, had shown Auerbach. "Hiring Dave was like Walter Brown hiring Red forty years ago," Hudson said. "It's going to change because the top men want it changed. To me, there's a tremendous opportunity here to make a point."

But since affirmative action speaks louder than words, there was little practical evidence of this new, revolutionary attitude in Gavitt's debut. No one forced Chris Ford into hiring a black assistant coach. When Hudson brought the broadcasting situation to the fore by pointing out the sham of having no black announcers, Alan Cohen demanded an explanation from Jan Volk. Eleventh-hour feelers were floated to former players like Quinn Buckner and Norm Van Lier. Both were booked, Buckner to other networks and Van Lier to Richard Lapchick's Reebok-sponsored study of racism in Boston-area schools. It was too little and too late. The broadcasting team remained all white, as it would in 1991–92 when another white, marginal former Celtic, Jerry Sichting, replaced Doug Brown. The coaching staff remained the same.

One day following media day, the Celtics announced they were removing Jim Paxson from the active roster. Unlike Dennis Johnson, whose future had been "clarified," the Paxson move was generously transacted as "mutual agreement." The Celtics now had an all-black backcourt, leaving Bird and McHale as the only two substantial whites. Joe Kleine was once an undeserving first-round draft pick of Sacramento's, but he was at least a legitimate backup center, no Greg Kite. There were indications, finally, that the Celtics were going to cast themselves from the same mold as the 72 percent–black league. "So what happens?" Ron Grinker said. "They keep the big Yugoslav kid and Dave Popson."

Vrankovic, who played the previous season for Aris of Thessaloniki in Greece, was the Celtics' consolation prize after Dino Radja spurned them for Rome. Vrankovic was the veritable long-term project, but at twenty-seven, no young prospect. Popson couldn't even claim that paradoxical status. A twenty-six-year-old journeyman cut the previous year by the Celtics, his resume included stays in Albany with the CBA Patroons and Monaco, a team he could boast of leading in rebounding in 1987. Now he had a place in the Celtic locker room along Larry Bird Row. On opening night at Boston Garden, November 2, 1990, Vrankovic and Popson took the seats at the end of the Celtic bench reserved for white roster fillers. The new era at Boston Garden began with the old persistent racial balance—six whites, six blacks—still intact.

Chapter 14

The Long Goodbye

D AVE Gavitt was tired of the bureaucrat's life. At fifty-three, with his two sons graduated from college and into their own careers, he didn't need to maintain the family home in Rhode Island anymore. He was no longer motivated by his work as Big East commissioner, making huge sums of network money for Syracuse, St. John's, and the rest of the booming conference. Inside every old coach beats the heart of a mechanic with the undying passion to fix a broken machine. The man hailed in recent years as a marketing genius wanted the opportunity to rebuild a broken-down fast break.

The Boston media anointed Gavitt "Celtic CEO," but he wanted to sink his teeth into more than the bottom line, which was Cohen's territory. In his first weeks on the job, Gavitt listened to the incumbent Celtic brain trust, studied films of the 1989–90 team, and picked the brains of every pro basketball contact he had. After a while, he decided that Boston had suffered a collective atrophy of its basketball senses. It was the only city in America that failed to understand that the quick had inherited the hardwood. "The conventional wisdom of this town, when I took this job, was that our problems were caused by the age of Bird, McHale, and Parish," Gavitt said. "After about a month, I got my nose into it and found this quite humorous.

"When you match Larry, Kevin, and Robert relative to people who play their positions, they're fine. We broke down everywhere else. People were penetrating at will. We weren't able to put any pressure on the ball. We never triggered transition offense. You'd see Larry backing the ball in on every crucial possession on the left side. That's not his game. You won't remember him posting up. You'll remember him hitting the open man, coming off the screen, coming down on the break and touch-passing to some guy on the side."

The Celtics were philosophically, not physiologically, outdated. They were stuck in some romantic fantasy with Bird in the role of white knight. If the Chicago Bulls hadn't yet won a championship with unstoppable Michael Jordan orchestrating an entire offense, then the Celtics certainly couldn't recapture one with the soon-to-be-thirty-four-years-old Bird. Healthy, he remained one of the true wizards of the sport. But Gavitt decided the Celtics could no longer treat Reggie Lewis and Brian Shaw as if they should feel honored merely playing on the same parquet floor with Bird. These players needed expanded roles. Bird needed to be downgraded from celestial presence to aging superstar.

This was going to take some doing. Bird was not as intuitively flexible as John Havlicek had been. NBA stars of Bird's generation, approaching global, rock-star status, weren't prepared for a deescalation of influence. More important, Bird's quotations in Boston were held in biblical esteem. With the mighty coalition of media and fan support, he was a capable back-room politician. He was also not above a public demonstration of rebellion. Early during Jimmy Rodgers's second season as head coach, Rodgers had the nerve to suggest that Bird reduce his field goal attempts. Bird responded in the next game by refusing to shoot. He made his point—in a fashion that would have labeled many lesser lights as spoiled brats. Rodgers backed off. It was quite clear who was in charge.

Proud and stubborn, Bird didn't want to hear that the Celtic post-up game was obsolete. Nothing, nobody, was obsolete. He clung to former teammates and to old styles like a boy to his tattered teddy bear. To Bird, the old players were always best. Wilt Chamberlain was better than the players from Bird's own generation. Bird's own generation was better than these spry whippersnappers. He didn't believe the Celtics were desperately in need of a young blood transfusion. "I'll take the talent of the old players over the new any day," he coldly said on media day. Asked about the departure of Dennis Johnson, he snapped, "Personally, I think if D. J. were still here, he'd beat out Brian Shaw and Dee Brown. He'd still be starting. That's probably why they didn't sign him."

When he was promoted to head coach, Chris Ford was informed by Gavitt that it was time to begin weaning the Celtics from the Bird lifeline. "Probably the groundwork should've been laid a few years ago," Gavitt said, in an unusually frank, private interview. On November 17, the day after the Celtics opened their exhibition season by hammering the NBA champion Pistons in Hartford, Alan Cohen got a telephone progress report in his New York office from Gavitt. They were two kids with a new toy, a better teddy bear. "We ran all night. Chris put in this play where they clear out for Reggie along the baseline," Cohen raved to a visitor. "Things are going to be very different this year. We're going to let these young kids play." Would Bird accept this? Cohen winked. "Ford's a tough guy, and he's got Dave's support. Just watch."

The day following the Piston exhibition, a still-skeptical Bird told reporters, "We always start out running, but it's only a matter of time before we'll be walking it up again." Ford recognized this as the moment of truth. If he was ever going to be a successful NBA coach, he now had to impose his will on Bird. That day at practice, he called the team together. He repeated Bird's quotes. "Anyone who doesn't think we're going to run all season is badly mistaken," he said. "Anybody who doesn't like it can get the fuck out of here right now." He looked over at Bird. "Do we understand each other, Larry?"

Stunned, Bird shot back, "Fuck you, Doc," addressing Ford by the nickname he'd earned years before as a player for windmilling the ball in the face of Dr. J., Julius Erving. The message got through to Bird. Later in the season, Bird told *USA Today*'s Peter Vecsey, "After we finished blowin' smoke, we got together by ourselves for five minutes and settled the whole thing. I told him, 'You tell me what to do, and I'll do it. There'll be no second guessing.'"

What emerged for the first half of the season was a wonderfully weird marriage of generations that looked as if it had been co-produced by the diverse coaching brains of Paul Westhead and Hubie Brown. After two lopsided losses in the first six games, Ford realized he couldn't hide Michael Smith in the starting lineup and sent him to the bench where he belonged. Here, finally, was Kevin Gamble's chance at small forward, with Bird moving to power for-ward—just the way Ron Grinker envisioned. Compared to the old Celtic brain trust, the agent looked like Nostradamus. Gamble was a perfect fit into the up-tempo scheme designed to create high-per-centage shots. Gamble was perhaps the best at knocking them down, shooting at a 60 percent clip. In one enlightening stretch, he made 91 of 130 shots, 70 percent. In a game at New York on Febru-ary 7, he took 20 shots and made 16. "The missing ingredient," as Ford called him, was nevertheless still making less than half of Joe Kleine's $875,000.

Three-fifths of the starting lineup, under the emerging leader-ship of Brian Shaw, was now skilled and speedy. Four-fifths was black. Dee Brown, proving to be a precocious rookie and the steal of the draft, was the quickest Celtic of all, a perfect jumpstart off the bench. Bird loved him. From the day Gamble was inserted, the Celtics won twenty-five of their next twenty-eight games, commenc-ing a season-long domination of the Atlantic Division. As they contended for the best record and top playoff seed in the Eastern Conference, experts rated them serious title material while casting a wary eye at their bench. Smith, Popson, and Vrankovic, one-quarter of the team, were liabilities, expensive tokens, and Joe Kleine wasn't much better.

Much of the time, Ford used a seven-man rotation. Six of these players, Kleine being the exception, were averaging between 12 and 20 points. Bird, though still leading the team in nearly every statistical category, was averaging slightly under 20 points for the first time in his career. The network highlight films were again filled with magnificent Bird touch passes on the break, or flicked inside to Parish, pick-and-rolling from a half-court set. Bird was no longer camping out in isolation on the left side, making things easy for the defensive geniuses of the league like Dennis Rodman. He wasn't burdening old legs that couldn't handle the weight or the scoring load. He left the infiltration of opposing defenses to Shaw, to Lewis, to the thin but muscular and beautifully proportioned legs that blew like breezes past opponents.

The young players sensed that this was now their team, too. Bird was no longer the center of the Celtic universe. Ford pulled Brown and Shaw aside at one practice and told them, "You push the ball up the floor and don't worry about the old guys. If they don't run with you, they won't get the ball because you're up the court and they're not."

Just weeks after being viewed with suspicion in Boston, these young, black Celtics were fast breaking through the color barrier and onto a national stage. In November, Lewis was asked by Reebok to market a basketball shoe in his own national commercial. By December, he was throwing down Reverse Jams on screens across America. One didn't have to be a media-certified superstar to rate this kind of endorsement from Madison Avenue anymore. It helped if you could dunk, leap high in expensive sneakers. Reggie Miller in Indiana and Gerald Wilkins in New York were other examples of second-tier NBA players, even black players, making hay with long hang times and the NBA marketing explosion. But the sight of a black man in Celtic green in living, commercial color was strange. Stranger still was a Celtic not only participating in but winning the slam dunk competition during All-Star weekend. Brown, with long arms and large hands that allowed him to hold a basketball as if it were a grapefruit, theatrically pumped up his Reeboks before every jump at McHale's suggestion, then stole the show by dunking one ball with one hand, knocking in another from the back of the rim with the other. By February 1991, Brown, too, had his own Reebok commercial. His agent in Chicago, Steve Zucker, had all kinds of endorsement offers on his desk.

Bird had once dominated the 3-point shooting competition, an artificial event held for the benefit of sponsor American Airlines and a few curious fans. He had endorsed sneakers, soda, his own restaurant. But now, with Brown, there was a fuss in Boston, an explosion of puritanism. Red Auerbach's Celtics were supposed to be above this form of tasteless commercialism. They were supposed to be basketball players, not high-wire acts. Dee Brown pumping up his sneakers on national TV? What was next? An exploding scoreboard for Boston Garden? Hip-shaking Celtic Girls? Probably not. Hudson defended Brown to his detractors. This was all part of the Celtics letting down their hair and adding some badly needed funk to their portfolio. Inner-city Boston would eventually notice. "Red's attitude was always, 'We don't need you, you need us,'" Hudson said. "Give 'em a winner, that's all. The difference between Dave and Red is like the difference between [former NBA commissioner] Walter Kennedy and David Stern."

It began to look that way. "We're living in a different time, a different age," Gavitt said. "The needs are different." With their stunning success and the emergence of Lewis, Shaw, Gamble, and Brown, Gavitt appeared to have transformed the Celtics overnight to meet those needs. The bench was laden with undeserving whites, but the young runners and the three front-line veterans made Boston one of the league's most interesting teams in recent years.

The Celtics almost deserved all their network exposure.

They seemed to be getting through on the local level, too, if only by osmosis. There was no new community outreach program. Larry Bird was not going to walk the streets of Roxbury and introduce himself. But some black fans were starting to notice the flashy play of the black starters. "I see some changes," Lewis said of his Dorchester neighborhood. "They may not be Celtic fans, but they say they're Reggie Lewis fans. That's a start."

The turnaround had happened so much faster than expected. One day in November 1990, sitting behind the desk in his office, Gavitt said, "We've worked hard to get this team moving in a different direction. We're happy where we're headed, but we don't kid ourselves. We have a long way to go." By December, that distance had shrunk considerably. The Celtics were challenging Portland for the best record in the league. They were toying with opponents. When he happened to be in town, Auerbach blew his smoke rings and accepted all praise for the ingenious stroke of hiring Gavitt. It was as if Walter Brown had sent Gavitt his spiritual blessing from the Mystical Celtic Beyond. Gavitt's retooled machine hummed like it was right off the assembly line. There were smiles, and enough credit, to go all around.

Then lightning struck, a bolt of pain down the franchise's spinal cord. Larry Bird got hurt.

Before the 1990–91 season began in Boston, there had been talk of this ambitious palace coup. King Larry was to be deposed. From Cohen to Gavitt to new coach Chris Ford, there had come the blasphemous, realistic notion that it was time for the Celtics to stop planning their basketball lives around a hobbling thirty-three-year-old ex-superstar.

Yet somehow, by winter, the Celtics were desperately, impossibly, figuring out a way to keep Bird pinned together for the season and beyond. In the face of public pressure and some short-term success, the organization's resolve had flagged. The Legend wanted to live on, and the Celtics now wanted him to. What had happened to *the plan?*

On January 8, 1991, the Celtics left for New York and a game against the Knicks. Bird remained behind in Boston with severe pain in his lower back. He was listed, in standard NBA-ese, as "day to day." Bird's back, like his surgically corrected heels, had been gradually worsening. He suffered from a compressed nerve root resulting from a bulging disk, a swollen joint, and a tiny congenital opening of the spine. He had been wounded by too many minutes in too many seasons; by a too-white, too-shallow Boston bench that gave him little respite over a long, hard decade. Yet Bird played on, the embodiment of Boston Garden. Storied but crumbling.

For the moment, there didn't seem to be any cause for alarm. The Celtics reported that Bird was experiencing spasms. And the Bird-less Celtics took care of the Knicks, then returned home to beat Milwaukee and the Los Angeles Clippers. The revival was in full blossom. They were 29–5, with enough youth and verve to weather this crisis.

It was naive, however, to think a sudden, prolonged absence by Bird would not create major adjustment problems. He was still the Celtics' top scorer, their best defensive rebounder, and by far the best passing forward in history. Despite offseason plans, nobody had informed the Celtic guards to distribute the ball more democratically. They had had no time to learn life without Larry.

"You don't lose someone who does as many things as Larry and not feel it," Shaw said. Bird's input on the team, it turned out, really hadn't been reduced before his injury. Without this catalyst at forward, without the self-confidence that comes of winning titles in overheated buildings, and with the town practically daring them to be great on their own, the young Celtics slipped several notches. They lost to teams they should have routed, Bird or no Bird. They fell to Golden State at home. The New Jersey Nets, a pitiful team on the road and only slightly better at home, won in Boston Garden two nights later. There were four straight losses, six in seven games, and seven in ten.

The more the Celtics slumped, the more the media turned its focus away from the court and onto the mysterious condition of Bird. Bird wasn't talking. Gavitt, facing his first test of patience and tact, reacted in vintage Auerbach manner. Upset by a front office leak on Bird's injury in the first place, he told everyone to get lost. There would be no progress reports on Bird. His totalitarian gag order barred any Celtic employee from discussing Bird's back. Gavitt explained that he was trying to stay focused on basketball, but the result was that Bird again was set apart from the group. There were rules that only applied to him. Gavitt had drawn a line between the organization and the public for what appeared to be no good reason. In his first crisis, he had fallen back on the old, arrogant Celtic methods.

With the comfort of Bird suddenly an issue, Gavitt went out and leased a custom-made jet, like seven other successful NBA teams. Bird was able to lay flat while soaring thirty thousand feet in the air to far-flung places like Portland and Utah. Here again, the perception was: anything for Larry Bird. Privately, the young players wondered if the Celtics would have been arranging arrival and departure times so carefully had the injured party been Reggie Lewis or Brian Shaw.

The Celtics were 8–7 without Bird, then began winning big when he returned. They went to the West Coast and took four of five, even though Kevin McHale was down with an ankle sprain. They beat the Lakers at the Forum. They lost only at Phoenix, where Bird missed 18 of his 23 shots. "I thought they were all going in," he said reassuringly.

As Bird settled back into the lineup, he resumed calling the shots. The team was winning again, but the old dependence on Bird had been reinforced by his absence. There was now a sense that the Celtics could only go as far as Bird could carry them. And Bird, more than anyone, believed that.

Late in a Sunday afternoon game at the Garden against Portland, Bird forced a wild 3-point shot that missed and sealed a close Trail

Blazer victory. On an earlier Portland possession, Clyde Drexler had taken and hit a low-percentage jump shot. The announcers, Marv Albert and Mike Fratello, immediately pointed out that Drexler had gotten away with a terrible shot. Nothing, however, was mentioned when Bird badly misfired.

Near immunity from such criticism was part of Larry's legend. He'd earned much of it. As the white superstar of his generation, he had also received a generous benefit of the doubt. Questioning Bird certainly wasn't the popular thing to do in Boston. It took no less a star than Kevin McHale more than a year to finally admit that he (along with Jim Paxson) had anonymously ripped Bird for a quick trigger beyond the 3-point line during the 1989–90 season.

As Bird reassumed more and more control of the offense, more of these whispers emerged. There were other egos, younger and still developing, on the team now. The Celtics still comfortably led the Atlantic Division. They'd face no challenge there. With Isiah Thomas injured and Detroit slumping, Chicago was the most serious competition in the conference. Opponents, however, didn't worry the Celtics. Bird's back did. The sight of Bird stretched out on his stomach in front of the Celtic bench during a February 24 game in Indianapolis was frightening and would become all too familiar. It was enough to give all of Boston heartburn. *How's Bird? Will Bird hold up? They don't win without Bird!*

The young players quietly resented this. But when the issue of Bird's apparent autonomy with the ball was raised in the press, again anonymously, Chris Ford raged. He said it was nonsense. The point shouldn't even be addressed. Everyone knew Bird was one of the great team players of all time. In the *Globe*, Jackie MacMullan said the issue of Bird's shot selection was hardly new. Bird was Bird. She labeled it a "non-story."

While Bird's feelings were dwelt on, the thoughts and insecurities of the younger players were ignored again by the coaches and the media. They began to feel this wasn't so much their team after all. The perfect transitional season was prematurely finished. Expectations for another championship, which would have been Bird's fourth and likely his last, had been raised early. Now the organizational mindset appeared to have shifted. The team and the town held their breath with Bird's every move. Legends, prejudices, and ancient methodology would die hard. Maybe Bird needed these energetic black kids to pump some life into the team, common wisdom dictated. But any fool could see they needed him more than he needed them. The Celtics of the early nineties would still rise or fall with Larry Bird. Boston would still see him as its white knight on the horse.

"We hear it every day, over and over, the same questions about Larry," Dee Brown said the day before the Celtics' first-round playoff series against the Indiana Pacers. Even this exciting rookie, so much in awe of Bird, acknowledged the Bird hysteria with a sigh. More back spasms had sidelined Bird during the last two weeks of the season. The Celtics stumbled badly toward the playoffs, experiencing several embarrassing blowouts on the road. Now, with Bird's status unknown, the city feared a third straight first-round playoff dismissal. Bird, of course, wasn't talking about the playoffs or commenting on a *Globe* report that he'd decided to undergo back surgery following the season. At Hellenic College, while the Celtics made final preparations for the big Indiana series, a media contingent carefully observed Bird on the stationary bicycle. The reporters symbolically turned their backs on the other players, who were out on the practice floor. Most of the local writers, sensing Bird would not play, picked the Celtics to lose.

Bird was the story, the only story. Playing in obvious pain, he dueled Indiana's brash, streak-shooting Chuck Person to a draw through four games, setting up a fifth and decisive game in Boston. In the second quarter, diving for a loose ball, Bird slammed the right side of his face into the floor. He stayed down for several seconds. Few had seen his face collide with the parquet, and most in the building believed the back had finally given out. Bird left the floor and did not come out to start the second half. The Pacers and

Celtics struggled on in a close game. Five minutes into the third quarter, Bird returned to the bench. The Garden fans stood and cheered for three minutes. Despite warnings by their coach, Bob Hill, to expect this drama, the Pacers nervously glanced over their shoulders and were soon giving futile chase to a rejuvenated Bird, who was soaring against all odds for 17 second-half points, 7 rebounds, and 4 assists. Boston Garden was wild. The television cameras found Auerbach nodding with approval. The Celtic Mystique was at work again.

Ford, meanwhile, wasn't wasting any more time with offensive diversity. As reported by courtside observer Steve Bulpett in the *Boston Herald,* Ford intuitively knew how to script this latest Celtic fairy tale, even as the Pacers rallied late in the game.

"Get the ball to Larry," he screamed from the sideline.

"Post Larry."

"Larry, Larry, Larry!"

This was pro basketball's version of *Hoosiers:* The home state team against its most beloved player. The Celtics held on. The headline in the *Herald* the next morning was more to the point: LEGEND OF LARRY LIVES ON. The city was positively giddy over Bird. But with the arrival of the defending champion Detroit Pistons the following afternoon came this sobering reality: The Celtics had only survived one round against a team with the seventh-best record in the Eastern Conference, a franchise without a single playoff series victory in its history.

The Celtics were still a struggling team. Worse, their young players, particularly Brian Shaw and Kevin Gamble, seemed to be shrinking amid the clamor over Bird. At least Ford understood their plight. "I think all the Larry stuff and the questions about whether the young guys can win without him do affect them," he said. "But it's a Catch-22. Until they win without him, they're going to hear the questions."

They would not be answered in game one against Detroit. Bird could not play, and the Celtics lost handily. Half of the Garden faithful had picked up and left with four minutes still remaining and the Celtics down a doable dozen. No Bird this night. No miracle. As the game wheezed its final breaths, as the players began stepping in the direction of the exit ramp, there came a terrifying glimpse into a Bird-less future. The remaining fans booed.

"Would they have booed if Larry had been out there?" a smirking Brian Shaw said, repeating the question by a reporter. "What do you think?" He knew. Celtic fans never booed in the presence of Bird. With Bird out, the Celtics instantaneously were denied their privileged status. They could be treated like any other NBA team.

In the fifth game of a deadlocked series back in Boston, with Bird playing ineffectually, the Celtics were behind by 18 points in the third quarter. Not so much as one boo was heard. The Celtics rallied behind Dee Brown, Reggie Lewis, and Bird, only to lose this pivotal game when Bill Laimbeer buried three late jump shots. The defender, Bird, could not move fast enough to get a hand in the Detroit big man's face. The Celtics were one game from elimination, and Bird had reached the point where he could contribute little more than moral support.

In Boston and elsewhere, he was justifiably hailed for his courage. Less fanfare, however, was given to Isiah Thomas's heroism. Thomas was attempting to play through a multitude of painful injuries, including surgery on his shooting hand. But there seemed to be room for only one John Wayne in this series. "People keep talking about Bird, and rightly so," Piston assistant coach Brendan Malone said. "But our guy wasn't supposed to be even practicing until this week. Surgery on his hand. Pulled groin. Sprained ankle. There is nobody tougher than Isiah."

Weeks later, it was another veteran, Magic Johnson, who would play on badly stretched, swollen knees through the NBA finals. He would ice them for up to an hour after each game, limping about the locker room in obvious pain. Nobody seemed to notice. One martyred superstar, preferably from Boston, was enough per season.

It was Thomas, appropriately, who would finally put the Celtics to sleep in overtime of game six with several clutch plays, including a 3-point bank shot as the twenty-four-second clock expired. As in game five, the Celtics, now playing without Robert Parish and his badly sprained ankle, staged a valiant second-half comeback. The emerging Dee Brown played like a six-one Michael Jordan and Lewis sliced up the Piston defense. Brown had clearly moved ahead of Shaw, who rode the bench with fellow starter Gamble.

With Bird unable to assert himself on the defensive boards, with Detroit's Dennis Rodman, John Salley, and Vinnie Johnson climbing all over the glass, Ford did not have the luxury to play Gamble in what invariably became a slower, more physical half-court game. Gamble was never a physical player. He needed the quicker flow to get his shots, to shoot his 60 percent. This should not have been startling news, but Gamble was treated like some massive playoff flop. Quick substitutions ensured he'd never be a factor. Despite his fine season, Gamble averaged just 6 points and 1 rebound during the playoffs. One thing was certain: The Celtics would be armed with these numbers when contract time came. Bird's injury, the age of the front line, the inability to rebound and get the ball out on the break, and the second-round elimination were likely to come out of Gamble's next paychecks. Indeed, Gamble was unsigned through the end of the 1991 exhibition season, moving even Parish to state that his friend was being "nickeled and dimed" by the Celtics.

Similarly, Shaw's ill-timed slump probably resulted more from intramural pressure from Brown than from any opponent. The unusual circumstances surrounding Brown's rookie season—from facedown on the Wellesley street to high above the rim in Charlotte at the All-Star Game—had made him an electric entertainer, and a sympathetic one as well. When the *Herald* conducted a poll asking fans to vote on their preferred point guard starter, Brown won easily over Shaw.

Every time Shaw started slowly in the playoffs, Ford would go to Brown and stay with him. It was difficult to make an argument against Ford's strategy, or against Brown, but Ford might have rescued Shaw from his woes by playing him with Brown in the back-court and swinging Reggie Lewis to small forward. Of course, that would have meant reducing Bird's minutes. And right to the bitter end, it was Bird's call on when he played and for how long.

As game six progressed, Bird became an alarmingly paler ghost. His shooting was way off. He couldn't jump for rebounds. He couldn't defend. The Pistons, too, were staggering at the Auburn Hills Palace, desperately trying to avoid a return trip to Boston for game seven. One more quick defender to trap the Detroit guards, one more active body to reach for a rebound or a loose ball, one more healthy player in Bird's place might have made the difference. But Ford could not get himself to do the unthinkable—to tell Bird, even this lame and pitiable version, to sit down with a Celtic playoff series on the line.

Impossible. Ford used the same lineup for the final nineteen minutes of game six. Considering Bird's condition, this seemed an incredibly obstinate approach. To Ford, to Boston, a gimpy, bent-over Bird was still preferable to anyone else. He dared to be great. He wanted the ball. If he didn't have it, then, of course, he would just go out and steal it.

But this was not 1987 anymore. The Celtics lost, never got the series back to Boston. In the aftermath of Boston's defeat, a tired and frustrated McHale talked of retiring, though few believed he would. Bird, meanwhile, underwent back surgery June 7. In discussing the procedure, Dr. Arnold Scheller, the team physician, said he believed Bird would return some time during the 1991–92 season, perhaps early. Bird's back problems were not solved. His condition had been treated to alleviate the pain from a bulging disk and constant wear and tear.

Scheller said Bird would be hospitalized for three days. Bird left the hospital after one day. It was widely reported that he walked out with no assistance. The chants of "Larry ... Larry" reverberated throughout New England.

Epilogue

BY THE TIME Larry Bird is finally, officially gone, the Celtics possibly, finally, will be playing in a new Boston Garden. They will pay nothing in rent until at least 2004. They will still dodge their taxes and air their own broadcasts. They will move the parquet floor, piece by piece, and find a cranky organ to fill the breach. They will hang the championship banners—probably still sixteen of them—and the retired numbers. The same faces will slide into their press row seats. But will the new, elusive building always be jammed the way the old one is now? Will there be waiting lists and lines for seats to games against the worst teams in the league? For the Charlotte Hornets? The Miami Heat?

"Once Larry's gone, whenever that is, it's going to be interesting to see what happens," Lewis said one night before a home game in December 1990. "If we're a winner, they'll probably still come. Whether it's still like this, sold out every night, that's hard to say. A lot of these people love Larry more than they do the Celtics."

According to the blueprint, there will be about four thousand additional seats to fill at the new Boston Garden. In Ken Hudson's noble, idealistic world, a good number of them would fall into the hands of Boston's black population. The current patrons would not hassle them, even if these new spectators deigned to root for the Knicks or the Bulls. They would come out in even greater numbers for a team whose big names are Reggie Lewis, Brian Shaw, and Dee

Brown. To continue their extraordinary run of sellouts, to maintain their unparalleled popularity, the Celtics would not have to search every corner of the globe to locate the next white hope; the next Cousy, Havlicek, Cowens, or Bird.

If this should happen, then a new era of the Boston Celtics really will have begun. Then Dave Gavitt will be a sportsman to celebrate. Hudson believes this is possible. Jo Jo White does not.

"I believe Russell was the last black superstar in Boston," White said. "Since Russ retired, they've always had to have their white superstar. If they don't have it, they'll go out and get it. In Boston, it's a must. And the league needs it in a place like Boston, too."

From White's perspective, this racial arrangement was a convenient get-rich scheme for the Celtics and the NBA, one that both organizations always understood completely. Both knew their audiences. The Celtics knew white Bostonians. The NBA knew white Americans. There was dual complicity in the marketing of a white team in a predominantly black sport. The Celtics were a team with tentacles reaching deep into the league's burgeoning corporate structure. They were a team with major white stars, a statistically astounding racial balance, and an administrative army of safe, white faces speaking directly to fashionable Boston neighborhoods and its affluent distant suburbs.

Only the Celtics could tie all the green ribbons around this lucrative package. They had Auerbach, embodiment of the powerful and unchallenged system. They had Bird, the ultimate tactical weapon. They had a powerful media machine to disseminate Celtic propaganda in the name of Celtic Pride.

In the eighties, in Reagan's and Bush's America, unchecked economic growth took on a moral righteousness. Greed was not only justifiable, it was admirable. The Celtics were good at it, and they were winners besides. Questioning their tactics was akin to burning the flag—those sixteen championship flags. The message to those who didn't always agree, to Cedric Maxwell and Gerald Henderson, was to love it or leave it. The Celtic idea of a social consciousness, of doing the right thing, was to make the finals as often as possible.

In Dave Gavitt's first year, there were a few attempts to change the face of the Celtics, to treat agents, players, and outsiders with some dignity. But Gavitt was just scratching the surface. It would take far longer to outgrow the deep-seated Auerbachian attitudes. It would take courage, financial risk, and some sharp criticism to drag Boston forward into the NBA of New York, Los Angeles, and Philadelphia.

Beyond the Celtic Mystique and the sixteen championships, there was another legacy passed on to Gavitt and his aides. The Celtics were a basketball franchise with few or no ties to a black community. They were not alone in this, but in no other city haunted by the misery and tragedy of urban America was professional basketball such an exclusive province, such a country club, for the white fan.

The word on the streets of Roxbury has been out for years, and Gavitt has yet to change that perception. The Boston Celtics are still for whites. Whites are still for the Boston Celtics. The cigar smoke is still in the air and business is just great.

Index

ABA (American Basketball Association), 58, 63, 67–68, 71, 82

ABC (American Broadcasting Corporation), 67, 100

Abdul-Jabbar, Kareem, 16, 78–79, 82, 118, 224

Adidas sneakers, 197

Agents, 15, 63–64, 68, 69, 115, 126–27, 228. *See also name of specific agent or player*

Ainge, Danny: and the Celtic fans, 49; and Henderson negotiations, 149, 150, 151, 154, 155, 157; joins the Celtics, 44–45; and Jones (K.C.), 129, 138; and Maxwell, 121; as a player, 119, 121, 149, 150, 167–68; and race relations, 122, 149, 233, 237; and Rollins, 167–68; salary of, 149, 150, 154, 155; trading of, 60

Archibald, Tiny, 43, 81–82, 107, 131, 234–35

Armato, Leonard, 2, 5, 6–7, 12, 17

Attendance: and Bird, 116–17; and the Boston Garden ownership, 209–10; and the Celtic business ventures, 209; and community relations, 176–77, 182; and the future of the Celtics, 257–58; and race relations, 51, 75–76, 117, 123, 135, 154,

176–77, 182; and the stock sale, 206; and wins/losses, 77, 116–17

Attles, Al, 24, 54, 137, 158, 187

Auerbach, Red (Arnold Jacob): and agents, 63–64, 68, 69, 115, 126–27; and Celtic arrogance, 18, 25, 34; and the Celtic fans, 145; and the Celtic Mystique, 42; and the Celtic owners, 39–40, 49–50, 64, 205, 218, 219–22; and the Celtics' purchase of radio/television stations, 208; characterizations of, 6, 23–24, 25, 29, 33, 40–41, 52; cigars of, 18, 25, 32–33, 34, 38–40, 46, 49–50; and community relations, 186, 187; contract negotiations for, 49–50, 220; and the defeat in his last game, 141–42; and the Egg Game (1961), 29; and financial matters, 205, 214, 219–22; and injuries, 224; joins the Celtics, 46–48; as a legend, 38–46, 47, 140, 141; loyalty to, 12, 57, 231–32; and the media, 2, 9, 71, 75, 85, 116, 151, 152, 191–92, 193, 226, 253; and the Nationals, 27, 32–33; and the NCAA scandals, 100–101; personal background of, 46, 219; and the Philadelphia 76ers, 34; and the Players Association, 67–68, 221;

Auerbach, Red (*cont.*)
    power/control of, 63–64; recreation
    fund in the name of, 173; and refer-
    ees, 25–26; retirement of, 51; and
    salaries of players, 6, 62, 71, 73, 155,
    221–22; salary of, 49, 205, 220; stat-
    ue of, 38–39; strengths of, 42; and
    the visitors' locker room, 21, 22–23;
    and women, 52–53; writings of, 38,
    52–53, 56. *See also* Celtic arrogance;
    name of specific person

Barkley, Charles, 91, 116, 124, 171, 237
Barksdale, Don, 53, 55
Barnes, Marvin, 81, 107, 115
Baylor, Elgin, 27–28, 67
Beard, Butch, 136, 191
Bedford, William, 155–56
Bianchi, Al, 28, 31–32, 112, 141, 142,
    165, 172–73
Bias, Len, 12, 140, 155–56
Biasone, Daniel, 26, 27, 28, 32–34, 48
Bickerstaff, Bernie, 132, 138, 139
Bird, Larry: and agents, 228; and atten-
    dance, 116–17, 177; and Auerbach,
    41, 42, 90, 93, 107–8, 115, 116, 224;
    and the Bird complex, 160, 161–62,
    164; and black domination of the
    Celtics, 240; black players' reactions
    to, 160–63, 164–65, 167, 250, 258;
    and the Celtic–Braves franchise
    exchange, 107–8; and the Celtic
    fans, 77, 178, 179, 243, 251, 252,
    253–54, 257; and Celtic intimida-
    tion, 168; and Celtic loyalty, 153;
    and the Celtic Mystique, 253; as a
    Celtic player, 20, 43, 156, 231,
    242–56; and Celtic Pride, 94; and
    Chamberlain, 244; and Cohen's pur-
    chase of the Celtics, 204; as a col-
    lege player, 87–91, 92–94, 96,
    104–6; and the commercialization of
    basketball, 113, 114, 115; and com-
    munity relations, 173, 178, 179, 180,
    182, 196, 232–33; contract negotia-
    tions/drafting for, 86, 90–93, 107–8,
    115, 116, 153, 228; dependence on,
    249–50, 252; endorsements of, 197,
    247; and the future of the Celtics,
    257; and the Henderson negotia-
    tions, 153; injuries of, 62, 137,
    164–65, 224, 248–56; and Johnson
    (Magic), 88–90, 93–94, 96, 104–6,
    113, 114, 147, 157, 196; and Lee
    (Spike), 195; as a legend, 16, 39,
    251, 253, 256, 258; and the McAdoo
    trade, 86; and the media, 94–95,
    111, 148, 159, 161–62, 167, 182,
    195, 229, 232–33, 244, 245, 249–50,
    251, 252, 253; and the MVP award,
    159; and Newman, 141–42; personal
    background/personality of, 94–95,
    105–6, 162, 236–37; and the Piston
    rivalry, 157, 158–59, 160; and the
    Players Association, 67; and referee
    calls, 25; and Rodman, 163–64;
    salary of, 45, 62, 63, 116, 216, 229;
    scouting of, 41, 90–93; and stealing
    the ball, 143–44, 147, 178; and
    stereotyping, 164–65; and style of
    play, 133; tenure with the Celtics of,
    59; and the Thomas incident,
    160–63; and Woolf, 115. *See also*
    names of other Celtic members
Bird complex, 160, 161–62, 164
Black Coaches Association, 101
Black players. *See name of specific player*
    or topic
Bonus trade clause, 151
Boston area: Celtic community relations
    in the, 170–82, 183–97, 232–33,
    239–40, 248, 259; Celtics as a pre-
    cious resource in the, 211; gangs in
    the, 171–72; Haitian community in
    the, 181; Portuguese community in
    the, 180; race relations in the, 39,
    56–57, 75, 123, 126, 170–82,
    183–97, 226–29, 232–33, 237–40,
    258, 259
Boston Celtics Communications Limited
    Partnership, 208, 213
Boston Garden: ambience of the, 19–20;
    and community relations, 177–78;
    the new, 209–13, 257; as obsolete,
    39; and television contracts, 212–13;
    and the visitors' locker room, 20–23,

24, 30, 31

Boston Globe, 14, 116, 149, 151, 152, 153, 182, 191, 192, 213, 252. *See also name of specific reporter*

Boston Herald, 145–46, 191, 192, 255

Boycott, players, 67

Bradley, Bill, 109, 115–16

Brannum, Bob (Beeb), 28, 33, 55

Broadcasters, 189–91, 240. *See also name of specific person*

Broudy, Nat (Feets), 108–9

Brown, Dee: agent for, 2; and Bird, 244, 245, 246, 247, 252, 254, 255; and the Celtic fans, 247, 255, 257–58; and community relations, 171, 175, 184–85, 187; endorsements by, 247; and the future of the Celtics, 257–58; joins the Celtics, 226; personal life of, 184–85, 187, 226–27; as a player, 125, 244, 245, 246, 247, 252, 254, 255; and race relations, 171, 175, 184–85, 187, 223, 226–27, 236, 237

Brown, Eleanor, 123, 154–55

Brown, Hubie, 130, 133–35, 245

Brown, John Y.: and Auerbach, 39–40, 218, 221; and the Celtic–Braves franchise exchange, 81, 107–8; as a gambler, 217; and the McAdoo deal, 40, 43, 85; and the media, 40; as an owner, 39–40, 45, 46, 81, 214, 217–18, 219–20; and politics, 217, 218; and salaries, 221; and White, 40, 60

Brown, Larry, 99–100, 125

Brown, Walter, 46–52, 54, 64, 67, 179, 180, 220, 222

Bulpett, Steve, 191, 253

Campanis, Al, 37–38, 164

Carlisle, Rick, 122, 125, 152, 164

Carr, M. L. (Michael Leon): and the Celtic fans, 239; and community relations, 172, 187–89; joins the Celtics, 43; and the Lewis negotiations, 15; Maxwell's views of, 121; as a player, 148, 188; and race relations, 172, 187–89, 233, 239; retire-

ment of, 188; and Sampson, 168; as a scout, 187, 188; and the Shaw negotiations, 187

Carroll, Joe Barry, 43–44, 89

CBS (Columbia Broadcasting System), 82–83, 97, 110, 135, 157, 167–68, 190

Celtic arrogance, 10, 11, 12, 18, 21, 22–24, 25–26, 29–30

Celtic–Braves franchise exchange, 81, 107–8

Celtic fans: in the 1950s and 1960s, 23, 29; and Celtic intimidation, 32, 158, 168–69, 178; and the commercialization of basketball, 247; graciousness of the, 31; and the Lakers, 171; and the Philadelphia 76ers, 31; and the Piston rivalry, 158; and race relations, 75–82, 86, 154, 158, 171, 177–79, 193, 239, 257; and referees, 30–31, 32; and the Shaw negotiations, 9; and the stock sale, 206–7. *See also name of specific player*

Celtic intimidation, 24, 28–29, 32, 158, 168–69, 178

Celtic jackets, 232

Celtic Mystique, 41, 42, 149, 197, 227, 239, 253, 259

Celtic Pride, 1, 8, 42, 63, 73, 94, 200, 227, 258

Celtics: founding of the, 50; future of the, 257–59; modernization of the, 231–41; as the most hated team, 194; and the stock sale, 200–201, 204–5, 206–7, 220, 222; value of the, 213, 214–15, 216, 222. *See also name of specific person or topic*

Centers, 115–16

Chamberlain, Wilt, 34, 36, 54, 77, 78, 118, 144, 167, 218–19, 244

Chaney, Don, 70–72, 120, 132, 137

Cheerleaders, 52–53

Coaches: as celebrities, 134; clipboard, 131–32; and college sports, 99, 101, 102; and the media, 132; morality of, 133–34; and race relations, 101, 126, 129, 130, 132, 136, 137, 160–61, 195, 233–36, 240; and salaries, 130, 131; salaries of, 132;

Coaches (*cont.*)
  stereotyping of, 137; system,
  133–34. *See also name of specific
  person*
Cohen, Alan: and Auerbach, 203, 220,
  221; and the Boston Garden ownership, 210–11, 212–13; and community relations, 232; and Gavitt, 244;
  and Jones (K. C.), 138, 140; as a
  lawyer, 202; and Madison Square
  Garden ownership, 201, 203–4; and
  the modernization of the Celtics,
  244; and the Nets, 201–2, 203; as an
  owner, 200–205, 206, 207, 208,
  210–13, 214, 216, 220, 221, 222; and
  the purchase of radio/television stations, 207, 208; purchases the
  Celtics, 201, 203–4, 214, 216; and
  race relations, 123, 126, 240; and
  the Shaw negotiations, 2, 5, 6, 9, 10,
  12; and Stanley, 2, 10; and Stern,
  109, 201, 204–5; and the stock sale,
  200–201, 204–5, 206, 213
College sports, 96–106
Commercialization of basketball, 47, 58,
  109–16, 247
Commercials. See Endorsements
Community relations. *See* Boston area
Continental Basketball Association, 61,
  149, 229–30
Converse sneakers, 197
Cooper, Chuck, 47, 50–51, 52, 53, 55
Cousy, Bob: and Auerbach, 42, 47–48,
  50, 51, 53; as a broadcaster, 51, 190;
  and Brown (Walter), 64; and the
  Celtic fans, 33, 47, 49, 75; as a
  coach, 131; and community relations, 187, 196; contract negotiations of, 47–48, 64; and Jones (K. C.),
  139; and the Nationals, 31, 33; personal life of, 187; as a player, 48, 49,
  65, 214; and the Players Association,
  65–66; and race relations, 51–52,
  55, 56–57, 123, 187, 196, 233;
  retirement of, 51, 54; tenure with
  the Celtics of, 59; and the Tri-Cities
  Blackhawks, 47
Cowens, Dave: and Auerbach, 74; and

Bird, 93; and the Celtic fans, 76–77,
  78–79, 81; as a coach, 80, 81, 82,
  85–86; and community relations,
  172, 187, 195–97, 238; end of era of,
  86; leave of absence by, 79, 80; and
  the McAdoo trade, 85–86; and the
  media, 76, 80; personal life of, 187;
  as a player, 41, 44, 72, 73, 77–79, 80,
  81, 83, 196; and the Players Association, 196; and race relations, 62,
  78–79, 170, 172, 187, 195–97, 233,
  238; and Russell's qualities, 41;
  salary of, 62, 73; and Silas, 74, 81;
  tenure with the Celtics of, 59; and
  White, 81, 82
Cunningham, Billy, 25, 26, 34

Daly, Chuck, 158, 181
Dantley, Adrian, 159, 160
Dartley, Michelle, 185–87
DeBusschere, Dave, 46, 109
Deferred money, 215
Delaware North, 211, 212
Detroit Pistons. *See* Pistons
Divac, Vlade, 114, 131
Downing, Steve, 91–92, 108
Drugs, 82, 113, 141, 155–56, 201–2, 217,
  236
Dumars, Joe, 154, 158
Dunleavy, Mike, 130, 131, 132
Dupee, Paul, 203–4, 205, 214, 221, 222

Egg Game (1961), 29
Elmore, Len, 81, 191, 193
Endorsements, 121, 197–99. *See also
  name of specific person*
Erving, Julius, 82, 111, 118, 188, 235–36,
  245
ESPN, 97, 100
Ewing, Patrick, 14, 67, 84, 91, 124, 171,
  194, 238

Falk, David, 13, 14
Fast break, 33
Ferry, Bob, 15, 191
Ferry, Danny, 3, 4, 155
Fitch, Bill, 43–44, 118, 126, 129, 131,
  146, 149, 232

Fitzsimmons, Cotton, 129, 139
Fleisher, Larry: and Auerbach, 69–70; and Celtic arrogance, 18; and the commercialization of basketball, 113; death of, 114; and free agency, 153; and the Hall of Fame, 114; and the Havlicek negotiations, 69–70; and the Henderson negotiations, 153; and the Players Association, 66–67, 113–14; and salaries, 63, 71, 113–14; and the Silas negotiations, 72
Fleisher, Marc, 10–11, 13, 17, 18, 114
Ford, Chris: and Auerbach, 12; and Bird, 244–45, 251, 253, 255, 256; as a broadcaster, 235; as a coach, 132, 137, 231, 233–34, 244–45, 246, 251, 253–56; and Gavitt, 244; and the McAdoo trade, 85; as a player, 43, 82; and race relations, 137, 232–33, 235, 240; retirement of, 235; and the Shaw negotiations, 10
Forwards, 115–16
Fox network, 207–9
Frazier, Walt, 23, 189
Free agency, 43, 72–74, 109–10, 123, 153, 215, 227. See also name of specific player

Gamble, Kevin, 120, 125, 174, 223, 229–31, 236, 237, 245, 247, 253, 255
Gaston, Donald, 2, 109, 203–4, 205, 207–9, 210–11, 214, 220, 221, 222
Gavitt, Dave: and Auerbach, 231–32, 247, 248, 250; and Bird, 250; and Brown (Dee), 226; and Cohen, 244; and community relations, 173, 186–87, 259; and Ford, 244; and the future of the Celtics, 258, 259; and the Il Messaggero peace offering, 17, 18; joins the Celtics, 140; and the Lewis negotiations, 14, 15, 18, 228, 231; and the modernization of the Celtics, 231–32, 242–43, 244, 247, 248, 259; personal background of, 140–41; and race relations, 173, 186–87, 232–33, 239, 240, 259; and the Shaw negotiations, 2, 10, 13, 18,

231; and the Smith (Charles) case, 186–87; and Stanley, 2, 14, 15, 18, 231; and television contracts, 97
General Utilities Doctrine, 205
Gibbons–Carr, Michele, 185
Gilmore, Artis, 122, 125
Glenn, Mike, 124–25, 136, 137
Globetrotters, 50, 51
Grantham, Charles, 136–37, 150–51, 178, 190, 204
Greer, Hal, 34, 54, 143, 145
Griffith, Darrell, 44, 89
Grinker, Ron, 118–19, 123, 230, 231, 233, 240, 245
Gruppo Ferruzzi, 8, 10, 17
Gulf + Western, 42, 201, 203–4

Haitian community, 181
Hall of Fame. See name of specific person
Hannum, Alex, 28, 34–36
Harris, Bob, 24, 28, 29
Hartford Civic Center, 210
Havlicek, John: and agents, 228; and Auerbach, 68–70, 74, 101, 146, 147; and Bird, 146; and Celtic arrogance, 24; and the Celtic fans, 68–69, 76, 81; and community relations, 187; contract negotiations for, 68–70, 228; as a legend, 143, 146–47; and the media, 76, 80, 145–46; and the modernization of the Celtics, 243; personal life of, 187; as a player, 31–32, 72, 81, 115–16, 143–47, 148, 243; and race relations, 54, 233; retirement of, 146; salary of, 62, 68–70, 71, 73; tenure with the Celtics of, 59
Hawks, 29, 54. See also name of specific member
Heathcote, Jud, 87–89, 93, 104
Heaton, Bob, 93, 94, 105
Heinsohn, Tom: and Auerbach, 38, 42, 61, 101; as a broadcaster, 190, 191; and Celtic arrogance, 24; as a coach, 38, 61, 80; and community relations, 187; and the media, 80; painting by, 34; personal life of, 187; as a player,

Heinsohn, Tom (*cont.*)
   41, 146;and the Players Association,
   66–67; and race relations, 191, 233;
   Russell comment by, 77; as a scout,
   90, 91; as Silk's roommate, 179;
   tenure with the Celtics of, 59
Henderson, Gerald, 101, 119, 143–44,
   147–54, 155, 156, 157, 183, 258
Henry, Conner, 122, 164
Hill, Bob, 130, 133, 253
Hodges, Bill, 94–95, 96–97
Holzman, Red, 33, 84, 108–9, 133
Hometowns, 213–14
Hudson, Ken, 75–76, 77, 232, 233–34,
   235, 236, 237–40, 247, 257, 258

Indiana Pacers. *See* Pacers
Injuries, 62, 224. *See also name of specif-
   ic player*
International Management Group, 114
Investors Funding Corporation, 219–20
Italy, 4–5, 14–17. *See also* Il Messaggero

Jimmy Fund, 173
Johnson, Dennis, 101, 133, 149, 158,
   168, 174, 178, 221, 225, 234, 235,
   237, 244
Johnson, Magic (Earvin): and Abdul-
   Jabbar, 82; and Bird, 88–90, 93–94,
   96, 104–6, 113, 114, 147, 157, 196;
   as a businessman, 219; and the commercialization of basketball, 113,
   114; and community relations, 196;
   and endorsements, 219; and the
   Henderson steal, 148; illness of,
   104; injuries of, 254; Maxwell's
   views of, 117; and the media, 95,
   148; and NBA television, 82,
   110–11, 113, 114; and ownership of
   NBA teams, 219; personal background of, 95; as a player (college),
   88–90, 93–94, 95–96, 104–5; as a
   player (NBA), 129, 130, 133, 254;
   and race relations, 124, 181,
   235–36; and Riley, 129, 130, 131
Johnson, Vinnie, 159, 255
Jones, K. C.: and agents, 126–27; and
   Auerbach, 12, 41–42, 57, 64,

126–27, 131, 138; and Celtic arrogance, 24; and the Celtic owners,
   221; as a coach, 81, 126, 128–32,
   137–38, 139, 148, 150, 151–52, 234,
   235; and community relations, 175;
   contract negotiations of, 64; and the
   Henderson steal/negotiations, 148,
   150, 151–52; leaves the Celtics, 129,
   139; low profile of, 126, 139; and
   McAdoo, 85; and the media,
   137–38, 139, 146; personal life of,
   175, 183; as a player, 129, 145, 146;
   and race relations, 53, 54, 56, 57, 81,
   123, 126, 137, 175, 183, 233, 234;
   salary of, 71, 130; tenure with the
   Celtics of, 59; as VP, 138
Jones, Sam: and Auerbach, 101; and
   Celtic arrogance, 24; and the Celtic
   fans, 76; and community relations,
   174–75; contract negotiations for, 9;
   as a player, 41, 68, 144–45, 146; and
   race relations, 53, 174–75, 233;
   salary of, 71; tenure with the Celtics
   of, 59; White as a successor to, 60
Jordan, Michael: agents for, 14; and the
   Celtic rivalry, 243; and the commercialization of basketball, 110–11,
   171, 194; and community relations,
   172, 181; contract negotiations for,
   67; and endorsements, 197, 198,
   219; and the media, 124; and ownership of NBA teams, 219; as a player, 91; and race relations, 124, 171,
   172, 181; and Thomas, 159; wealth
   of, 67
Judkins, Jeff, 120, 230, 237

Keenan, Diane, 123, 154–55
Kelley, Rich, 166–67
Kelser, Greg, 104, 105
Kennedy, Ted, 20, 68, 177–78, 207
Kennedy, Walter, 66–67
Kerr, Johnny, 28, 31, 33–34, 144
Killilea, John, 41, 90–93, 108
King, Bernard, 17, 21, 118, 119, 165,
   166, 188, 215
King, Bob, 96–97
Kite, Greg, 122, 125, 224, 240

Kleine, Joe, 91, 122, 226, 233, 237, 240, 245, 246
Knicks, 23, 82, 172–73, 189, 192, 201. *See also name of specific member*
Knight, Billy, 81, 107
Knight, Bobby, 91–92, 93, 96, 101, 234
Koncak, Jon, 91, 155

Laimbeer, Bill, 116, 157–58, 254
Lakers: attendance at the, 117; broadcasters for the, 189; and Celtic fans, 171; Celtic rivalry with the, 157, 194; and the media, 111; in Minneapolis, 27–28; move from Minneapolis to Los Angeles, 28; as a publicly held corporation, 205–6; and race relations, 122, 189; Short as owner of the, 27–28; style of play of the, 133. *See also name of specific member*
Lang, Scott, 149–50, 151–53, 154, 156
Lanier, Bob, 78, 113
Lapchick, Joe, 198–99
Lapchick, Richard, 101, 126, 198–99
Larry's Game, 196
Lee, David, 164, 178
Lee, Spike, 162, 193–95, 197, 198
Levin, Irv, 39, 74, 81, 107–8, 219–20
Lewis, Reggie: and Auerbach, 69; and Bird, 244, 246, 257; and the Celtic fans, 247, 257–58; and community relations, 171, 172, 174–75; contract negotiations for, 13–14, 15, 227–28, 231; endorsements by, 197, 246; and the future of the Celtics, 257–58; and Gamble, 230; and Johnson (Dennis), 234; and leaving the Celtics, 1–2; and the media, 228–29; as a player, 137–38, 231, 243, 244, 246, 247, 254, 255; and race relations, 63, 125, 171, 172, 174–75, 223, 227–29, 236, 237, 248; salary of, 228, 229
Lohaus, Brad, 120, 122, 155
Loscutoff, Jim, 24, 28
Luceri, Gianluca, 3, 8, 17

McAdoo, Bob: as an "All-Time Great,"

84; and Auerbach, 40, 85; and Beard, 136; and Brown, 40; and the Celtic fans, 16, 85; contract negotiations for, 40, 43–44; as a player, 16, 43, 78, 83–84; and race relations, 86, 226; trading of, 84–86; and West, 131
Macauley, Ed, 42, 48, 49, 50, 53, 55
McDonough, Will, 2, 14, 152–53, 228–29, 239
McGuire, Al, 96, 98
McHale, Kevin: and Auerbach, 120, 121, 224; and Bird, 162, 237, 242–43, 251; and Brown, 247; and the Celtic fans, 14; and community relations, 180; contract negotiations for, 42–44, 45–46; injuries of, 224, 250; and Maxwell, 119, 120–21, 122, 237; as a player, 44, 119, 128, 133, 156, 231, 237, 242–43, 250; and race relations, 122, 232–33, 237, 240; retirement of, 256; salary of, 63, 120–21; Shaw's views of, 5
MacMullan, Jackie, 191, 251
Madison Square Garden, 193, 201, 203–4
Malone, Karl, 84, 91, 116, 124, 160
Mangurian, Harry, 45, 107–8, 116, 204, 210, 214–16, 219–20, 221
Maravich, Pete, 117, 122
Maxwell, Cedric: and Auerbach, 37, 38, 41, 101, 118, 119–21; and Bias's death, 156; and Bird, 117, 118, 122; and the Celtic fans, 178, 239; contract negotiations for, 119–21, 153; and endorsements, 121; and the future of the Celtics, 258; and the Henderson negotiations, 153, 156–57; injuries of, 62, 119–20, 164–65; and Johnson (Magic), 117; and McHale, 120–21, 122, 237; and the media, 119, 120–21; and Parish, 119, 121; as a player, 43, 118–19, 121, 148; and race relations, 37, 38, 118, 119–20, 121–23, 164–65, 178, 225, 233, 236, 237, 239; and Russell, 121; trading of, 120–21
Meadowlands Arena, 202

Media: and Auerbach, 71, 75, 116, 151, 152, 191–92, 193, 226, 253; and Celtic Pride, 258; and Celtic rivalries, 159; and the Celtics' purchase of radio/television stations, 207; and coaches, 132; and community relations, 182, 191; and the McAdoo deal, 40; and pro teams as hometown entities, 213–14; and race relations, 38, 80, 95, 135, 160–61, 167–68, 182, 189–93, 239; and training camp, 223–24. *See also* Sportswriters; Television; *name of specific person*

Il Messaggero: Celtic feud with, 10–11, 13, 15–16, 17–18; and the Lewis negotiations, 15; and race relations, 4–5; and the Radja negotiations, 1, 17, 18; and the Shaw negotiations, 1, 3–5, 6, 7, 8, 9, 10–11, 12–13, 17; wealth of, 10, 17–18

Most, Johnny, 122, 145, 147, 190, 221, 235

Moulter, Larry, 211, 212

Mullin, Chris, 4, 165–66

Murdoch, Rubert, 207–9

MVP award, 159. *See also name of specific player*

Nationals, 26–34, 54

The National (newspaper), 190–91

NBA (National Basketball Association): ABA merger with the, 67–68, 82; black domination of the, 53–54, 82–83, 114, 122, 123–25; and blacks in nonplayer positions, 136–37; broadcasters for the, 189–91; and Brown (John Y.), 217–18; and the Celtic–Braves franchise exchange, 107–8; and Celtic intimidation, 24; Celtics relationship with the, 9, 24, 204, 258; and the commercialization of basketball, 58, 109–16; and community relations, 172, 175–76, 232; drafting in the, 92; economic problems of the, 58; and European players, 114; expansion franchises of the, 124, 213, 215, 217; as a family,

109; and financing the teams, 207, 215–16; and the Havlicek steal, 145; image problems of the, 82; and the integration of the teams, 47, 50–52, 53–54, 195; and the NCAA, 98; and the Players Association, 67–68, 113–14; and rep–player social relations, 4–5; and the Rodman incident, 163; and the Rollins–Ainge fight, 167; salaries in the, 58, 71, 154–55; and the Shaw negotiations, 8; and "stealing," 124; and television, 82–83, 110–12, 212–13; and the Thomas–Bird press conference, 161, 162. *See also name of specific commissioner*

NBC (National Broadcasting Corporation), 96–97, 110, 111, 112, 130, 131, 164, 190

NCAA. See College sports

Nelson, Don, 56, 59, 70, 76, 92, 101, 137, 156

Nets, 201–2, 203

New Boston Garden Corporation, 209–10, 212

Newman, Johnny, 141, 166

New York Knickerbockers. *See* Knicks

Nike sneakers, 197

No trade clause, 152

Nuggets, 205–6, 219. *See also name of specific member*

O'Brien, Larry, 67–68, 111

Ohen, Alan, 2, 10

O'Riordan, Brian, 180

O'Riordan, John, 180

Owens, Al, 173–74

Owners, 67, 196–97, 215, 216, 218–19. *See also name of specific person*

Pacers, 23. *See also name of specific member*

Packer, Billy, 96, 97

Parish, Robert: and Auerbach, 224; and Bird, 246; and the Celtic fans, 141; and community relations, 172, 238; contract negotiations for, 42–43; injuries of, 224, 255; joins the

Celtics, 43; and Jones (K. C.), 137; and Maxwell, 119, 121; and the media, 224; personal life of, 224; as a player, 5, 44, 128, 141, 156, 158, 224, 242–43, 246, 255; and race relations, 122, 172, 225, 232–33, 236–37; rumors about, 224–25, 226; and the Shaw negotiations, 5; as a superstar, 42–43; tenure with the Celtics of, 224

Paxson, Jim, 122, 156, 230, 240, 251

Payton, Gary, 98, 139

Pension demands, 67

Philadelphia 76ers, 25–26, 31, 34–36, 54, 117, 176. *See also name of specific member*

Pinckney, Ed, 174, 237

Pippen, Scott, 159, 163

Pistons, 24, 43, 116, 157–60, 175, 176, 224, 253–56. *See also name of specific member*

Pitino, Rick, 99, 100, 133, 165

Players Association, 65–67, 112–14, 196, 215–16, 221

Podoloff, Maurice, 48, 65–66

Popson, Dave, 126, 237, 240, 241, 246

Portuguese community, 180

Proposition 42 (NCAA), 102

Public relations directors, 136

Race relations. *See name of specific person or topic*

Radja, Dino, 1, 11, 13, 15, 17, 18, 240

Ramsey, Frank, 31, 58, 64

Red Auerbach trophy, 132

Reebok sneakers, 197, 198, 246, 247

Reed, Willis, 42, 78, 84, 137

Referees, 25–26, 30–31, 32. *See also name of specific person*

Reggie Lewis Foundation, 174

Reserve clause, 72–74

Retired Number Celtics, 59–60

Richardson, Michael Ray, 16, 84–85

Riley, Pat, 22, 129–30, 131, 133, 164, 191

Robertson, Oscar, 24–25, 41, 54, 67

Robey, Rick, 89, 121, 122, 233, 237

Rodgers, Jimmy, 92, 138, 140, 201, 221, 230, 234, 243

Rodman, Dennis, 20, 143–44, 159, 160, 163–64, 246, 255

Rollins, Tree, 135, 167–68

Rosensweig, Tod, 12, 173

Rowe, Curtis, 80, 81, 183

Royals, 24–25, 54. *See also name of specific member*

Russell, Bill: and Auerbach, 42, 48–49, 51, 52, 53, 55–56, 57–58, 73; and the Celtic fans, 53, 76, 77, 78, 145, 183, 239; and the Celtic Mystique, 41; and Chamberlain, 54, 77; as coach, 51, 54, 137, 195; and community relations, 174–75; contract negotiations for, 42, 48–49, 50, 73; and Cowens, 41; and the Hawks, 34–35, 48–49; and the Howell deal, 12; Maxwell's views of, 121; and the media, 38; and the Nationals, 31, 33, 34; personal life of, 183; and the Philadelphia 76ers, 34; as a player, 42, 53, 55–56, 65, 68, 77, 115, 121, 179; and race relations, 38, 51, 52, 54, 55–56, 57–58, 174–75, 183, 233, 236, 239; retirement of, 183; salary of, 68; as a superstar, 258; tenure with the Celtics of, 59

Ryan, Bob, 9, 120, 140, 159, 191, 226

Salaries: and Auerbach, 6, 62, 71, 73, 155, 221–22; and Celtic Pride, 73; and coaches, 130, 131; and the commercialization of basketball, 58, 113; in the NBA, 71; and the owners, 215, 216; and race relations, 58, 61–63, 71, 73, 74, 82, 154–55; studies about, 154–55; and television, 228. *See also name of specific person*

Salary caps, 13, 62, 113, 131

Sama, Carlo, 7–8, 10, 17, 18

Sampson, Ralph, 155, 168–69

Sanders, Tom ("Satch"): and Auerbach, 12, 41–42, 57, 64, 81, 146; as a coach, 80, 81; and community relations, 172, 196; contract negotiations for, 64, 74; and the Nationals, 27; as a player, 41; and race rela

Sanders, Tom (*cont.*)
   tions, 53, 57, 172, 196, 199, 233;
   salary of, 71; tenure with the Celtics
   of, 59
San Francisco Warriors. See Warriors
Scapecoats of management, 225
Schayes, Dolph, 26, 27, 28–29, 31, 33,
   34, 46, 54
Scott, Byron, 147, 148
Scouting, 90–92, 97–98
Seymour, Paul, 28–29, 30, 31
Share, Charlie, 47, 48
Sharman, Bill, 49, 59
Shaughnessy, Dan, 76–77, 149, 152, 238
Shaw, Brian: and Auerbach, 69; and Bird,
   244, 246, 249, 253, 254; and the
   Celtic fans, 177–78, 247, 254, 255,
   257–58; and community relations,
   174, 175, 177–78; contract negotia-
   tions for, 1–13, 15, 17, 227, 231; and
   free agency, 6, 7; and the future of
   the Celtics, 257–58; and Johnson
   (Dennis), 234; as a player, 243, 245,
   246, 247, 253, 255; and race relations, 125, 174, 175, 177–78, 187,
   223, 227, 236, 237
Short, Bob, 27–28, 67
Sichting, Jerry, 156, 168–69, 237
Siegfried, Larry, 64, 71
Silas, Paul: and Auerbach, 72–74, 81; as a
   coach, 173; and community relations, 172, 173, 174; contract negotiations for, 62, 72–74; and Cowens,
   74, 81; as a free agent, 74; influence
   on players of, 71; as a player, 32,
   72–74, 79, 118; and the Players
   Association, 72–74, 82; and race
   relations, 62, 172, 173, 174, 233;
   and salaries, 82; salary of, 71;
   White's comments about, 73–74;
   Wicks compared with, 79–80
Silk, John, 179–80
Slaughter, Fred, 15, 225, 234
Smith, Charles, 156, 185–87
Smith, Michael, 122–23, 126, 224, 230,
   237, 245, 246
Sneaker companies, 99, 197–99
Spiro, Richard, 123, 154–55

SportsChannel, 213
Sports Illustrated, 111, 197, 198
Sports (magazine), 118–19
Sportswriters, 111–12, 130, 191–92. *See
   also name of specific person*
Stanley, Jerome: and Auerbach, 1–2, 14,
   15; and black salaries, 63; and
   Cohen, 2, 10; and community relations, 174; and Gavitt, 2, 14, 15, 18,
   231; and the Lewis negotiations,
   13–14, 15, 227, 228, 231; and the
   negotiation process, 7; and race
   relations, 15, 228–29, 239; and the
   Shaw negotiations, 1–2, 5, 6–7, 8,
   9–10, 14, 227, 231
"Stealing", 124
Stepin Fetchit story, 37, 38, 118
Stereotyping, 162, 164, 166, 167–68
Stern, David: and the Broudy funeral,
   108–9; and the capitalization of
   NBA teams, 216; and Cohen, 109,
   201, 204–5; and college basketball,
   98; and the commercialization of
   basketball, 109, 112, 114; and community relations, 175–77, 232; contract for, 109–10, 204; and financing
   the Celtics, 204–5; and the Players
   Association, 112–13; and race relations, 114, 175–77; salary of,
   109–10, 204; and the Shaw negotiations, 10
Stirling, Scotty, 44, 165
Stock sale, 200–201, 204–5, 206–7, 220,
   222
Strom, Earl, 25, 26, 34, 144
Syracuse Nationals. *See* Nationals

Taub, Joe, 202, 203
Taxes, 209, 215–16
TBS, 135
Team "dee-fense," 33
Television: and Celtic rivalries, 157; and
   the Celtics' purchase of stations,
   207; and college sports, 96–97, 98,
   99, 100; and community relations,
   176, 182; and the NBA, 82–83,
   110–12, 212–13; and the new
   Boston Garden, 212–13; and the

Players Association, 66–67; and race relations, 81–82, 168, 176, 182, 189–93; and salaries, 228; and the stock sale, 206; and the value of the Celtics, 216
Tenure: with Celtics, 59–60
Thomas, Isiah, 28, 143–44, 154, 157, 158, 159–63, 164, 166–67, 225, 251, 254–55
Thompson, David, 82, 96
Thompson, John, 78, 101, 102, 125, 186
Thurmond, Nate, 54, 78
Ticket prices, 176–77, 193, 197, 204, 213, 216
Trainers, 136
Training camp, 223–24
Turner Network Television, 212–13
Twiss, Jeff, 19–20, 232

Unseld, Wes, 78, 132, 135, 137
USA Today, 112

Vecsey, Peter, 112, 245
Visiting teams: and Celtic arrogance, 25–26; Celtics' physical beating up of, 24, 28–29; and the visitors' locker room, 20–23, 24, 30, 31
Vitale, Dick, 43, 98
Volk, Jan: and Auerbach, 11–12, 141; career of, 11–12; and the Celtics' purchase of radio/television stations, 208; and the Henderson negotiations, 143, 149, 150, 151–52, 153; and Jones (K. C.), 138; and the Lewis negotiations, 14, 228; and Mangurian, 45–46; and the media, 191–92; personal background of, 12; and race relations, 240; and the Radja negotiations, 11–12, 13; and Rodgers, 138; and the Shaw negotiations, 2–3, 5–6, 7, 9, 10, 12–13; and Stanley, 15; as ticket manager, 76, 116, 177

Vrankovic, Stojan, 7, 126, 233, 237, 240–41, 246

Walker, Chet, 34, 143, 145
Walton, Bill, 96, 120, 122, 164–65, 233
Warm–up practice, 24
Warriors, 24, 28, 54
Washington, Kermit, 107, 167
Wedman, Scott, 122, 172, 237
WEEI (radio station), 208, 232
Wellesley, Mass., 184–85, 226–27
West, Jerry, 67, 130, 131
Westhead, Paul, 131, 133, 245
Westphal, Paul, 64
WFXT (Channel 25), 207–9
White, Jo Jo: and Auerbach, 61, 101; and the Auerbach legend, 40; and Bird, 93; and Brown, 60; and the Celtic fans, 76, 81, 239; and Celtic loyalty, 63; and the Continental Basketball Association, 61; contract negotiations for, 40, 61–63; and Cowens, 81, 82; and the future of the Celtics, 258; injuries of, 62, 164–65; joins the Celtics, 60; and the media, 40, 76; as MVP, 60; as a player, 60–63, 72, 73, 82; and race relations, 61–63, 81–82, 164–65, 233, 239, 258; salary of, 73; and Silas, 73–74; tenure with the Celtics of, 60–63; traded to the Warriors, 40
White role models, 160
White tokenism, 124–26
Wicks, Sidney, 79–80, 81, 115, 183
Wilkens, Lenny, 54, 132, 137
Willens, Robert, 200, 201, 205–6, 207, 209
WLVI (Channel 56), 207
Women: Auerbach's views of, 52–53
Woolf, Bob, 64, 68, 69, 115, 116, 228
Worthy, James, 21–22, 133, 143, 147, 148